King's Quest VII™

Authors
Peter Spear and Jeremy Spear

Editors
Willem Knibbe, Dan Brodnitz

Design and Production
s.w. artz, inc.

Vice President and Publisher
Ron Resnick

Infotainment World, Inc.,
951 Mariner's Island Blvd., Suite 700, San Mateo, CA 94404.

ISBN 1-57280-006-2

Printed in the United States of America

10 9 8 7 6 5 4 3 2 1

This book is dedicated to:
JB Compton and the Howling Larva
You know why.

Contents

Acknowledgments

Oodles of folks helped us out in various ways and made this book possible.

At Sierra On-Line:
Roberta Williams (forever and ever), Mark Siebert, Lorelei Shannon, Marc Hudgins, Jon Meek and the KQ7 QA wizards and wizardresses, Dan Rogers, Jerry Bowerman.

At Infotainment World:
Willem Knibbe, Ron Resnick, Pat Ferrell.

In various other places:
Bill Gladstone, superstar.
John Kilcullen.
CompuServe (for being there in the middle of the night).
America Online (for being there in the middle of the night).
Toshiba (for the loan of a swell quad-speed CD-ROM drive).
Mo, Melissa, Liz, Dave, Matt, and Squeaky Toy.
Virginia Soper (for always being there).

And especially:
Joe Escalle for his effort, dedication, organization, patience, and (especially) his screenshots. Sorry about that raise.

Read Me First! *Please...*

This book is not a hint book. This book is an *answer* book. Nothing is hidden. All the puzzles and secrets of King's Quest VII: The Princeless Bride are revealed. This is industrial-strength, direct, clear, and straightforward information. There is stuff in here you can find no place else.

Accept no substitutions.

Finding your way around

There are several different ways to use this book, depending on the level of help you feel most comfortable with.

Part 1 (The Stories So Far) has no game answers at all. It has story synopses of all six previous King's Quest games. If you have never played a King's Quest game before or want to be brought up-to-date on the continuing saga of the Royal Family of Daventry, start here.

Part 2 (Making It All Click) is a step-by-step, screen-by-screen, mouse-click-by-mouse-click, "just hold our hands, we're doing all the work" path from the beginning to the end of the game. It's organized the same way as KQ7: six chapters alternating between Valanice and Rosella. If you're stuck, just flip to that appropriate section for the correct answer or strategy.

Part 2 is also filled with a great deal of additional information about the game, some of our own observations and questions, and the occasional digression into the game's original design. They will give you a unique perspective on KQ7 that you can use to impress your friends, start conversations at cocktail parties, write a doctoral dissertation, or just plain enjoy.

When you've finished playing through to game's end, try reading through Part 2 to get a different feel for the game experience.

Parts 3 and 4 (From the Eye between the Worlds and The Princeless Bride) relate the adventures of Rosella and Valanice in story format. The Princeless Bride is a most curious piece of work as it purports to be the telling of actual and *true* events. Is it? Make up your own mind after reading both it and Part 3. The story itself also provides an accurate and complete walk-through the game. Read along as you play, or enjoy it by itself. The universe is *much* stranger than we imagine.

Part 5 (Where's Where) contains a complete set of maps for the game. Don't leave home without 'em. The maps also list what can be found in the various locations of the game. This chapter works great if you just need a nudge in some direction, or just can't seem to find something.

Part 6 (What's What) is a complete listing of all the objects found and/or made in KQ7. The list includes where and when these objects are discovered. It also tells their use, for those times you have something but just don't know what to do with it.

Part 7 (Who's Who) is our own little exclusive — the original artist sketches of many of the game's characters. This stuff is really neat, especially for those times when ten or twenty pixels worth of detail just doesn't seem to be enough. Up close and in pencil, you'll discover an entirely different view of dozens of familiar characters.

How to reach us if something needs fixing

We've done our darndest to pack as much interesting, useful, and accurate information into this book as possible. Especially accurate. But the one inescapable truth about writing books about computer games is that we normally deal with software that is continually being revised. No matter how carefully you sneak into the oddest corners of games, no matter how often you play them from top to bottom and from inside out, the occasional tidbit can get overlooked. Oftentimes, significant changes are made moments before a game is sent out to be duplicated and shrink-wrapped. Sometimes these changes can affect a problem's solution, the placement (or non-placement) of some critical item, or even how to get from point A to point B.

Before this book went to the printer, we checked it for accuracy one last time against the King's Quest VII shipping version. But this is not the most perfect of worlds. We still might have missed or misstated something. We might even be dead wrong someplace (but we don't think so).

If you find a mistake, uncover something neat that you think we might like to include in a later printing, or just feel like dropping us a line about the game, here are our preferred mail drops:

CompuServe: 75300,2374
MCI Mail: PSpear or 311-3280
ImagiNation Network: Box 1822
Snail mail: Infotainment World Books
951 Mariner's Island Blvd. Suite 700 San Mateo CA 94404

America Online: PeterSpear
Internet: PeterSpear@AOL.com

We'd like to hear from you. Enjoy!

Peter Spear Mill Valley, California January, 1995
Jeremy Spear Bennington, Vermont January 1995

Spear's Rules for Playing
KING'S QUEST VII

1. **DEATH IS YOUR FRIEND.**
   There are dozens of situations in which Rosella and Valanice can die in KQ7. However, the player is always offered the chance to "Try Again?" which allows one to continue playing from the point just before the commission of the fatal act. Don't worry when attempting death-defying feats — if your character dies, there is always a second (and third and fourth, etc.) chance at life. Digital death is so temporary here that you can use it to have more fun by watching the death scenes you might miss by playing smart and well.
   Die often. Die well.

2. **WINNERS ALWAYS QUIT.**
   King's Quest VII is different from other computer adventure and role-playing games in that players are prohibited from creating and hoarding a lot of saved games — places in the action where one can return if things aren't going well. KQ7 allows only one save per game, and it's automatically activated each time the player quits. It can be slightly annoying to have successfully played through an entire chapter or three without a stumble and then have to start over because of a computer crash or power failure.
   Quit often. Quit well. Then, after quitting, continue from where you were by choosing the "Continue Old Game" option.

3. **PAY ATTENTION.**
   There are clues everywhere, and not all of them are obvious. If you don't look and listen carefully, you'll miss plenty.

4. **TAKE GOOD NOTES.**
   Better yet, take *great* notes. You may need to know tomorrow what you learned today, and memory can be so uncertain. Write things down. Make sure you can read your own handwriting.

5. **KNOW WHERE YOU ARE AT ALL TIMES.**
   Avoid getting lost by making good maps or consulting ours. Not only will they show you where you are and where you've been, they'll also give you an idea of where you haven't been.

6. **MAKE THINGS CLICK.**
   If the game cursor either glitters or changes color, it means you can do something, see something, or talk with someone. Click the mouse button. Click on every nook and cranny of everything you collect or encounter. You never know what might happen.
   Sometimes the result might be disastrous, but hey, that's why we have Rule 1.

7. **EXAMINE EVERYTHING.**
   You never know what you might find. Once you have something in inventory, examine it again. You never know what you might find there, either.

8. **TALK TO EVERYBODY.**
   You never know what you might learn. And keep talking to everyone; they might have more to say — a lot more.

9. **COME BACK AGAIN LATER.**
   Do things over. People can have new things to say. Things might change. New opportunities might be presented.

10. **THINK CREATIVELY, BUT DO THE OBVIOUS.**
    Not all problems are solved by using logic. Many are solved by using *illogic*, but that doesn't mean you shouldn't do the obvious. Something as mundane as giving a dog a bone can be so obvious as to be overlooked, yet can yield great results.

11. **WALK AWAY FROM YOUR PROBLEMS.**
    Sometimes, the answer just won't come. Other times, the answer won't come because you're looking too hard. Let your brain clear; go away and do something else. Forget about the game and come back later.

12. **ASK FOR HELP.**
    When all else fails, yell "Help!" A befuddlement to some is the obvious to someone else. And, of course, there is this book. Who gave you all the answers to everything, anyway?

13. **REMEMBER, IT'S ONLY A GAME. HAVE FUN.**

PART ONE

The Stories So Far

The King's Quest games are stories. Good stories. Stories not about shooting or kung-fuing things up, or hacking monsters to taco-sized bits with the magic sword of Whatchamicallit, but stories about people and their magical adventures. Their heartbreaks and their triumphs. Stories anyone — old, young, in-between, or non-commital — can enjoy. Let us relate to you a story about the games themselves.

The first time we ever heard about King's Quest was in December of 1984 when we were mooching some review software from John Williams of Sierra On-Line.

"Listen, kid!" John said. "We've got this revolutionary new game that you gotta see. It's called King's Quest, and it's just like an animated cartoon. Trust me." Understand something, John is not now and, to the best of our knowledge, has never been a snake oil salesman. He doesn't even talk like one. Not in our presence anyway. But hype is often an alternate spelling of "extolling the wonders of the latest computer game." Except in the case of King's Quest, John may have been understating his case.

King's Quest VII: The Princeless Bride was released in November 1994, the 10th. anniversary of the release of the original game. Over this period of time, the King's Quest series has become the best-selling computer game series in history. By the time you read this, it will have sold more than 3 million copies, most during times when any game selling even 100,000 units was considered a megahit. One can also make a good guess that another 15 million to 20 million more copies have been illegally duplicated and (presumably) played.

Two things made King's Quest revolutionary in the beginning. First, the game was fully animated. King Graham (the hero) actually moved from place to place; a dragon's flames needed to be avoided, a bean stalk needed climbing, and a lake needed to be swum. Watching where Graham stepped became as important as figuring out what to do next and how to do it. No one had ever done this before in a full-blown graphic adventure game. There were plenty of action games on the market, but there were no animated cartoons until King's Quest.

The second revolutionary aspect was that the game was written to run on the IBM PC. King's Quest was the first major game to be written for a computer that most people considered to be a serious business tool. OK, so it briefly came out first in black and white, although there were color versions for other types of "home" computers. But, at the time, color cards were rare on PCs. King's Quest *demanded* them and, over the years, better and better ones. They were still years away from being called "video" cards.

The King's Quest games were also "interactive multimedia" games from before the term was invented. Over its first 10 years, the King's Quest games (along with other Sierra titles) have ignited the popularity, and now necessity, of color graphics in better and better clarity and resolutions. The series set, and keeps setting, higher standards for animation and graphics. It was the first major product to champion sound cards. Along the way, King's Quest V was one of the first major CD-ROM hits. And with King's Quest VII, the series introduces animations as smooth and clean as traditional Hollywood cell animation.

We must also point out that the creator, designer, and writer of that first King's Quest game was a woman named Roberta Williams. Although Roberta had been designing hit adventure games for some years prior to King's Quest, the games' enormous successes played a big part in bringing more and more women into what was once a heavily male-dominated line of work. This a not a shabby lists of achievements.

We guess John was right when he said, "Trust me!"

This is all interesting stuff, in its way, but what really keeps people coming back by the millions are the stories. They're the real magic of King's Quest. Stories about a family, the royal family of a kingdom known as Daventry. Stories of people you can care about. Stories that make you laugh and cry. Stories of wonders and magical deeds.

Stories to make you rush on in excitement and scratch your (preferred body part) in puzzlement. Stories that make you think. It is said that when a preview of *King's Quest IV: The Perils of Rosella* was first shown to an invited audience, a person wept when King Graham apparently collapsed and died.

King's Quest VII: The Princeless Bride tells the dual stories of Princess Rosella and Queen Valanice as they quest through the land of Etheria. You don't need to know anything at all about what happened in the earlier six adventures in order to enjoy this one. Still, you might be curious about what has been going on in Daventry over the years, so here is the story so far:

King's Quest I: Quest for the Crown (1984) (the original title was plain ol' King's Quest) tells the story of a young knight of Daventry named Graham. He's summoned by his monarch, King Edward, who had no heirs. Graham was tasked to find the three great, and now lost, treasures of the realm before invaders overran the kingdom. He is promised the throne of Daventry as a reward if he is successful.

Suitably motivated, Graham tromped off, defeated a fire-breathing dragon to retrieve the Magic Mirror, fiddled around a bit with some leprechauns to get back the Magic Shield, and climbed to the top of a really big beanstalk to get the ever-full Chest of Gold from a giant. The dragon, broomstick witch, sorcerer, troll, hungry wolf, nasty dwarf, and riddlesome Rumplestiltskin he encountered along the way kept life interesting for him.

When Graham, quests completed, finally returned to Castle Daventry with the treasures, good King Edward was true to his word and gave Graham his crown. Then the ex-monarch dropped dead on the spot, immediately eliminating any of the inconveniences that are possible when an ex-king is hanging around while the new kid on the throne is trying to rule.

King's Quest II: Romancing the Throne (1985) begins a year or two later. Graham has become comfortable in the king business except for one tiny detail. He needs a queen. That decision made, he checks out the magic mirror and, Lo!, he sees a beautiful maiden held captive in a Crystal Tower. She has been kidnapped by a wicked witch named Hagatha, and is crying out for rescue.

If you were a young king — and a single one at that — what would you do?

Graham decided to stop kinging it for a bit and try his hand at the rescuing-fair-maidens business. He travels to the land of Kolyma where he finds the wicked witch in question. The princess, however, is somewhere else. To free her, Graham needs to find three keys, each opening a magical doorway that is on the far side of a bottomless chasm. The bridge between is a killer.

To find the three keys, Graham needs to visit King Neptune beneath the waves, duck out on Hagatha's cuisine, pay his respects to Riding Hood, fly a magic carpet, and accompany Death to Count Dracula's castle so he can stake out a certain coffin. The mermaid, genie, jewels, and occasional grandma along the way help take his mind off of another mean dwarf and the big, bad wolf.

Through the final door and across a lavender ocean, Graham at last finds the object of his quest. It's love at first sight, of course. A simple kiss later, King Graham and Valanice are married.

King's Quest III: To Heir is Human (1986) jumps ahead nearly 20 years after Graham and Valanice's wedding. They are nowhere to be seen.

In the land of Llewdor, there lives an evil magician named Manannan. How evil is he? Instead of employing servants to cater to his peculiar needs, he keeps a slave, just one, a young boy whom he kidnaps and then raises from infancy. When the slave reaches his 18th birthday, there is no party — Manannan kills him and starts over with another boy. Now that's evil!

Gwydion is Manannan's current slave. He's three days shy of 18 and needs to escape. His plan is simple and dangerous. Each time his master either naps or poofs off someplace, he explores. First he breaks into the wizard's secret laboratory and discovers a spell book. In Manannan's study, he discovers the magic wand needed to create the spells. From then on, whenever possible, he will rush down from the mountain top, where the house sits, to gather ingredients for the magic spells.

One spell lets Gwydion understand what the small animals chatter between themselves. From them and a neighborhood oracle, he learns that he is really a kidnapped prince. He also finds out that he has a sister, a twin. Oh, by the way, she's soon to be sacrificed to a three-headed, fire-breathing dragon. Happy birthday.

Surviving close calls with Medusa, some nasty bandits and the Three Bears, Gwydion is finally able to turn Manannan into a cat and escape. Free at last, he goes into town and is kidnapped by a band of pirates who could recognize a country bumpkin when they saw one.

The brigands transport Gwydion across the sea, but just before they reach land, he is able to dive overboard and escape. From there he travels over the mountains, past an abominable snowman, down cliffs of sudden death and arrives in, of all places, Daventry.

The kingdom is in ruins; a dragon has been wreaking havoc for years. Gwydion meets Rumplestiltskin (or a close relative) and discovers that he is Prince Alexander of Daventry. His sister, Rosella, is at that very moment being sacrificed to the dragon. She had been sent there by her — their! — father, King Graham.

Alexander isn't about to let any little old monster disturb the family reunion. He defeats the dragon, rescues his sister, and arrives in Castle Daventry in triumph. Upon meeting his son, King Graham passes the torch of adventuring to his children by throwing his adventuring cap to them. The story ends with the cap still in flight.

King's Quest IV: The Perils of Rosella (1988) picks up at the very moment the prior game ended.

Before Graham's adventurer's cap touches the floor, he collapses as if dead. The good fairy, Genesta, appears to inform Rosella that the only way to save her father's life is to travel to the land of Tamir and bring back a magical fruit she will find there. Rosella agrees, Genesta poofs them to Tamir, and then tells the princess that she won't be able to take the fruit home unless she first recovers the fairy's magic Talisman from the evil (surprised?) Lolotte. And you thought used-bridge salespeople are a tad liberal with the entire truth.

Undaunted, but perhaps a bit miffed, Rosella quests on and finds the magic fruit. In the great tradition of both her mother and brother, however, she gets herself kidnapped by Lolotte, a wicked witch down to the green of her skin. Her son Edgar leers, drooling, over her shoulder. Lolotte demands Rosella bring her a unicorn in order to escape death.

After escaping from the belly of a whale in order to satisfy Lolotte's demand, Rosella returns with a unicorn.

The ungrateful witch demands a second gift, the hen that lays golden eggs. For this, Rosella needs to escape a princess-eating ogre. A *hungry* princess-eating ogre. And his wife.

Mission accomplished, Lolotte is still not finished with Rosella. This time she wants Pandora's Box.

Rosella is not pleased, of course, but three deadly crones, one mummy, a couple of ghosts, and a graveyard filled with hungry zombies later, she staggers back with the required item. Lolotte is ecstatic. But instead of freedom, her reward is to be marriage to Edgar — a fate worse than death. She is imprisoned in Edgar's bedroom.

A small noise is heard at the door, and a rose is slipped under it. It's a rose concealing the key to her prison. Rosella escapes the room and finds her way to Lolotte's bedroom. She opens the door and is able to shoot an Arrow of Love through Lolotte's black heart. The witch melts, and Rosella is able to recover Genesta's Talisman.

Rosella makes her way back to Genesta's castle with the Talisman and magic fruit. There she discovers that the rose had been slipped to her by Edgar, who really wasn't as bad as he was set up to be. Genesta rewards Edgar by transforming him into a beautiful prince. Rosella is returned in a flash to Castle Daventry where the magic fruit restores King Graham to full health and provides a happy ending to the game.

King's Quest V: Absence Makes the Heart Go Yonder (1990) takes place some unspecified time after The Perils of Rosella. King Graham returns home after a morning's stroll to find a hole where Castle Daventry once stood.

From a near tree comes the voice of an owl named Cedric. Familiar to the wizard Chrispinophur, Cedric explains that the castle was whirled away by an evil wizard, Mordack. Graham's family had been take along for the ride, kidnapped together this time.

Cedric flies Graham to his master in Sernia to seek answers and help. Help means giving the king a magic wand in need of a charge and Cedric for company.

Graham adventured through Serenia, gathering and trading the supplies they would need for the journey eastward to Mordack's island. By the time they were provisioned, they had escaped the endless desert and its blood-thirsty bandits, given aid to the kingdoms of both the ants and the bees, defeated the obligatory evil witch and found the needle in a haystack.

Across the mountains they ventured. Captured and threatened by the Ice Queen, Graham bests a Yeti in its lair so as to save Cedric's life. Reunited, the two make their way to the sea and sail still farther east in quest of Graham's family and Mordack's castle. Then, tragedy struck. On the first island they come to they are attacked by harpies. Cedric is left for dead.

Graham finds aid for the near-lifeless owl, but he must continue onward alone to the castle. Once there, he emerges from Mordack's basement maze (doesn't everybody have one?) and befriends the captured Princess Cassima, kidnapped by Mordack from the Green Isles for refusing to marry him. Graham finally confronts Mordack in his laboratory. As all seems lost for the monarch, Cedric arrives in the nick of time and saves Graham from sure death. The king is able to use Crispinophur's recharged magic wand to defeat Mordack in a duel of magical spells.

As the smoke clears in Mordack's laboratory, Crispinophur arrives to restore Graham's family to their normal size and Castle Daventry to its home. Prince Alexander and Cassima meet fall in love at first sight. She invites the prince back to her place in the Green Isles. Crispinophur wraps things up by teleporting everybody home. Arm in arm, the Royal Family of Daventry returns to their castle.

King's Quest VI: Heir Today, Gone Tomorrow (1992) continues the story of Alexander and Princess Cassima.

The prince is moping about the throne room one day when the image of Cassima appears in the trusty old magic mirror. She is staring out a tower window, looking troubled. Alex immediately hires a ship and heads off for the land of the Green Isles. The trouble is, nobody is quite sure where they are. No matter, the prince had read the star pattern in the sky above Cassima and is sure he can navigate to them. After a long voyage, the expedition is wrecked on rocks. Alexander is the only survivor. But he had made it to the Green Isles.

At the palace of Cassima's parents, King Caliphim and Queen Allaria, he meets the vizier Alhazred and learns that they have died. Cassima, he is told, is in mourning and cannot see him. Anyway, she's going to marry Alhazred soon. Alex is shown the door and told to leave the isles.

The trouble is, there is no way off the islands and no ferry between them. And the rulers of the different islands have grudges against each other; war seems inevitable. As Alexander is learning this, and throughout this adventure, he is followed by Alhazred's personal genie, who keeps attempting to lure him to his death.

Alex is sure that something is wrong with Alhazred's version of events. Using a convenient magic map, he travels between all of the islands and sets things right.

The winged rulers of the Isle of the Sacred Mountain are sure that the Isle of Wonder has stolen its greatest treasure, the Golden Fleece. Alexander is sent into the catacombs there, but he earns Lord Azure and Lady Aerial's eternal gratitude by defeating the minotaur that lived there and rescuing their daughter.

The inhabitants of The Isle of Wonder, which is full of visual puns and nonsense, are sure that their great treasure, the Singing Stone, has been made away with by the ruler of the Isle of the Beast. Alex brings peace between its two rulers, the Red and White

Queens, by ensuring they both have identical lumps of coal to give as wedding presents to Cassima.

The Beast who ruled over the self-named Isle is angry at those from the Isle of the Mists, blaming them for the loss of his jeweled coat of arms. The Beast lived under a curse that would not be lifted until a bride would come to him of her own will, despite his animal exterior. Alexander earns the Beast's friendship by bringing Beauty to him, thus restoring him to manhood.

The druids of the Isle of Mists are convinced that their Sacred Oak is in the possession of the winged folk of the Sacred Mountain. By casting a spell to bring rain and fertility to their island, the druids point the prince to the Isle of the Dead where, they think, it might be possible to restore Cassima's parents to life.

Beyond the gates of death, Alexander challenges the Lord of Death himself, making him cry. Caliphim and Allaria are released to again join the ranks of the living. They head off to assemble the other rulers of the Green Isles, and Alexander dashes off to free Cassima from what he now knows is imprisonment.

Back at the castle, Alex is able sneak inside. In one room he discovers all of the stolen treasures of the islands — Alhazred had been the true thief. In the vizier's study was written proof that not only had Alhazred killed the king and queen, but he intended to kill Cassima after marrying her. Alexander stops the ceremony, discovering that the genie is impersonating Cassima. He chases the fleeing Alhazred to the top of the highest tower and barely prevents him from killing her. In the climactic sword fight, Cassima's bravery allows Alex the opportunity to prevail.

Alexander and Cassima lock eyes. He proposes. She accepts. Her parents relinquish their titles so that Alexander and Cassima marry and become king and queen of the Green Isles. They throw a great wedding reception.

PART TWO

Making It All Click

The people who design computer adventure games have a name for a step-by-step, action-by-action, screen-by-screen written path through their creations. The list of all the mouse clicks and actions necessary for the completion of a game are known as "click-throughs." It's a no-brainer document that lets the game's production team and testers move quickly, top to bottom, through the game to make sure everything works as designed. Click-throughs are sometimes referred to as "walk-throughs" by many people, but we're going with Sierra's terminology. We like it because it suggests both an image of a switch-clicking on the light bulb over our heads when we get stuck, and the sound of the key piece of a puzzle finally falling into place.

Click.

Oh, so that's how it's done!

Our click-through of King's Quest VII follows a straight path through the game. We'll pause as we go along in order to explain alternate solutions to the problems that have them, prepare for what is ahead of us in each chapter, drop special tips, and insert the occasional editorial remark.

Every puzzle and problem is solved in this click-through. To use it, just flip to the game chapter where you need help, and the answer will be there. Use as few, or as many, of the answers as you wish. If you've finished playing, read all the way through to discover some things you might have missed.

But always remember that while seeing the plot unfold and reaching the end of the game is exciting, most of the fun is in the playing. Try figuring out what's going on by yourself first. Discover if you're as clever as those dang-blasted game designers who think they're smarter than you are.

After all, the idea of an adventure is to overcome all obstacles, isn't it?

BUT BEFORE WE CONTINUE

The Princeless Bride begins with an animated cartoon that sets up the coming action. You should watch it at least once. When it's finished, you will be allowed to start the game at the beginning of any of its six chapters.

While this is good in theory, it is best to choose either Chapter 1 or 2 because the story of Valanice picks up in one and Rosella starts in two. Better yet, as the Red Queen commanded in Wonderland, "Begin at the beginning and continue through the middle until you reach the end. Then stop!" This is the path we're following. If you choose a different order, just flip ahead to the game chapter in question and pick up there. Each section of KQ7 is complete in itself; both the paths through the chapters and the solutions to the game's problems stay the same with but a few minor exceptions. We'll point those out as we arrive at them.

It is most important to keep in mind that, despite being able to choose a starting point, The Princeless Bride is a quite linear game. While Rosella and Valanice can move around quite a bit within their virtual worlds, almost everything that happens or that they can do depends on something else happening first. A good example of this is in Chapter 2: Rosella needs to put a troll to sleep. It's not enough just to find the certain item and figure out how do it, however - the troll will never sleep, *even if you do everything else correctly*, unless Rosella overhears a specific conversation about how it's done. In other words, *the order in which you experience things in KQ7 is as important as the things that needs to be done.*

Things that must occur prior to something else happening are called "triggers." King's Quest VII has a lot of triggers, many of them quite obscure. For example, Rosella will never even see the cat needing rescue in Chapter 4 unless she gives a totally unrelated item to a totally unrelated character. She might not even know that the cat's in the game. Because of all these triggers, be careful to follow this click-through step-by-step when you need help. If you're looking for a specific solution to a specific problem, you may have to read back a bit to make sure the proper triggers have been pulled. Strict linearity does have the advantage of ensuring that people pay attention to the game's dramatic thrust, plot, and dialogue to proceed. This, in turn, makes playing The Princeless Bride more like playing a true interactive movie than just another computer adventure game.

THE STORY BEGINS

Valanice, queen of Daventry and mother of Princess Rosella, is attempting (not for the first time, we assume) to talk her daughter into marriage with some prince or another. Rosella's friends are all doing so, Valanice reasons, and Rosella is almost 20 years old, so it's about time that she begins settling down. Perhaps Valanice's anxious to become a grandmother.

Rosella is not too pleased with the idea, preferring to run away from the everyday life of being a beautiful princess, have adventures, and visit fairy tale castles in the sky. She sings of her dreams as her mother drones on, then dives into a looking-pond to follow a tiny dragonet that suddenly appeared, as if from those very dreams.

Valanice hears the splash and sees Rosella disappear under the water. Stopping but to pick up Rosella's comb, the queen jumps in to rescue her daughter. Just as their hands are about to touch, a mysterious arm appears, snatches the princess' arm, and vanishes — along with Rosella.

What's a mother to do?

Chapter One

Where the Blazes Am I?

Goal of the Chapter:

In the first chapter of King's Quest VII, you play the part of Queen Valanice. The goal of this chapter is for Valanice to discover a way out of the desert in which she finds herself stranded and trapped. And stay alive, of course. To do so, she must find two pieces of turquoise that, when put together, form a key that opens a doorway through a colossal stone head.

How to do It:

When the opening cartoon has finished, we find Valanice deposited by a sandstorm into a somewhat barren desert. **(Figure 1-1)** She immediately manages to rip her petticoat on a cactus and then is nearly run over by a rampaging, half-jackrabbit, half-antelope critter known as a jackalope — talk about a great way to start your day.

Figure 1-1

INSIDER INFO: *Replays happen. If you want to replay a particular sequence over (such as the jackalope sequence), it can be done. Either press the ALT and F4 keys at the same time, or click on the Close button at* *the top left corner of the KQ7 window. Select Close. When the message, "The game has not been saved" appears, click on Yes. To replay the sequence, restart the game and continue on from your save. This method only works if you follow Spear's Rule 2 (Winners always quit).*

As soon as the game gives you control of Valanice, look around. Next to Valanice is the cactus, which is still holding fast to the remains of her petticoat. Make note also of the jackalope's path between the two large cacti; you might need to set a jackalope trap there later.

Check your inventory — it's the stuff in the long window at the bottom of the game screen. **(Figure 1-2)** You'll find that, for the moment, Valanice's only possession is Rosella's comb. If you click your cursor on the comb, the cursor will turn into the comb. Now click the comb on the icon that looks like a large eye. This will give you a close-up view of the comb. If you click on the comb now and hold down the left mouse button, you can turn the comb around. Try it. Now close the comb window by clicking the Close box in the upper-left corner of the window.

Figure 1-2

INSIDER INFO: *It is very important to examine everything you find in King's Quest VII this way. As soon as something appears in inventory, move it to the eye icon for a close-up look, and then rotate it. Lots of times — repeat, lots of times — doing this will reveal something important that you'll need, or need to know, to complete your quest.*

There is one more thing to try before we get on with the action. The cursor now should still look like a comb. Click the comb on Valanice. After she has finished crying, return the comb to inventory by clicking the cursor back on the inventory window. To use an inventory item in KQ7, merely click the cursor on it. The cursor will change. If you pass the new cursor over something and the cursor glitters or changes color, then you'll know the item can be used at that time.

Grab the piece of petticoat off of the vicious desert vegetable and proceed to the west (the left side of the screen).

(Figure 1-3) West of the jackalope run is a small pool of salt water and the massive

Figure 1-3

statue of an ancient god. Lying next to the pool is a big stick. Take the stick by clicking your cursor on it, then look into the pool (click on it).

(Figure 1-4) You'll see an idol at the pool bottom, though, unfortunately, there is no way to reach it just yet. The camera pan up from the idol to Valanice is nice, though.

Figure 1-4

Click on the pool again. Salt water. Yuk. Check out the gleaming white salt crystals (the sparkles) at the front of the pool; click on them to pick one up.

INSIDER INFO: *You don't really need to take the salt at this time since Valanice will not be needing it until Chapter 3 and will be returning to the desert then. But, hey, we're here, so take it now, anyway.*

(Figure 1-5) Next, look at the hieroglyphics on the base of the statue. These are the clue to tell you how to turn the salt water in the pool into fresh, drinkable H2O. The translation works out to something like (from left to right):

Hmm. So you have this pool of bad water. Cry into a bowl. Mix in some of the bad water. Put an ear of corn into a hand. Now the water is safe to drink.

Figure 1-5

Or something like that.

Anyway, you can't make the fresh water without having read these symbols, even if you've been reading ahead here and already know how to do so.

Figure 1-6

(Figure 1-6) Look at the statue's blue necklace until you see a close-up (this might take two tries). Notice that the beads move around if you click on any of the empty holes, and that there are four different holes to which each bead can be moved. Retain this information for future use. If you click a bit high on the statue, its head will rotate, changing its visage from water deity to sun god. If this happens, click the head again to set it aright for now.

Once you've done all this, walk south.

Figure 1-7

(Figure 1-7) South of the statue is the beginning of a desert that continues endlessly to the south, west, and east. Wander around if you want, but it is very easy to get lost, and Valanice will die of thirst after she's been there a few minutes (our time).

INSIDER INFO: *This is the Desert Spirit problem. Although we will describe how to meet the ghost, quench his thirst, and receive the stuff made available to Valanice as a result of doing this, we must point out to you that this problem is entirely optional. You don't need to do it. If you choose not to, you don't have to make fresh water. However, Valanice must return to the desert in Chapter 5, and her teleporter drops her in at the spirit's skeleton, and she'll have to walk out. If you solve the Desert Spirit problem, you'll learn the route back to the temple. And you'll have a bit more KQ7 to enjoy.*

(Figure 1-8) *But if you prefer to avoid the desert, you might still need to get the horn. It is in the skeleton screen, two screens south of where Valanice starts the game. If she hasn't given the*

Figure 1-8

water to the skeleton, there will be a whirlwind in this screen when she arrives. The horn will also be there. Click on the horn to get it — it might take a few tries.

Now you can play on without worrying about making water or chatting with the Desert Spirit.

The best way to handle the desert is to walk into it and wait a few moments at the top of the screen. **(Figure 1-9)** What you're looking for is a man in dun clothing — the Desert Spirit. As soon as Valanice sees him, click on the Spirit to start a conversation. Otherwise, he'll wander off the screen and you have to search some more. If the Spirit doesn't appear, step back north, then try again. Do the same if he get away from Valanice. The game randomly decides when to generate his appearance, so he should be there after a few tries. Repeat as often as necessary until the spirit arrives. The thirst timer is reset each time Valanice leaves the desert screen.

Figure 1-9

INSIDER INFO: *We call this technique* ***the edge-of-the-screen trick.*** *It can be used not just to find someone, but to avoid them as well. This trick will come in handy several time throughout KQ7, so keep it in mind.*

Figure 1-10

The Desert Spirit is the ghostly

remains of a traveler who lost his way in the trackless wastes and died of thirst. He'll tell Valanice that he is terribly thirsty and that the only way out of the desert is through a giant, sealed stone head. When the conversation is finished, walk back to the statue. From the statue, walk another screen north. **(Figure 1-10)** Valanice is now at the stone head of which the Desert Spirit spoke.

When you reach the stone head, stop and look around. Paths lead to the south, east, and west, and to the right of the head there is a prickly pear bush. There are some footprints on the ground; look at them. Look at the head, then look again just below it's mouth where the cursor sparkles. The second look allows you a close up view of the head. There, you can see an empty space for an arrow shaped key. Exit the close-up to return to the desert wasteland.

Here we go round the prickly pear. **(Figure 1-11)** Look at the prickly pear bush. There's a fruit on it. Use Valanice's stick to hit the bush and knock the thorny delicacy to the ground. Put the stick back in inventory, pick up the pear, and walk east.

Figure 1-11

Stop east of the colossal head and look around again. **(Figure 1-12)** Several thing need to be examined: there is a cave entrance to the north, a vine with gourds and a patch of damp sand on the left of the screen, and some more hieroglyphics scribed on the rocks to the west.

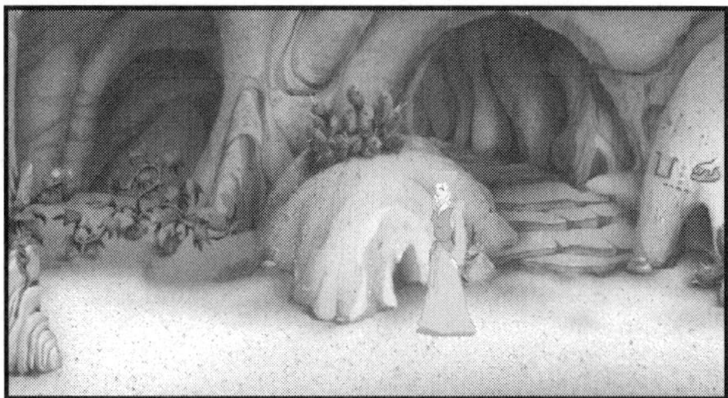

Figure 1-12

Look at the gourds. Look at the ground between them and the large cave, and you'll discover that the sand is wet. Check out the hieroglyphics above the smaller cave (which you can't enter).

(Figure 1-13) The glyphs are telling you how to drain the pond by the statue. The translation (from left to right):

At the pool of bad water
Three blue beads should be lined

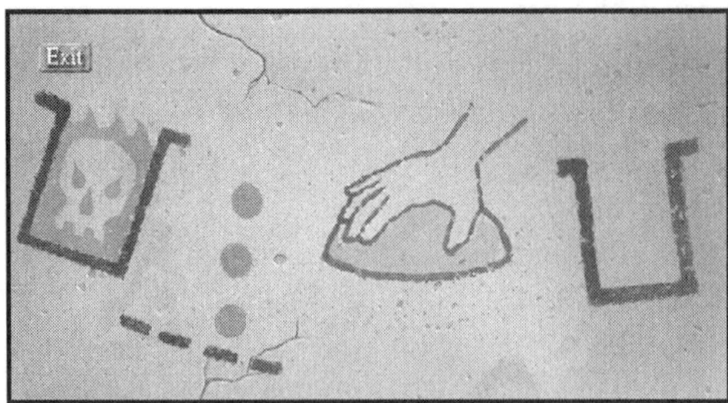

Figure 1-13

Figure 1-14

Figure 1-15

up just so.

Turn the hand holding a bowl over
And the pool will empty.

You can't do anything with the hieroglyphs except appreciate their dubious artistic worth. Walk north into the big cave.

You'll find a small basket on the ground and a row of four clay pots sitting on a ledge. **(Figure 1-14)** Pick up the basket and look at it in inventory. Open the basket by clicking on its lid. Rotate the open basket and remove the kernel of corn you find inside.

(Figure 1-15) Now, one by one, try to take each of the four pots. The first three will shatter and crumble into dust (no matter what order you do it), but Valanice will be able to hold on to the fourth. Since you've now exhausted all of the possibilities for mischief and mayhem inside the cave, go back outside.

(Figure 1-16) Back outside the cave, click the kernel of corn on the wet sand next to the gourd patch. There must be some really good fertilizer in that soil because the little kernel of corn immediately grows into a full, healthy cornstalk, complete with fresh ears of corn. Take an ear so you can make fresh water, then walk one screen east.

INSIDER INFO: *This really is an*

amazing corn stalk. While Valanice is only allowed to carry one ear of corn at a time, she can always go back for another. Make more fresh water, get another. If you possess a high boredom threshold, or are just the kind of person who enjoys doing things like this, the cycle can be repeated endlessly.

Figure 1-16

(Figure 1-17) East of the gourd patch is a small shop named Rare Curiosities and a pair of holes in the ground. The holes are the home of our obnoxious friend, the jackalope. Go ahead, look in one. After Valanice gets startled by the jackalope, walk over and knock on the door of the shop. When the door opens, talk to the proprietor. We assume he's a packrat, although Sierra refers to him as a Kangaroo Rat. Either way, he's not too happy.

Figure 1-17

The rat tells Valanice that the Jackalope has stolen his glasses and that he won't trade with her until he gets them back. The jackalope will then appear to taunt the both of them; when this is over, walk one screen west back to the gourd patch.

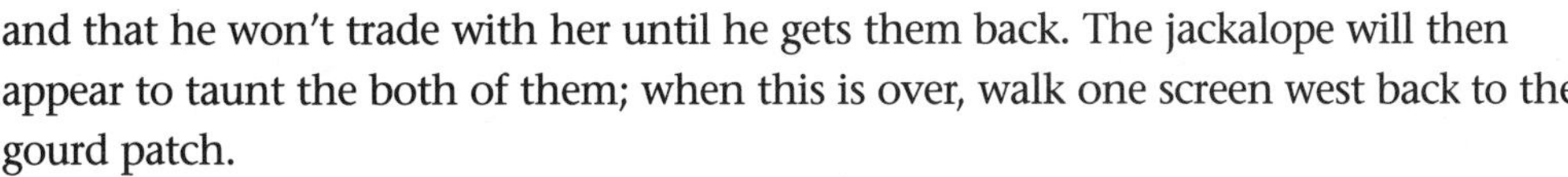

Check out the gourds again. One of them has split open; click on it to take the seed that's inside, then walk back to the statue by the pool.

INSIDER INFO: *Once Valanice has seen the gourd vine, the seed itself will not appear until she has planted the corn, leaves the vine screen, and then returns. This is the game itself playing a variant of the old edge-of-the-screen trick; if you step off the screen and immediately return, the seed will be waiting. KQ7 is observing you, not the opposite.*

When you arrive back at the statue, read the hieroglyphics again. As we translated earlier, what they tell you to do is:

Figure 1-18

1. Cry into the statue's bowl
2. Pour salt water into the bowl
3. Place an ear of corn in the statue's hand

You'll have potable water in no time. Almost as easy as turning on a faucet, eh? Let's do it.

(Figure 1-18) First, click Rosella's comb on the statue's bowl to make her cry into the bowl. If Valanice hasn't clicked the comb on herself and cried already, this won't work, so do that if you're having a problem. Click the clay pot on the salt water. If you now look at the pot in inventory, it will read, "Salt Water." Click the pot of salt water on the bowl. Finally, click the ear of corn on the statue's hand.

With luck, the bowl will glow momentarily, and then you'll have fresh water. If it doesn't, you've done something wrong. Go back and get another ear of corn and try again.

Click the cursor on the bowl. If everything went OK, Valanice will exclaim "Mmm. Fresh!" Dip up a pot full of water and walk south into the desert again.

South of the statue, use the old edge-of-the screen trick to look for the Desert Spirit. When you see him, talk to him again — don't click the pot of water on him, talk first. If he doesn't appear, walk back to the statue, turn around, and try again.

Once you've engaged the Spirit in meaningful conversation, give him the fresh water to quench his eternal thirst. He'll offer to help. At this point, Valanice will automatically follow the Spirit to the final resting place of his earthly remains.

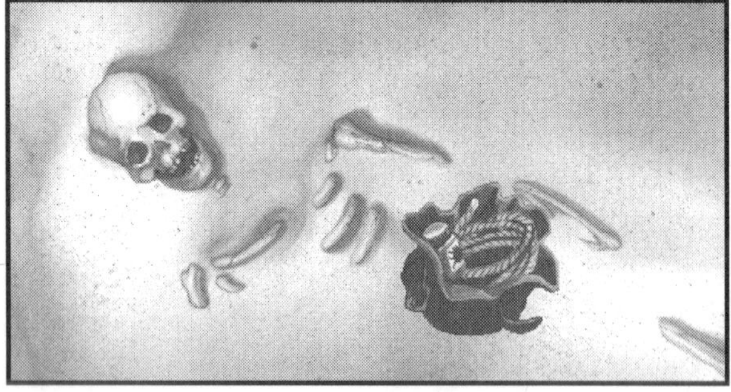

Figure 1-19

(Figure 1-19) At the Desert Spirit's skeleton, the grateful phantom offers Valance a gift. There are two to choose from, and the only information you'll have to go on is what we're writing here. The vial on the left is a bug-reducing powder; the rope on the right is just a rope. While each one has its advantages, taking the bug powder is the better choice.

If you take the rope, you do not get the horn, and you are forced into clothes-lining the jackalope later in order to return the rat's glasses to him. You are also forced to overcome the scorpion in the temple by a means that can lead to Valanice's death if she's not quick enough.

If you take the powder, you get the horn, you retrieve the glasses by blowing the jackalope out of his hole, and the solution to beating the scorpion is faster and safer.

We prefer faster and safer.

Choose whichever item you like. If you take the powder, the horn will be available for Valanice to take after the Spirit disappears. Take it (if available). Walk two screens north. You are now back to where Valanice started the chapter.

Figure 1-20

(Figure 1-20) Walk two screens to the east, and Valanice will be in front of an ancient temple. If you took the rope from the desert spirit, Valanice must now make a flag by clicking the piece of torn petticoat on the stick while they're in inventory. If you have the bug-reducing powder, skip this step and go right on in.

INSIDER INFO: *The temple is really a pyramid, but because of the problems of getting the correct scale between the heights of Valanice and the pyramid, the top was cut off in order to make her entry into it seem more natural.*

Figure 1-21

(Figure 1-21) Valanice will be confronted by a giant scorpion inside the temple, an event that is sure to bug you as well. Click either the flag or the reducing powder on it. The bug-reducing powder shrinks the nasty thing and renders it harmless. If you use the flag, the scorpion will strike at it and embed its stinger in the

Figure 1-22

Figure 1-23

Figure 1-24

wall. If this is the case, you must work fast so Valanice can leave the temple before scorp frees its appendage. And if it does, the queen of Daventry will be killed. This is why we prefer to take the bug powder in the desert.

(Figure 1-22) Once the bug is dealt with, look at the idol at the back of the temple. It sits upon a rune-graven altar. Click on the central rune, the one that looks like a large upside-down teardrop. The rune will turn, allowing a ray of sunlight to strike the idol and causing three colored gems to rise up out of the altar.

Click on the bluish gem and place it in the idol's upraised hand, put the yellow gem in the idol's outstretched hand, and put the red gem on the circular platform to the right of the idol. **(Figure 1-23)** This will cause causes the first piece of the key to the stone head to rise up from the left side of the altar. Take the piece and leave the temple.

It's time to go jackalope hunting. If you have the rope, walk one screen west from outside the temple to where Valanice began the chapter. **(Figure 1-24)** Click the rope on the left of the two cacti that straddle the jackalope's path. Tie the rope between the cacti to trip the jackalope when he shows up. Sure enough, the jackalope comes running along, trips, and leaves in a rather bad mood. **(Figure 1-25)** He also leaves behind a piece of his mangy hide and the packrat's glasses. Take both (look carefully for the fur) and walk back to the packrat's trading post.

Figure 1-25

If you didn't take the rope, click the skeleton's horn on Valanice in order to blow the dust from it. Click it again on the jackalope's hole. **(Figure 1-26)** The somewhat dazed jackalope leaps out of his hole, then falls back inside, leaving behind the packrat's glasses and a piece of the hair off his behind. Take both.

Figure 1-26

INSIDER INFO: *The glasses-jackalope-fur problem is one of only three puzzles in KQ7 that has more than one solution. What you trade with the rat in this sequence is the second. The third problem is how you defeat the scorpion.*

However you obtained the glasses, knock on the rat's door and talk to him to find out that he trades stuff. If he closes his door on Valanice, click again. Click the glasses on the rat to return them to him. The rat will now happily trade with Valanice. Give him the gourd seed you picked up a while back; he will give a blue glass bead in exchange. When you have the bead, leave the trading post and walk back to — you guessed it — the statue.

INSIDER INFO: *If you are taking the "no water, no desert" path through Chapter 1, feel free to trade the corn kernel to the rat. It's the only other thing that he'll trade for the necessary bead. But if you change your mind later and want to grow corn, another kernel will appear in the basket if you look for it.*

Figure 1-27

Figure 1-28

Figure 1-29

It's time to drain the pond.

First, click on the statue's head. This will change it's face to that of a sun god.

Next, click on the statue's necklace. **(Figure 1-27)** This will give you a close-up of the necklace and the three blue beads that are set in it. There are empty spaces next to the beads where they can be moved. Move the beads until they line up like the ones in the screenshot; this order is the same as the blue beads in the hieroglyphic clue above the small cave. We did suggest you pay attention to it.

Finally, click on the hand of the statue that is holding the bowl. It will tip over, and the water will drain out of the pond. Walk Valanice into the empty pool.

(Figure 1-28) Kneeling at the bottom of the pool is an idol holding an offering dish. Look at it; Valanice will see two shapes made out of turquoise. Look at it again in the close-up, and the close-up goes away. Look at the bowl again in the long shot. Place the rat's blue bead in the offering dish — if Valanice hadn't looked the second time, the game would not allow the bead to be placed into the bowl. The second look is the trigger here.

(Figure 1-29) Take something from the bowl; take one, any one. On second thought, of the three objects now on the plate, you want the one that is shaped like the letter "V"; it is the second part of the key needed to open up the colossal stone head. *If Valanice takes either piece without having first placed the bead on the dish, she will be killed.* Take the second key puzzle piece, put the two pieces together in inventory, and leave the pool.

INSIDER INFO: *This is as good a time as any to remind you once again that death is your friend in KQ7. Go ahead, let Valanice get killed just to see what happens to her. Since the game always lets you try again after death, why not satisfy your curiosity?*

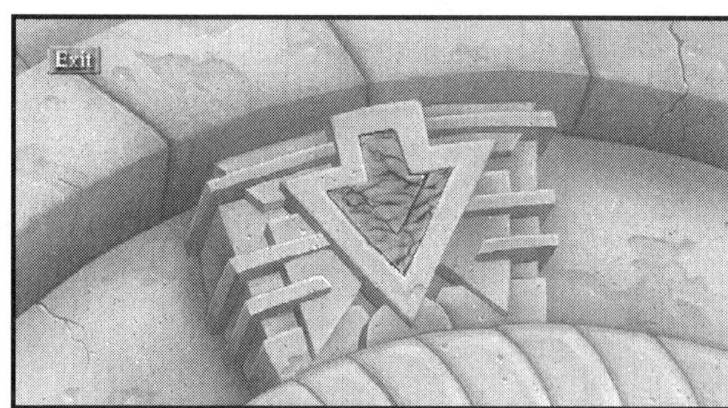

Figure 1-30

When Valanice is back topside, walk north to the stone head. **(Figure 1-30)** Look at the face (just above its lip), and place the completed key in it's slot when the close-up appears. This causes the mouth of the head to grind open, allowing Valanice to enter. Inside is a cave, where Valanice is confronted by an enormous, hungry gila monster.

Chapter 1 abruptly ends in a shameless cliffhanger.

Chapter Two

A Troll Is as a Troll Does

Goal of the Chapter:

In the second chapter of King's Quest VII, you play the part of Princess Rosella of Daventry. The goal of the chapter is for Rosella to escape the Troll Underground and imminent marriage to the Troll King, and to be transformed back into her human form. To do so, she will have to collect the ingredients of a magic potion and discover the details of a foul plot afoot in the land.

How to do It:

Chapter 2 begins with Rosella being dragged through a magic mirror by the king of the trolls. As if that's not bad enough, but she comes through the mirror transformed into a troll. Worse still, she is engaged to be married to King Otar, the Troll King! While this is happening, look closely at the color of the king's eyes. They're green. This is an important detail to remember.

Figure 2-1

The animation ends with Rosella sitting dejectedly in her room in the troll caverns.

Look around. There's nothing to do here right now except look in the mirror or stare at the Troll King's portrait. **(Figure 2-1)**

Notice the king's eyes in the portrait; they're *not* green at all. They're a bluish purple. Did he have a bad night before the portrait was painted? Or is something more sinister?

How did you guess?

INSIDER INFO: *There is a low stool, a cushion, and a small bedside table in Rosella's room. There is nothing you nor Rosella can do with them now, and the cursor will not sparkle when it is moved over them. It would be a mistake to assume this will always be the case.*

Open the door to the west and exit into the great hall.

(Figure 2-2) Upon entering the great hall, Rosella is immediately challenged by Mathilde, King Otar's former nursemaid. She recognizes that Rosella is not a real troll and offers to help make her human again by means of a magical potion. Of course, there are a few ingredients she'll need to gather first. Hmm! (as her mother might say). The required ingredients are:

- Silver Spoon
- Gold Bowl
- Crystal Dragon Scale
- Baked Beetles
- Water of Emeralds (green water)

Figure 2-2

Figure 2-3

(Figure 2-3) After the conversation with Mathilde is finished, a troll child comes in, acts obnoxious, drops a wind-up toy rat on the floor, then leaves for dinner. Take the rat and look around.

One passage leads northwest back to Rosella's room, another leads north to the mud baths. One tunnel goes west to the blacksmith's forge and two lead east: the one at the top of the screen goes to the kitchen and the one at the bottom of the screen leads to the mines.

Figure 2-4

Figure 2-5

Figure 2-6

There is a nasty-looking spiked shield hanging on the north wall, just to the left of the Troll King's throne. Take the shield down and look at it in inventory. Click on the shield to remove the central spike. Now, walk east to the kitchen (use the passage at the top of the screen).

(Figure 2-4) The first time you enter the kitchen, you can't do anything but watch the animation and get thrown out by the cook. However, before Rosella gets pitched back into the great hall, you'll hear that the cook is looking for a nice, juicy rat for his stew. Yummy, yummy!

Back in the great hall, you'll get caught up in another animated sequence, and Rosella will automatically walk north to the mud baths, where a pair of trolls are lounging and talking. **(Figure 2-5)** A tall, imposing woman in black and pink walks by and snorts at them, then leaves. The woman is Malicia, the UBG (Ultimate Bad Gal) of the game, and you'll be seeing a lot of her later on in the story. For now, talk to the trolls to learn a little bit about Malicia — she's supposedly an evil fairy. That done, walk one screen northwest back to the great hall, then back to the kitchen.

When you enter the kitchen this time, click the wind-up rat on the cook and watch him chase the unexpected delicacy out of the room. Don't worry, the rat comes back to you after the cook is gone. **(Figure 2-6)** Put the mechanical rodent back in your inventory and look around.

Check out the stove for mooseburgers.

Against the north wall is an open cabinet full of dishes and bowls, and there's a large box that looks suspiciously like a candy vending machine. First off, take a gold bowl out of the lower shelf of the cabinet. **(Figures 2-7 and 2-8)** Look at it in inventory. Keep it if it has a stamp on the bottom reading "14K gold." If it doesn't, it's the brass bowl. Put it back and take the one on the shelf above it.

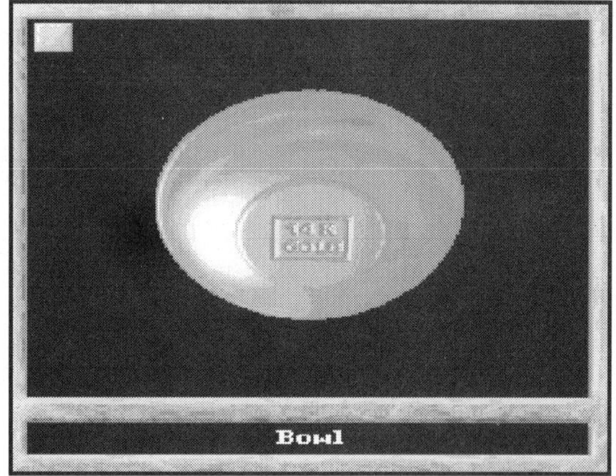

Figure 2-7

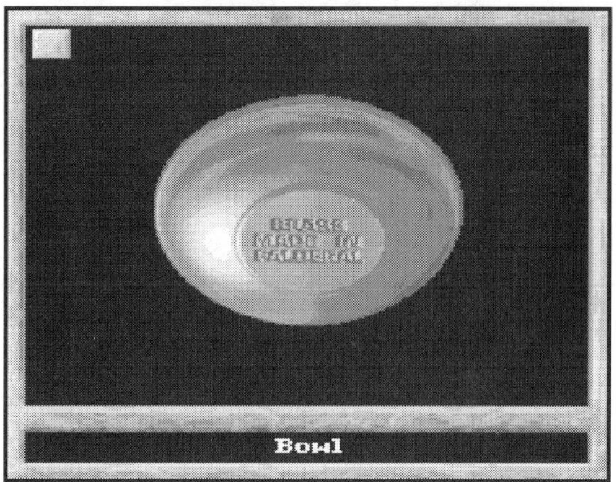

Figure 2-8

Once you have the bowl, click on the brown box-like vending machine to get a handful of baked beetles for your potion. After you have the beetles, walk back to the great hall.

(Figure 2-9) Return to the hot mud bath. There will be two troll women chatting and gossiping. Listen to them as they talk about wet sulfur and sleep. Talk to them a bit, then leave.

INSIDER INFO: *We've written earlier about the triggers in KQ7. You have just pulled an important one by listening to the troll women. If Rosella doesn't make this visit, the wet sulfur sleeping pill will not work later. Does this make sense? From one point of view, Rosella would have no way of knowing what to do with the sulfur if she hadn't overheard. Fine. On the other hand, just because Rosella doesn't hear about it from the women doesn't mean she didn't know about it from some other prior source. And in either case, if the sulfur works at all, it should work even if Rosella stumbles upon the trick completely by accident.*

Figure 2-9

Figure 2-10

Figure 2-11

From the great hall, walk one screen to the lower west, and Rosella will be in the blacksmith's forging area. **(Figure 2-10)** At the 'smith's, look around. Passages lead back north the way you came and down into the sulfur pits. The only thing to do here is talk to the smithy and the jeweler, who also happens to work here.

Talk to the buff blacksmith. Nice guy, for a sexist pig. When he's done hitting on Rosella, talk to the jeweler. He is a much friendlier (and less slimy) chap. The jeweler will tell Rosella that he wishes he had enough money to leave the troll kingdom and lead a civilized life. When she's through speaking to the trolls, follow the passage leading down.

(Figure 2-11) Rosella is now in the sulfur pits. Look around. An old mining lantern hangs on the north wall, and there are several pools of green-tinted water close at hand. A deep crevice — the Pit of Winds — bisects the chamber, and across it, on the top left corner, is a patch of wet sulfur. Getting to it is the problem. Here's the route:

(Figure 2-12) Walk to the point closest to the pit near the screen's center. This will take you two tries.

(Figure 2-13) Jump to the little island in the middle of the pit.

(Figure 2-14) Jump to the safe spot at the top left corner. You've made it. Click on the wet sulfur to retrieve a lump, then carefully return the way you came.

Back across the pit, take the lantern off the wall. Finally, click the gold bowl from the kitchen on the pool nearest the entrance to fill it up with the "water of emeralds." Now that you're done looting the sulfur pits, return to the blacksmith's forge. Once Rosella has returned to the forge, notice that the blacksmith is pouring silver into a spoon mold. Click the wet sulfur on the fire in the forge. The blacksmith will breathe the sulfur fumes, get giddy, and fall asleep. As soon as he's snoring, look at the mold on the table next to the troll and notice that it's too hot to touch. Grab the tongs off the tool rack against the north wall — they're the ones at the far left.

This will give you a "tongs" cursor, not an inventory item. **(Figure 2-15)** Use the tongs to pick up the spoon mold and dump it in the bucket of water next to the anvil. Rosella now has the silver spoon that was in the mold. Return the tongs to their place on the wall. Return to the sleeping troll and pump the bellows at the forge to make the fire leap and throw sparks. When

Figure 2-12

Figure 2-13

Figure 2-14

Figure 2-15

Figure 2-16

Figure 2-17

this happens, click the lantern on the leaping flames to capture a spark. Whew! That was a lot of stuff to do. Return to the great hall.

From the great hall, walk east into the mines (take the passage at the bottom of the screen). **(Figure 2-16)** Look around. An inoperable bucket lift leads up into Ooga Booga Land — check it out. A decrepit mining cart with a missing wheel sits in the mud to the north — look at it, too. There is also a bridge crossing a lava river.

Attempt to cross the bridge. When you do, a toll troll crawls out onto the bridge and won't let Rosella pass. Talk to him. Ignore what he demands. Walk back to the broken mining cart and look at it again.

(Figure 2-17) Click the shield on the cart to replace the missing wheel. Click the spike on the shield wheel to hold it in place. Select the Ride option. Whee! Off Rosella goes. The cart barrels into the troll and knocks him off the bridge, leaving the way across open. After the dust and bits of cart settle, walk two screens to the east to the crystal dragon.

(Figure 2-18) In the dragon's chamber, have Rosella talk to the overgrown lizard (this will take several clicks). She'll learn that the dragon has lost her will to live — she needs to find her spark. Give the dragon the spark from the blacksmith's forge by clicking the lit lantern on it. **(Figure 2-19)** The joyful dragon rewards Rosella with an enormous diamond and flies off before you can get one of her scales. But that's easily rectified.

Walk back to the forge and give the jeweler the dragon's gem. He, too, will rejoice, then give Rosella his old hammer and chisel before he heads off to see the world and join the ranks of civilized society.

Once you have the jeweler's tools, walk back to the dragon's lair. The dragon will be back and sound asleep by now. Click on the dragon to talk with her. No answer.

Click Rosella's hand on the dragon's tail. Click the hammer and chisel on her tail to — Stop! Don't use the hammer and chisel right away. Rosella can die if the dragon's tail hits her as she attempts to remove a scale. **(Figure 2-20)** Look closely at the screenshot. Wait a bit until the dragon's tail slaps the floor and stays. Click the hammer and chisel on Rosella to safely get a scale. Rosella now has all the ingredients necessary to concoct the magic potion.

Figure 2-18

Figure 2-19

Figure 2-20

Figure 2-21

Return (again!) to the great hall and talk to Mathilde. Give her the gold bowl full of emerald water. Then give her the baked beetles, the silver spoon, and the crystal scale in any order you like. She'll whip up a potion, and after a few mishaps, Rosella will be human again. The silver spoon melts in the process, leaving Rosella with a silver pellet as a souvenir, an essential item for later in the game.

INSIDER INFO: *Mathilde does not have a lot of patience. If Rosella takes too long giving the stuff to her, she'll end the magic potion sequence and sit down. If this happens, just click the next ingredient on the nursemaid and she'll pick-up where Mathilde left off. The scene is played this way in case a player would rather give Mathilde each of the items as they are discovered.*

(Figure 2-21) As soon as Rosella is her true self again, Malicia and the Troll King appear, and Rosella is teleported back to her room again, accompanied by the threat that Malicia will soon be back to "take care of her." Doesn't that make you feel so much better?

Figure 2-22

Look around in Rosella's room. Check out the portrait of the Troll King that graces the north wall — it now has steam coming from out of it's nostrils, a sure sign that there is something hidden behind it. Notice again that the king's eye color is not green. You need to climb up and remove it.

(Figure 2-22) To do so, make a stack of furniture. You have one nightstand, a footstool, and a cushion to work with. As we noted before, these were immovable objects the first time

Rosella was here, but not now. Place the nightstand on the ground beneath the picture. Next, put the footstool on top of the nightstand. Finally, drop the cushion on top of both of them. Rosella climbs up, removes the portrait, and climbs inside.

Figure 2-23

(Figure 2-23) When Rosella is inside the airshaft, she will automatically peek through a hole in the wall and spy on a conversation between Malicia and the Troll King. **(Figure 2-24)** The two evil-doers are discussing how to start a volcano to bury Ooga Booga and the kingdom of Etheria as well. Nice folks. Notice again the king's eye color — green. But in the portrait it was not green. Something must be amiss.

Figure 2-24

As soon as their conversation is over, crawl east, toward the light at the end of the tunnel. Rosella will fall out of the airshaft and tumble into the great hall.

When Rosella lands in the great hall, she knocks something down from its perch on the back of the throne. It's the king's pet dragon toad. Pick up the toad, then try to re-enter Rosella's room. Before Rosella can do so, Malicia appears and starts threatening Mathilde, who responds in kind. Before things get too ugly, Malicia is scared by a bat and leaves, screaming that one day she'll destroy all rats and bats. Apparently she isn't a rodent fancier.

Leave the great hall, then immediately re-enter it. Talk to Mathilde, then show her King Otar's dragon toad. Rosella tells Mathilde that "Otar" is an impostor and that the real Troll King is imprisoned somewhere above in Ooga Booga. Mathilde gives Rosella a magical snake rope to fix the bucket lift to Ooga Booga.

Figure 2-25

Walk east to the bucket lift. Malicia will appear again and threaten Rosella. Click the trusty old wind-up toy rat on Malicia (she really doesn't like rodents!). Malicia taken care of, walk east to the bucket elevator.

(Figure 2-25) When Rosella reaches the bucket lift, click Mathilde's snake rope on the lift to repair it. Click on the lift again to start upwards toward Ooga Booga. As the lift ascends, the shaft begins to collapse about Rosella's head.

Talk about a real downer.

Thus endeth Chapter 2.

Chapter Three

The Sky Is Falling!

Goal of the Chapter:

Chapter 3 picks up where Chapter 1 left off, with Valanice being menaced by a giant, hungry, gila monster in a narrow cave. Her goal (other than surviving her immediate predicament) is to learn all she can about where Rosella might be.

How to do It:

(Figure 3-1) Feed the prickly pear to the gila monster and it will go away — whether it's because of a full stomach or a mouth full of spikes is unclear. Once the oversized reptile has departed, walk northwest out of the cave.

Figure 3-1

INSIDER INFO: *KQ7 allows players to start the game at the beginning of any chapter. If you jump to Chapter 3 without having either played or finished Chapter 1, Valanice won't have the prickly pear or the grains of salt in her inventory. Since they are most needed now, the game allows Valanice to escape back to the desert to obtain them before them monster chomps her. If you don't know how to get the items, refer to page 17.*

Figure 3-2

(Figure 3-2) Valanice emerges from the cave into a beautiful forest glade. A rather unattractive mud-choked stream bed crosses the glade. The stream is flanked by a pair of statues — one holding a jug and the other a cornucopia. The mud is straddled by the span of a shattered marble bridge. A patch of heavenly smelling flowers sprouts from the rocks on the west edge of the stream, though these are far out of Valanice's reach.

Look around. For the now, the only ways out are west or south in the direction you came. The only thing to do here right now is leave. Go west.

Figure 3-3

(Figure 3-3) West of the glade is a massive oak tree bleeding sap from the vicious spike stuck in its trunk. Beneath the tree sits a stag (Attis). He rises and warns Valanice that the woods are not safe to travel through. Talk to him to learn his tragic story. Keep talking to him until he has absolutely nothing else to say. You need to hear his entire story, including the part about the Rock Spirit, to make the River of Life flow later.

Click Rosella's comb on Attis to ask about Rosella. He will say that he has heard that she is to be married to King Otar, the Troll King. He also tells Valanice that the only entrance to the Troll King's realm is to the west, past the were-woods. To pass through the were-woods, he adds, Valanice must visit a merchant in the town of Falderal. Once she is done speaking with the stag, walk one screen west.

INSIDER INFO: *What is it about trolls that makes many people dislike even the thought of them? At the beginning of the game, Valanice was nagging Rosella getting married. Now, we can understand why Rosella might be put off by the Troll King once she's met him, and once she's* *been **told** that she's to be his bride. After all, a girl should get some say in the matter. And, up close and personal, Otar might have been quite off-putting.*

*But Valanice's reaction puzzles us. She wanted Rosella married to one prince or another, and by the tone of her remarks, it didn't seem to matter much which one. So when Attis tells Valanice that Rosella is to be married, and to a **King**, why does she react so negatively? It can only be the mere fact of his trollness.*

Figure 3-4

(Figure 3-4) West of Lord Attis and his oak tree is a nondescript patch of forest with paths leading north, west, and east. There is nothing to do here, but be warned: Do not go any further west or Valanice will be in the were-woods where (no pun intended) she will be eaten by a were-bear. **(Figure 3-5)** Valanice needs a special salve to survive the woods and won't obtain it until Chapter 5.

Figure 3-5

Now that you know this, eschew the western route and walk one screen north.

North of the entrance to the were-woods are the head waters of the dysfunctional stream. **(Figure 3-6)** Stepping stones lead north across it's muddy expanse, and a very large spider web is barely visible on the other side. Carefully (Valanice can sink and die in the

Figure 3-6

Figure 3-7

mud) walk across the stepping stones one stone (one click) at a time.

(Figure 3-7) At the spider web, you will see a spider struggling with a frantic hummingbird. Quickly click the basket on the spider to catch it. Click on the hummingbird to free her from the web. This also gets rid of the web, which blocks the path to Falderal. The birdie will thank Valanice and leave, but don't worry, she'll be back when you need her. Now that you've done your good deed for the moment (there are *a lot more* good deeds ahead), walk northwest. This will take Valanice to the gates of Falderal, otherwise known as Nonsense Land.

Figure 3-8

(Figure 3-8) At the main gate of Falderal, Valanice will be denied access by the archduke's guard. However, there are two gates into Falderal; just click on the small door to the right of the main gate to enter Nonsense Land despite the guard's rather absurd threats.

INSIDER INFO: *For some folks, the guard's badgering (so to speak) can grow old fast. There is a way to bypass conversations in cases where there is no fast-forward option. If you click your mouse during a speech, the game will jump to the end of whatever line of dialogue is being spoken. So you can click through, line by line, any conversation you don't want to endure again.*

(Figure 3-9) Inside Falderal, Valanice will be confronted by a real dog of an archduke who tells her that she has no business in the town. Click Rosella's comb on him. Sympathetic to the point of tears, the archduke will now allow Valanice to wander freely around town. Ignore Chicken Petite (Chicken Little's separated-at-birth twin), who's running around yelling, "The sky is falling!" Notice a path leading west out of town, a path leading east, and entrances to both a China Shop and Town Hall to the north. Town Hall has a sign on the door which you can't read right now, so walk into the China Shop.

(Figure 3-10) Talk to the proprietor. He might be a real load of a bull, but everything he says is true. He's depressed and wishes that his stolen china bird, Treasure, would come back. Listen to his story. Look at the mask on the cabinet on the right side of the screen. Leave the shop and walk one screen to the east.

(Figure 3-11) East of Town Hall, at the far end of Falderal, is the wagon of the snake-oil salesman. Go there and look around. There is a fountain containing a mockingbird in a nest and a covered cage sitting to the right of the salesman's wagon. There is also an entrance to the Faux Shop, a place that is best taken with a grain of salt.

Click on the mockingbird to talk to him. Talk to him as much as you like — he has dozens of one-liners and put-downs for Valanice. Actually, let's rephrase that: Talk to the bird as much as you can *stand*.

Talk to the snake-oil salesman. He will tell Valanice that he can sell her a magic salve that will get her through the were-woods in safety. In exchange, he wants a magical statuette that is in the archduke's mansion.

Figure 3-9

Figure 3-10

Figure 3-11

Figure 3-12

Figure 3-13

Figure 3-14

(Figure 3-12) After you're done talking to the snake-oil salesman, click on the cage to the right of the wagon to uncover it. Inside is Treasure, the china bird. Click on the cage again to open it. Click on Treasure to talk to her and get her to leave the cage. Once you have the china bird along for the ride, return to the China Shop. Give Treasure back to the proprietor. In return, he will give Valanice the fine china mask. Once Valanice has the mask, leave the shop — it's time to go crash the archduke's masquerade ball.

Once outside the China Shop, watch the guests entering Town Hall, then look at the announcement on the Town Hall door again. Click the mask on Valanice to have her put it on, then click on the door another time. This time, Valanice will be allowed into the party.

(Figure 3-13) At the ball, ignore the archduke and the happy party-goers. Click on the tapestry on the north wall to move it, revealing the entrance to a passageway. Valanice will automatically follow this passageway north.

(Figure 3-14) The next room consists of two sets of very weird stairs, one leading up and the other leading down. Follow the stairs leading down. Keep following them down (no matter what Valanice's orientation) until you come to the door to the powder room in the far right corner of the screen.

Click twice on the door. The first time, Valanice will get socked in the face by a powder puff. The second click will allow her to enter.

The powder room is furnished in a tasteless, garish, and painfully bright fashion. There is a statue of Cupid on one table. Look at the plaque at its base; it's so tarnished, it can't be read — by Valanice, anyway. Rosella will take a shot at cleaning it in Chapter 4, but remember it's there.

(Figure 3-15) Ignore the other prominent aesthetic nightmares and focus instead on the three mirrors on the north wall. Click on the third one to the right of the door. An upside-down image of Valanice will appear and drag her through the mirror and into the archduke's study.

(Figure 3-16) Look around inside the archduke's study. Open the desk drawer and take the statuette from inside it.

(Figure 3-17) Click Rosella's comb on the statuette; Valanice will then have a vision of Rosella in the sinister land of Ooga Booga. Pop the statuette into inventory,

Figure 3-15

Figure 3-16

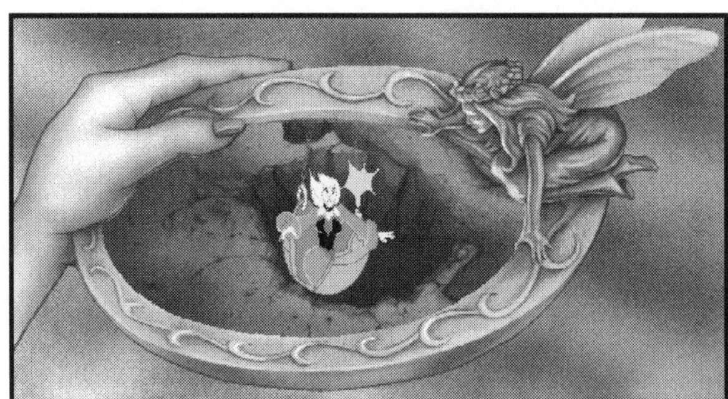

Figure 3-17

Figure 3-18

click on the door in the east wall, and leave the study. Ah, the stairs once more. Just keep moving forward and exit to the bottom center of the screen, the way she came in.

Once Valanice is back at the party, leave Town Hall and walk back to the snake oil wagon.

(Figure 3-18) It turns out that Chicken Petite was right after all. When Valanice enters the wagon room this time, the moon will fall from the sky into the fountain, scaring away the mockingbird and hopelessly traumatizing Chicken Petite. Attempt to get the moon by clicking on the fountain.

INSIDER INFO: *Valanice will be unable to trade for the book in the Faux Shop sequence unless she attempts to get the moon out of the fountain first.*

Look in the mockingbird's nest to get a wooden nickel.

The snake-oil salesman is taking a break and will not return until Chapter 5. Drat.

Attempt to enter the Faux Shop. Click the salt crystals on Valanice and try again. She'll eat the salt and will be able to enter the shop. That's taking things with a grain of salt, indeed!

(Figure 3-19) Once inside the Faux Shop, take the time to click around to look at the weird stuff. Talk to the shopkeeper, a mock turtle, of course, then give him the wooden nickel. Valanice will get a book.

Figure 3-19

Look at the book in inventory; it's titled "The Wit and Wisdom of Falderal." Click on the book, and it opens to reveal the wit and wisdom of that odd city. Empty platitudes all. Next, offer the china mask and receive a rubber chicken in return. Look at the synthetic fowl in inventory; click on it to get a feather — don't ask us how it got there. You now have everything Valanice needs to get from the Faux Shop. Leave the shop. Leave Falderal.

INSIDER INFO: *We have already pointed out that there are only three problems in King's Quest VII that have more than one solution. In the following sequence, Valanice will attempt to return the stag Attis to his true form by restarting the River of Life. What makes this puzzle unique is that while it has one solution, Valanice has more than one opportunity to solve it — now in Chapter 3 or later in Chapter 5. If you'd like to hold off until later, please do. We're going ahead with it here, and you can meet up with us when we're finished.*

From the gates of Falderal, walk three screens east. **(Figure 3-20)** You should now be at the resting place of the Rock Spirit, who happens to be a moss covered bunch of rocks in the shape of a head. He's truly a monster of rock. And he snores.

Figure 3-20

Tickle the Rock Spirit's nose with the rubber chicken feather. The Spirit will awaken and tell Valanice that she can restart the River of Life by pouring sacred nectar into the jug of one of the river statues, and that by placing sacred food in the other statue's cornucopia, she will restore Attis' wife, Ceres. Not bad for one rubber chicken feather.

Once you have heard the Rock Spirit's instructions, walk two screens west and one screen south to the stepping stones. Cross them carefully again. Go one screen south and two screens east (passing Attis along the way), back to the ruined bridge and the river statues.

Figure 3-21

Figure 3-22

Figure 3-23

At the bridge/statue room, click on the patch of flowers growing on the rock escarpment on the west side of the screen. These are the source of the nectar about which the Rock Spirit spoke. **(Figure 3-21)** The flowers are far out of Valanice's reach, but the hummingbird she freed from the spider web will fly up and offer to retrieve some nectar for her. When the bird asks if Valanice has a vessel to hold the nectar, click the clay pot on her, and she will proceed to fill it with nectar.

(Figure 3-22) After the hummingbird has left, click the pot on the statue holding the jug. The jug will fill with nectar and start the River of Life flowing again. The broken bridge will be mended with a rainbow, and Attis the stag will appear, drink from the River of Life, and become human again. Attis will go to the oak tree to pull out the spike that wounded the tree to try to heal it. He will not be able to until Valanice refills the cornucopia in Chapter 5.

When the animation with Attis and the tree is over, walk one screen east, one screen south, and one screen southeast. Valanice will be back in front of the giant stone head in the desert. Walk east to the rat's trading post. Knock on the door and offer him the book from the Faux Shop. Valanice will get a shepherd's crook in return. Once you have the crook, walk all the way back to the snake-oil salesman's wagon in Falderal.

It's a long walk, but you should know the way by now.

(Figure 3-23) Back at the salesman's wagon, click the shepherd's crook on the pond to fish the moon out. No, there's no stated, nor logical, reason for Valanice to do this, but what the heck, do it anyway. It triggers another cliffhanger ending.

As soon as Valanice has her hands on the moon, the archduke and his guard arrive to arrest her for stealing it. With Valanice's fate left hanging, Chapter 3 is now done.

Chapter Four

Will the Real Troll King Please Stand Up?

Goal of the Chapter:

In the fourth chapter of King's Quest VII, you pick up the story of Rosella as she attempts to escape from a collapsing elevator shaft. The goal of this part of the game is for Rosella to escape (and survive) Ooga Booga Land, free the real Troll King, and make her way to the room where the soon-to-be-exploded volcano is controlled.

How to do It:

As Chapter 4 begins, an ominous man with a large shovel is standing over the helpless Rosella. **(Figure 4-1)** Will he attempt to kill her as she hangs from the edge of the collapsing shaft?

Figure 4-1

As soon as you have control of the cursor, click on the shovel. The gravedigger will help Rosella from the hole, then return to his trade. As this happens, the shaft collapses in the background.

(Figure 4-2) Talk to the gravedigger; he will measure

Figure 4-2

Rosella for a grave. Talk to him some more and he will tell about his grave-digging machine and rat. Keep talking until he has nothing else to say. The conversation about the rat is a trigger for something to come.

(Figure 4-3) Look at the doors to the crypt when the gravedigger stores his machine. The skull, bat, and spider symbols are the solution for a later puzzle. Remember them because they are a lock combination Rosella needs later.

Figure 4-3

INSIDER INFO: *Warning! Rosella cannot afford to linger here or in any other outdoor location in Ooga Booga. The Boogeyman is lurking about underground and will, without warning, jump out and kill her. Depending on how close to Rosella the B-Man is when he pops up, Rosella can survive the encounter if you immediately walk her off to another screen. But if the two are too close, death is inevitable. Consider yourself warned.*

The best strategy in Ooga Booga is to do what needs to be done as efficiently as possible, then get on to the next room. If the Boogeyman is there when Rosella arrives, step back out at once, then return. If he shows up and she can escape, just walk right back in; he'll be gone. This is another application of the old edge-of-the-screen trick.

INSIDER INFO: *Both here and elsewhere in Ooga Booga, find the time to read the inscriptions on the tombstones. Besides being somewhat amusing, they are a direct reference to King's Quest IV: The Perils of Rosella where our heroine needed to read a lot of tombstones in order to survive the adventure. The ones here are optional, but fun. That's why we play games.*

Move west one screen. **(Figure 4-4)** Rosella is now in front of a ruined old house. Look at the graffiti on the wall — it's the lock combination again, just in case you need a reminder. The dog with glowing red eyes is of no concern to Rosella. Walk south through the gate.

Figure 4-4

(Figure 4-5) This is the tomb of the Headless Horseman, although Rosella will never learn this fact. Once Rosella begins walking, he'll fly overhead. The sobbing woman is the grieving shade of his wife, Elspeth. Do not — DO NOT — click on her at all; Rosella will die. Valanice will deal with the Woman in Black in Chapter 5. Rosella must avoid her. Walk east to the undertaker's house.

Figure 4-5

(Figure 4-6) The first time Rosella's here, there will be an animation of the ghoul kids spray-painting the house and bedeviling the undertaker's black cat. When it's finished, look at the mailbox. Great name. If you look at the gate, Rosella will close it for no particular reason. Open it again and click on the door. Dr. Cadaver will let Rosella inside.

Figure 4-6

Once the good doctor has finished his opening remarks, talk to him some more. Keep talking until he has nothing more to say. **(Figure 4-7)** Look around the

Figure 4-7

Figure 4-8

Figure 4-9

office. There are a few gags here, but if you look at the coffin-couch, you will be given a clue as to how Valanice will need to use it in Chapter 5.

Now that Rosella knows the Doc needs a backbone, leave the office through the door you came in. It is the only exit.

Outside, walk east to the creepy treehouse.

INSIDER INFO: *Now that we've mentioned Valanice's connection to Ooga Booga twice, it might seem superfluous for us to note that mama will be spending a lot of time amongst the tombstones. You're right. It is.*

Now it's time now for a major dose of the edge-of-the-screen trick. Rosella needs to get up into the treehouse to get the backbone. However, if the kids are at home when she gets up there, she's a goner.

(Figure 4-8) When Rosella arrives in this screen, she will see one of two things: a ghoul kid climbing up and going inside or no kids at all. If the climbing sequence appears, step back off the screen and return. If you see it again, back off again. When they're not climbing, it's safe to go up.

However, it is not safe for Rosella to climb the way the kids do. There is a rope to the left of the climbing web; click on it, and another bucket elevator will take Rosella inside.

(Figure 4-9) We know that we collect some weird stuff, but this place has us beaten. Look around inside the treehouse but *do not click on the thing-in-a-box* at the lower center of the screen. It's death.

The backbone is on the floor in a package between the *thingy* and the tiny coffin. Take it. Take the foot-in-a-bag from the tiny coffin. Click on the big mummy for laughs. Click on the shrunken heads on the back table, too. By now, the ghoul kids might know there's a burglar. It's time to make an exit. To get out of the treehouse, either click on the elevator rope, or climb through the window near the top of the screen. Whee!

Figure 4-10

Return to Doc Cadaver's office. Knock. Give the Doc the backbone, and Rosella will get what every young girl wants more than anything in the whole, wide world — a weird pet in a box. Leave Doc to his studies and return to the treehouse — weird pets need weird homes. Rosella will not be able to return to the undertaker's office now until she frees the Troll King.

(Figure 4-10) The animated rhyming sequence that begins this treehouse visit is a clue for when Rosella will attempt to enter the Boogeyman's home in a bit. This scene will not happen until Rosella has returned the backbone.

INSIDER INFO: *The clue translates as follows:* ***There is a branch shaped like a snake in the deadfall screen.***

If the branch points down, Rosella won't die when the deadfall is cleared away.

If the branch points up, she will meet the boogie, man. Fatally.

Figure 4-11

When you have control of the cursor again, click on the kids to talk with them. When they lower the elevator and invite Rosella to their room, do not accept. Click the weird pet on the rope. After a bit, something will fly out of the treehouse. Rosella has received the gravedigger's rat.

Guess where she's going now? Walk north by northwest back to the gravedigger. **(Figure 4-11)** Give the rat to the gravedigger. Rosella is given a horn and offered a free grave. Now *that's* what every young girl wants! Once the gravedigger's machine is fired up, leave the screen and return. Rosella will now see the shovel, which the gravedigger has discarded. Take the shovel. Return to the treehouse. Yes, again.

INSIDER INFO: *Just how is Rosella carrying the horn and shovel, not to mention the sooty lantern and the like? For that matter, where does Valanice hide her stuff? It isn't as if the horn from the desert is small or the prickly pear is of the non-stick variety.*

This is the classic problem of computer adventure games. For us, it reached its logical extreme in Sierra's Leisure Suit Larry V: Passionate Patti Does a Little Undercover Work when, in a pre-release version, it was pointed out that in one sequence, Patti was forced to ride down glass elevator completely naked, but still carried a full load of inventory stuff.

The solution to the Classic Problem of Computer Adventure Games is simple: Don't worry about it. It's only a game.

Figure 4-12

It's always party time with the ghoul kids.

(Figure 4-12) This time Rosella finds them torturing Dr. Cadaver's cat and preparing to bury it alive. This scene will not occur until Rosella has returned the rat.

Once the kids have left, use the hammer and chisel to free kitty. The cat tells Rosella where the real Troll King is imprisoned. She also gives Rosella an Extra Life. Since The Princeless Bride is not an arcade game where extra lives come with the territory, we'll have to assume that somebody will need to be brought back to life later.

Rosella is finished with the ghoul kids.

Walk two screens west to the tomb of the Headless Horseman.

Walk one screen south.

Rosella is in the Deadfall room where the B-Man makes his permanent home under the big pile of branches. It's time for the edge-of-the-screen trick again.

(Figure 4-13) The snake-like branch the clue refers to is in the left-center of the screen, and there is nothing to set it apart from any of the other branches. It's colored purple, not blue. The cursor will not change at all to indicate it's even there. The best way to figure out which branch it is is to look at the screenshots we've provided. **Figure 4-14** indicates that boogey is not home.

If the B-Man is in when Rosella arrives, leave the room and return. Continue as often as necessary until it's safe.

Click on the deadfall. Cool move. Blow the gravedigger's horn by clicking it on Rosella. He'll show up, clear the deadfall, and dig a hole. Click on the hole to enter it.

At the bottom of the hole is a great coffin. **(Figure 4-15)** Click on the lock to bring up the close-up of it. Remember your lesson in Ooga Booga graffiti. Click in this order: skull, bat and spider. The lock will open and reveal the true King Otar. Take a moment to notice his eye color — the real king's eyes in the portrait are not green, and neither are this Troll King's. Otar is the True Troll King! Huzzah!

Figure 4-13

Figure 4-14

Figure 4-15

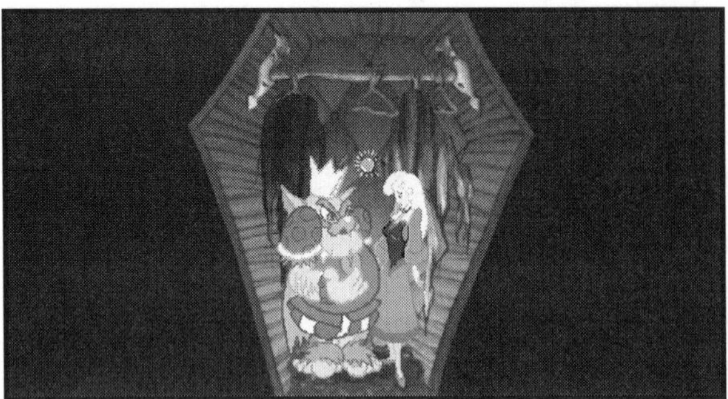

Figure 4-16

Of course, Malicia would choose this moment to appear, wouldn't she?

(Figure 4-16) When cursor control is finally passed back to the player, click the dragon toad on the king. Click the hammer and chisel on the king. This sequence has a timer attached to it; if you take too long to use the toad, the Boogeyman will get Rosella. And her little Troll King, too.

Figure 4-17

(Figure 4-17) Rosella and king Otar emerge in the cemetery. After some chatter, the game automatically will put King Otar — now a scarab beetle — into her inventory. It also will add a magic wand so that Rosella can turn Otar trollish again. And, of course, it will be used transform the appearance of the mystery guest star of the game (who has yet to make a real appearance).

When Otar tuns into a scarab, a black veil will materialize out of thin air. Take the black veil; it's a disguise. Click it on Rosella so she can wear it. Rosella is now disguised, and the Boogeyman won't attack her as long as she is like this. Also, if the ghoul kids see her like this, she'll scare them away.

INSIDER INFO: *"So," you may think, "Rosella will never see B-Man again?"* ***Au contraire!*** *Boogey will still pop up, but instead of jumping on Rosella, he'll mistake her for the Woman in Black and pester her about leaving her husband for him. Showing admirably keen taste, Rosella will treat him as a lecher and tell him to kiss off. Way to go, Rosella!*

(Figure 4-18) Look at the magic wand in inventory. Rotate it. The bulbish business-end should have the letter "T" inscribed on it.

(Figure 4-19) Find the glitter point on the wand's grip and click. Revolve the wand again. **(Figure 4-20)** The inscription should now show the letter "F."

The magic wand has two settings:

T turns someone (even if they're a scarab) into a troll.

F turns them into a faerie.

For the time being, forget we ever mentioned faeries. Reset the wand to **T**.

INSIDER INFO: *While the wand allows Rosella to turn the scarab Otar into the troll Otar nearly anywhere, there is only one place she can do this safely without getting terminated by a gargoyle.*

Transform Otar now, if you'd like, to see what happens.

It doesn't get any better with repetition.

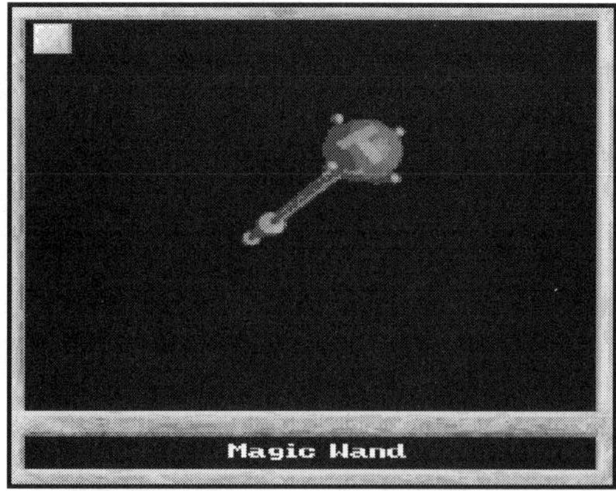

Figure 4-18

Figure 4-19

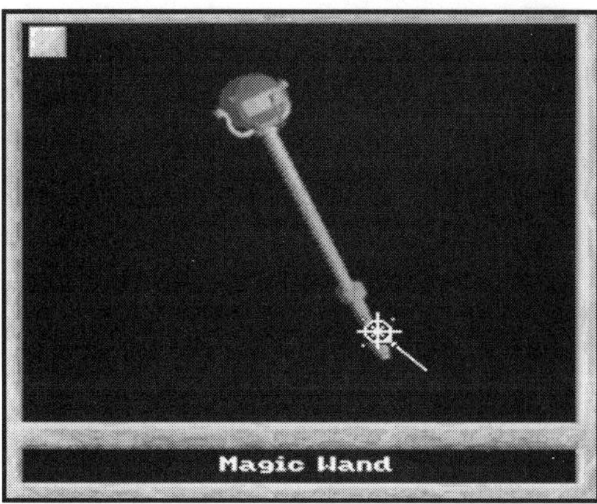

Figure 4-20

Go north from the cemetery being careful not to step into the open grave. Rosella will be back at the undertaker's house. Enter the house. Talk to Doc and receive an atomizer of defoliant. Look around a bit, then leave.

From Doc's place, walk east to the treehouse, then south to the gates of the cemetery.

If you haven't noticed by now, Ooga Booga Land is a cemetery. Rosella is now standing outside of it. **(Figure 4-21)** A swamp thing will immediately attack her. Spray the defoliant on the mossy creature to defeat it.

Click on the singing flowers to talk with them, but stay back. They're man-eaters, but they're not as sexist as their description, and their behavior, might make one believe — they'll eat women as well as men. **(Figure 4-22)** There is a red, fragrant flower at the base of the plants that Rosella will need. Click the foot-in-a-bag on the plants. Yum! While

Figure 4-21

Figure 4-22

Figure 4-23

they eat, click on the flower to take it.

Follow the path east to the front of the ominous stone building.

(Figure 4-23) Rosella has arrived at Malicia's house. Attempt to continue walking. After Otar is finished talking, follow the path east some more but exit the screen to the north, not the east.

Warning: *Don't even think about knocking on Malicia's door.*

Don't even think about clicking on the gargoyle.

Trust us on these.

INSIDER INFO: *This is the same gargoyle that attacks Rosella if she transforms the Troll King at the wrong time.*

(Figure 4-24) The way into Malicia's is from the back of her house. This screen is it. If Malicia's little dog is barking when Rosella gets here, step back to the last screen and try again. Do not attempt the following if Cuddles is making noise.

Click on the vine growing from beneath the house, then click the shovel on Rosella. The shovel will not work until Rosella has looked at the vine first. Click on Rosella to crawl into the house.

(Figure 4-25) If all is well, you will see Rosella sticking her head out of a trapdoor in Malicia's bedroom. When the cursor is yours again, place it over Rosella, and you will see an arrow pointing down. Click the cursor so she'll get out of sight. Your point of view changes to that of Rosella looking up through the hole. Immediately select the defoliant, and as soon as Cuddles begins to appear, zap the mutt with it. After a bit of animation, mutt and mistress will go elsewhere.

Click the cursor to climb into the bedroom. **(Figure 4-26)** Take Rosella to Malicia's dresser on the right side of the screen and click on it to begin rooting through her drawers. Keep clicking until Rosella finds the Malicia blasting device (called a Mysterious Device in the inventory close-up). It's in third drawer down. Once Rosella has the device, click on the pile of clothes and undies in order to put them back. A stocking (possibly clean, but that's unlikely) will drop to the floor. Take it. Climb back down under the floor.

Outside, don't forget to pick up the veil and quickly disguise Rosella again. At this point, she would prefer not to boogie with the man. (Ouch! Please forgive us for that last remark.) Suitably disguised, return Rosella to the front of Malicia's house.

Before we take Rosella

Figure 4-24

Figure 4-25

Figure 4-26

anywhere, go into her inventory and combine Malicia's stocking with the silver pellet. Rosella now has a sling. Armed and ready for trouble, walk due east. Trouble is waiting there.

INSIDER INFO: *If Rosella stands in front of Malicia's house too long, the gargoyle in front will begin to smell her, thus bringing back Malicia. Maybe its the stocking. Anyway, don't dawdle too long here.*

(Figure 4-27) "There" is the were-woods. "Trouble" is the were-bears that inhabit the place. Begin walking. When Rosella's disguise is ripped off and the wear-bear confronts her, click the sling on the bear. Victory is hers. *Sans* disguise, continue east; Rosella will not be needing it any longer anyway.

Figure 4-27

(Figure 4-28) The path through the were-wood takes our heroine to a clearing in the woods south of Falderal. It's the same place we warned you not to take Valanice beyond in Chapter 3. Turn north. Cross the stepping-stones and continue north to the town gate. If the river is already flowing, Rosella will have to take the long way around by going west to the rainbow bridge. Cross the bridge, hang a left, keep going, then turn north in the spider web room.

Enter Falderal — however you get there.

Figure 4-28

(Figure 4-29) As he seems to do all strangers, the archduke greets Rosella as soon as she enters town. He'll tell her that Valanice has already been there and been arrested, but the town likes her now. Rosella is given free-run of the town, but mama is nowhere to be found.

INSIDER INFO: *Time and causality*

seem to operate a smidgen differently in KQ7. You undoubtedly noticed that when the archduke greeted Rosella, he informed her that Valanice had already been released from her imprisonment. Even though the game player has not reached this point with Valanice, it is understandable that the two women are moving in slightly different time frames.

Figure 4-29

*However, in our click-through, when Rosella crossed the River of Life, it wasn't flowing. And if you have explored around a bit, you've noticed the Rainbow Bridge in ruins again also. Didn't Valanice set this situation aright **before** she was arrested?*

Rosella should visit at least one of the merchants to ask about the secret entrance to the underground. The owners of both the China and Faux Shops suggest that she should visit Town Hall (even though the bull refers to it as the "palace of the archduke," he is speaking of Town Hall.)

To visit the Faux Shop, Rosella needs to get some salt from the desert pool, and there's nothing to stop her from going there. She can even drop in on the rat and jackalope. Make it a point to visit the mockingbird in the tree in Falderal, just for fun.

After Rosella's finished goofing around, enter Town Hall and go to the Powder Room. After being poofed, enter the room.

(Figure 4-30) There is a statue of Cupid on a table. Rosella still has Malicia's stocking; click the stocking on the plaque at the bottom of the statue. **(Figure 4-31)** Clean now, the inscription on the plaque can be read. The message says to give it some fruit.

Look around the room. There are some golden grapes attached to the upper-right decorative column. Click on the grapes. Next, click the hammer and chisel on them to get a grape.

Figure 4-30

(Figure 4-32) When you click the gold grape on the statue of Cupid, a secret passage opens in

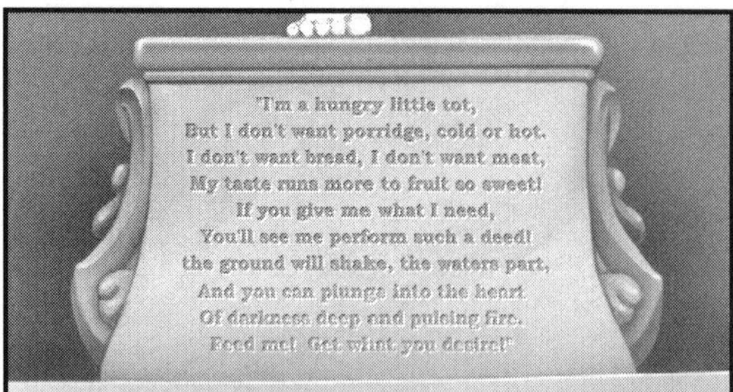

Figure 4-31

Figure 4-32

Figure 4-33

the middle of the room. Combine the magic wand and scarab inside inventory. King Otar will resume his normal form and leap down into the underground. This is the only place in KQ7 where Rosella can safely transform the king back into a troll.

Click on the passage for Rosella to follow.

(Figure 4-33) Rosella and Otar arrive in an underground tunnel outside the door to the room that controls the volcano — the room Rosella spied on in Chapter 2. Carefully watch as he manipulates the opening mechanism — this happens quickly after he speaks, so grease up your eyeballs. On the other hand, the following combination has been known to work:

Left eye
Right eye
Middle lever

Remember the sequence for use in Chapter 6.

Rosella and the king rush into the mechanical room and discover the false Troll King. The chapter ends as the two kings begin to roll about fighting for their lives and the throne of the Troll Underground.

Chapter Five

Nightmare in Etheria

Goal of the Chapter:

Valanice's goal in Chapter 5 is to escape her imprisonment in Falderal and discover a way to the land of Etheria (Cloudland and Dreamland.) There, she needs to free Mab in order to get to the summit of the Mountain of Winds, where she can summon Oberon and Titania and trigger KQ7's final chapter.

How to do It:

(Figure 5-1) Chapter 5 begins with Valanice's silly trial and sentence. She needs to put the moon back in the sky.

All Valanice needs is a slingshot. Outside Town Hall, click the rubber chicken on the tree. Click the moon on Valanice — you don't need to do this, but she hasn't had a bite to eat all game. **(Figure 5-2)** Click the cheese on the rubber chicken. The moon is taken care of. By the way, if you forgot the take the feather from the rubber chicken earlier, it is left behind here for your adventuring convenience. Don't forget to pick it up, if necessary.

Figure 5-1

After the archduke gives Valanice both thanks and pardon.

Figure 5-2

She is now free to leave Falderal.

Walk past the tree to the snake-oil salesman.

INSIDER INFO: *You might have asked yourself way back in Chapter 3 why Valanice, desperate to find her daughter, would go all the way back to the desert in order to attempt some sort of a trade. She didn't even know what the rat had to trade. Plus, she had little love for the jackalope, the rat's next-door neighbor. We wondered the same ourselves. The answer is simple, although a trifle expedient, and really belongs in this part of the click-through.*

The only purpose of Valanice's trade was to get the crook.

Why? So that Valanice could be arrested when she used it to hook the moon.

Why? So there would be a way to end Chapter 3 and begin Chapter 5.

After her arrest, the moon was not taken from Valanice, and shooting the moon back into the sky does nothing at all to advance the plot other than pull an extraneous trigger or two. The entire book/crook/moon sequence is left over from KQ7's original design, which was different than the finished product. But when KQ7's size was edited, and the original problem deleted, this particular series of events had to be left in so that there would be a cliff-hanger ending for Chapter 3. The beginning of this chapter depends on it.

We thought you might enjoy this piece of King's Quest trivia.

Figure 5-3

Now that Chapter 5 has begun, the snake has returned to trade some were-beast slave to Valanice in exchange for the magic statue. Click on the snake to talk with him. Click the magic mirror on the snake. The snake will explain how the salve works. Valanice is allowed to make this trade before doing the moon, but this order saves a few steps. Valanice is now finished with Falderal forever. Leave town. Don't look back.

Figure 5-4

Go to the clearing in the forest just before the were-woods. Click the jackalope fur on the salve. **(Figure 5-3)** To the eternal embarrassment of the were-bear, Valanice dashes through the woods like a wascaly wabbit. **(Figure 5-4)** The trouble is, she ends up in front of Malicia's. Worse, another swamp monster appears to make a meal of Valanice.

(Figure 5-5) Just when all appears lost, Attis appears out of the air to save Valanice. Whew!

Warning! *Don't even think about knocking on Malicia's door. Don't even think about clicking on the gargoyle.*

Figure 5-5

INSIDER INFO: *Trust us on these. This goes for Valanice as much as for Rosella. And while we're on the "like daughter, like mother" theme, don't forget the B-Man. He has a thing for older women. Fact is, we think, he's got a thing for any woman — dead or alive. Don't leave Valanice in any one place too long.*

Figure 5-6

Go west toward the cemetery gate, stop a moment to chat with the plants, then go inside. Once properly greeted by the ghoul kids, head west the undertaker's, south to the cemetery screen, and west to the deadfall. Watch out for open graves along the way.

(Figure 5-6) The black cat Rosella saved will meet Valanice at the deadfall and tell her about her

Figure 5-7

Figure 5-8

Figure 5-9

daughter, the Kingdom of Etheria, and the volcano. Afterwards, go two screens north to the ruined house. The black dog that growled at Rosella in Chapter 4 will take a much more menacing approach to Valanice now and will not let her pass. Exit to the south.

Return to the treehouse via the route Valanice just used. Click on the elevator rope to get up into the house. If the rope is not visible, leave the screen and return.

There is only one item needed from the treehouse. **(Figure 5-7)** Look at the mummy; it is holding something now which it wasn't when Rosella visited. Take the something, it is a femur — a large bone. Click on the mummy's hair. Click on the elevator rope to exit, or Valanice can jump out the back. In either case, once on the ground, go two screens west and one north to the ruined house.

The devil dog, hound from hell, or whatever you'd like to call it, still won't let Valanice pass. **(Figure 5-8)** Give the dog the bone as soon as you're given the chance. When the creature begins munching, click on it to talk. Keep talking until the dog gives Valanice the Headless Horseman's medal. Go south.

(Figure 5-9) The Woman in Black is still sobbing outside of the tomb of the Headless Horseman.

Click the medal on the woman, and she'll go away. Click on the tomb's inscription to read it. Click on the tomb's lock to find the crypt securely locked.

Walk back to the treehouse. The kids are chasing the poor cat with firecrackers. **(Figure 5-10)** Pick up the firecracker they drop on the ground. Immediately go back to the tomb and click the firecracker on the lock. Kaboom!

Figure 5-10

INSIDER INFO: *Firecrackers do not have long fuses, and this one is live. Valanice has 2 minutes or so to blow the lock on the tomb. It's plenty of time, but if she doesn't blow it, the firecracker will blow her.*

Figure 5-11

Move the cursor over Valanice until it turns into an arrow. Enter the tomb. **(Figure 5-11)** Click on the lid of the sarcophagus to move it. Click inside the sarcophagus to get the Headless Horseman's skull. Go outside.

Figure 5-12

(Figure 5-12) Stand in the middle of the path. Repeat: the middle of the path. This brings the Headless Horseman flying into the scene. As the Horseman soars down on Valanice, click the skull on him. If you're not fast enough, Valanice will be trampled. This may take a few tries, but death is soooo temporary in KQ7.

After the tender reunion

Figure 5-13

Figure 5-14

Figure 5-15

between the count (formerly the Headless Horseman), Elspeth (formerly the Woman in Black), and the family pooch, Black Valiant (formerly the black devil pooch), Valanice will be given the Horseman's fife — a musical horse whistle. Valanice will also be given a lift to Etheria.

(Figure 5-13) Necromancer drops Valanice off in Cloudland in the pastel paradise of the Rainbow Bridges. The four rainbows are shortcuts that will swiftly transport Valanice down to the four other main areas of the game. Here's how they work:

The northwest rainbow takes you to the skeleton in the desert.

The northeast rainbow takes you to Main Street in Falderal.

The southwest rainbow takes you to the path outside cemetery gates.

The southeast rainbow takes you to the statues in the woods.

Since Necromancer will always give Valanice a ride from the ground up to Etheria when she blows the fife, this makes for a very convenient teleportation system. Be grateful for it; Valanice has a lot of bouncing around ahead of her. Go east one screen. **(Figure 5-14)** This is the dragonet meadow. Click on them a few times. You will hear a very faint melody. This is a clue. Walk north. We hope you like dragonets — they will sing to Valanice a lot.

(Figure 5-15) Valanice finds a large harp with what looks like a crystal ball atop it. Click on the globe. It makes a musical tone. This is a clue. Click on the harp. It can make music. That's all for the moment. Return to the dragonet meadow, then go east.

(Figure 5-16) Valanice is at the base of the Mountain of the Winds. Follow the path north and keep walking until Valanice's off of the screen.

INSIDER INFO: *The Mountain of Winds lives up to its name. If Valanice stays on any one screen too long, a white wind-steed, Sirocco, can fly by and knock her on her backside, or back down the mountain. The injury is not fatal.*

The path ends next to the cave of the Dream Weaver. Do not click on the cave at this time. There is also a convoluted tree in the picture, and something glitters at the very end of its trunk. It's ambrosia, but Valanice cannot reach it from the ground. **(Figure 5-17)** Click on the tree to begin Valanice climbing. Click on the end of the trunk to get the ambrosia. Click on the ground to climb down.

INSIDER INFO: *Ill winds blow*

Figure 5-16

Figure 5-17

Figure 5-18

adventuresses no good. There is a particular ill wind known to fly around in this scene with fatal consequences. His name is Borasco. If Valanice's up the tree when he appears, the queen is really out on a limb.

Ambrosia in hand, return to the dragonet meadow and feed some of the stuff to the little flying dragons. They will change their tune with Valanice (so to speak). Listen carefully to the first four notes of their melody. Tune in mind, return north to the harp.

Valanice needs to enter into the sphere at the top of the harp. It won't be as tight a squeeze as it looks if she knows the right song to play. Obviously, it's the dragonet's song.

(Figure 5-18) Look at the harp in this screenshot. It contains six strings. With the longest string on the left side being string 1, play the tune by clicking the strings 1, 5, 6, then 4.

For the more musical among us, the notes are C, A, B-flat, and G.

After the first four notes have sounded, the harp will play the rest of the melody itself. The sphere will pulsate a few times. Click on the sphere to journey inside.

(Figure 5-19) The three Fates await Valanice. Click on one of them to begin chatting. Answer their question. When they're

Figure 5-19

Figure 5-20

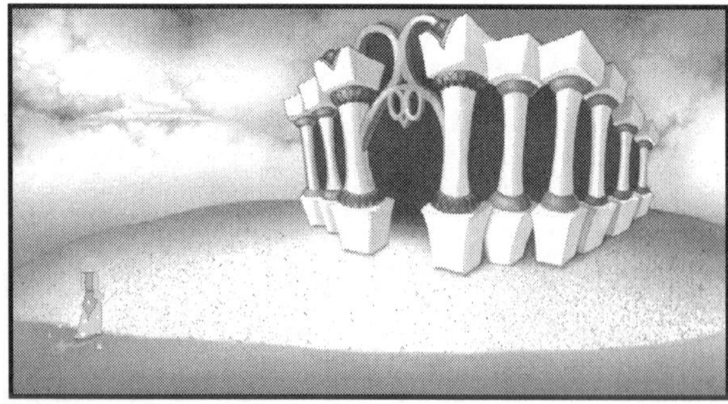

Figure 5-21

finished dispensing the relevant info about going to Dreamland, Valanice is returned outside. Go the meadow of the rainbows and click on the lower left (southwest) one.

Valanice is deposited on the road between Malicia's house and the cemetery gates. Walk west toward the gates. When the flesh-eating plants chime up, always feel free to chat. Even click Rosella's comb on them if you'd like. Just don't get too close — one measly foot-in-a-bag during Chapter 4 did little to satisfy their appetites.

Enter the cemetery and make Valanice's way to Doc Cadaver's. Click on the gates to open them. Knock on the door. Inside, talk to Doc, and he'll allow Valanice sleep on the couch. Valanice falls asleep and enters Dreamland.

(Figures 5-20, 5-21 and 5-22) Valanice's dream is a nightmare, with her being chased by a monster. At its end, she enters Mab's Temple and finds Mab frozen in a block of ice. There are no Ginzu knives around with which to free her.

Valanice awakens and is shown the door. When she's standing outside, blow on the fife. She is returned to the meadow of the rainbows.

Return to the harp. Play the same four notes as before. Enter

Figure 5-22

Figure 5-23

Figure 5-24

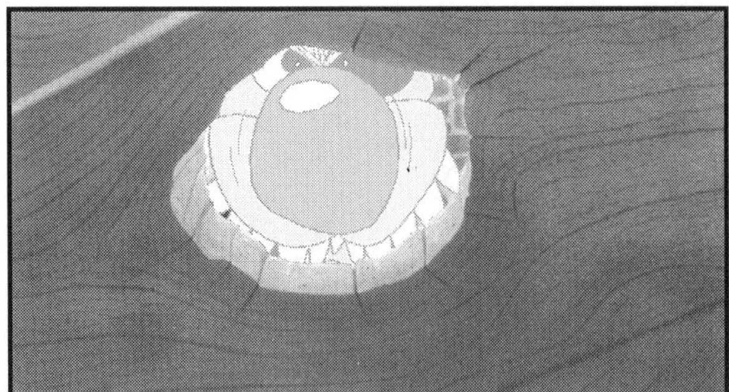

Figure 5-25

Figure 5-26

the sphere. Learn she must restore Ceres (the wife of Attis) to her true form. Return to the meadow of the rainbows and click on the lower right (southeast) one. Whoosh! Valanice's at the statues in the woods.

(Figure 5-23) Walk to the statue holding a cornucopia. Click the ambrosia on the statue. Take the fruit that appears in the cornucopia; it's a pomegranate. Cross the river and walk west one screen to visit Attis. Talk to him.

Click the pomegranate on the oak tree. **(Figure 5-24)** Another joyful reunion!

After Attis disappears, talk to Ceres. Talk to her some more after she's begun reforesting. She'll tell Valanice to get a crystal shaft and a beam of sunlight to take to Dreamland in order to free Mab. Ceres also tells Valanice to visit the three Fates. Again? Yes, again.

Fine. Use the fife. Ride the horse. Land. Deal with the dragonets. Go to the harp. Play. Climb in again. Talk. Learn how to free Mab. This time through, the Fates give Valanice a dream catcher. Leave the sphere. Deal with the dragonets. Return to meadow of rainbows. Click on the lower left (southwest) rainbow. Walk Valanice east, then to the rear of Malicia's house. Click on the hole that Rosella dug to enter beneath Malicia's bedroom.

Valanice pops up from the trapdoor in the floor. When cursor control returns to the player, place it over Valanice. Click the arrow to hide, and bring up the knothole view. **(Figure 5-25)** When Cuddles comes sniffing for Valanice, click the ambrosia on it. Soon, Malicia will leave. And her little dog, too.

Click the up arrow. Click on Valanice. **(Figure 5-26)** Click on Malicia's lamp in the lower right corner of the screen. Valanice now has the crystal shaft. Click on trapdoor and out. Go to the front of the house.

Valanice needs to get a shaft of sunlight, and, if you remember, there is one shining on the altar in the desert temple. We don't know about you, but we don't feel up to another long walk. Here's the shortcut:

Blow the fife and return to the meadow of the rainbows.

Click the top left (northwest) rainbow.

(Ouch! You are now at the desert skeleton)

Go two screens north, one east.

Look familiar?

Figure 5-27

Enter the temple. Don't worry about the scorpion because it is no longer in residence. **(Figure 5-27)** Click the crystal shaft on the beam of sunlight. Instant thaw machine.

Go outside. Fife. Horse. Land. Deal with the dragonets. Go to harp. Play. Climb in again. Talk. Are we repeating ourselves? Learn of the home of the Dream Weaver in the cave on the mountain. Leave the sphere. Deal with the dragonets.

Figure 5-28

Walk Valanice up the Mountain of Winds to the outside of the cave. **(Figure 5-28)** Click the dream catcher on the cave, then on the nightmare that emerges. Enter the cave.

(Figure 5-29) Welcome to the Dream Weaver's — purveyor of the finest fantasies and the whispers of memories. Click on him to talk. Again. Click the dream catcher on the Dream

Figure 5-29

Figure 5-30

Figure 5-31

Figure 5-32

Weaver, and Valanice receives the tapestry of dreams.

Use the tapestry on Valanice.

(Figure 5-30) As Valanice enters Dreamland, a nightmare attacks her. Click the dream catcher on the nightmare. Got it! Flee south. Go east to Mab's Temple and inside. Click the sunlight-filled shaft on the block of Mab. She'll promise Valanice sweet dreams, buts poofs her off to capture the wind horse, Sirocco. In the process, Valanice will acquire a magic bridle.

Valanice is returned to the base of the Mountain of Winds. **(Figure 5-31)** Climb back to the ambrosia tree and have Valanice hide in the right part of the screen, as in the screenshot above. It turns out that the wind horse that has been bugging Valanice is Sirocco himself. The next time it flies by, click the magic bridle on the horse.

(Figure 5-32) Captured, Sirocco will fly Valanice to the very top of the mountain, where she is surrounded by the winds themselves. King's Quest VII: The Princeless Bride then goes on animated autopilot until Valanice is left alone — and stranded! — at the very top of Cloudland with no way of escape.

Chapter Six

Ready, Set... Boom!

Goal of the Chapter:

In the final chapter of King's Quest VII, you again play the part of Princess Rosella. The goal is for Rosella to stop the volcano from erupting and destroying everything, defeat Malicia (and her little dog, too), and save the life of the handsome, young, charming prince who makes a sudden, and surprising, visit.

How to do It:

Chapter 6 is the shortest episode of KQ7, and most of it is presented in pre-packaged animations. However, Rosella has some important deeds to accomplish before the final boffo ending.

(Figure 6-1) Chapter 6 begins the same as chapter four ended; the two troll kings rolling around the floor of the volcano control room (the mechanical room to the game designers) fighting each other.

Figure 6-1

Rosella must first click the magic wand on the false troll king in order to change the dastard back to his true self. Ah! But which king is true? Which is false?

What is *not* the color of the true

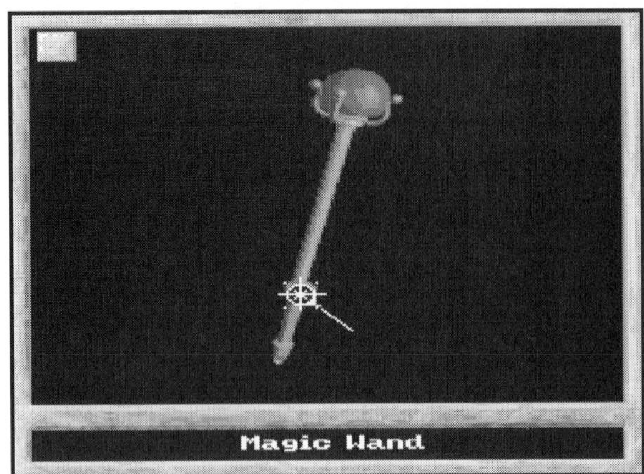

Figure 6-2

Otar's eyes?

All together now, "They are *not* green!"

Wait until cursor control is passed to the player. Open up Rosella's inventory and rotate the magic wand until you can see the letter inscribed on its head. It should be **T**. Rosella needs it to be **F**.

Rotate the wand again until it is pointed nearly straight up and down. **(Figure 6-2)** If you pass the cursor over the wand's handle while it is in this orientation, it will sparkle at the handle. Click on the wand's handle. Rotate it again to make sure you have F active. Return to the action.

Figure 6-3

While pummeling each other, both kings are pleading with Rosella to transform their opponent. Listen for the line, "No, no! Get *him!*"

The next king to land against the back wall after this line has been spoken is the one with green eyes (Fig. 6-1). Click the magic wand on him at once. Do this quickly before Malicia poofs in and spoils everything.

Zap! Instant Edgar. **(Figure 6-3)**

INSIDER INFO: *Who is Edgar? If you have never played a King's Quest game before, especially if you haven't played KQ IV: The Perils of Rosella, you might not know that Edgar was the ugly, deformed son of the wicked witch Lolotte. Edgar helped Rosella escape imprisonment and was rewarded by being transformed into a handsome young man — a beautiful form to reflect his beautiful soul. Despite not knowing Rosella at all, nor having been introduced to her properly, he immediately asked Rosella to marry him. She, of course, refused. Handsome stud-muffin or not, a woman does like to know something about the man she marries.*

Their relationship (including Rosella's gracious refusal) lasted all of about thirty seconds before

Rosella was magically transported home to her family.
Oh, that Edgar.

INSIDER INFO: *Who is Gregor Samsa? If the wrong king is clicked on in the volcano control room sequence, it sounds like the real Otar exclaims, "In the name of Gregor Sampson!" What is actually being said is "Gregor* ***Samsa.****"*

The Troll King is referring to Gregor Samsa, the protagonist of ***Metamorphosis,*** *a short story by Franz Kafka. He transformed into the form of a cockroach for the sin of wasting his life. And as a cockroach Samsa died.*

INSIDER INFO: *Why does the magic wand need to be set to F in order to transform Edgar? Good question. If you listen very carefully during Chapter 5, Valanice learns that Oberon and Titania are searching for their missing son. In Chapter 3, the snake-oil salesman mentions in passing to Valanice that Titania is queen of the faeries. Of course, Rosella doesn't know this.*

Since we will learn a bit later that Edgar is the son of O & T, it becomes obvious, although in hindsight, that the F setting returns faeries to their true forms, just as T does for trolls.

On the other hand, why does setting the magic wand on F not matter a whit when transforming Otar? It very much does matter when dealing with Edgar. Why, oh why? Because it's a ***magic*** *wand. Or something like that.*

Rosella and Edgar don't have very much time to enjoy their sudden reunion. Malicia poofs in anyway (although less fatally now), zaps the Troll King, and blows Edgar away. She has somewhat warmer regards for Rosella.

Figure 6-4

(Figure 6-4) Our heroine finds herself stranded on a narrow ledge inside of the volcano. The lava is rising.

KQ7 now quickly cuts between Rosella and Valanice, who is still stranded atop the Mountain of Winds. **(Figure 6-5)** A mysterious figure swoops out of the sky astride the Headless Horseman's steed and sweeps her off of her feet.

Meanwhile, back inside the volcano. The lava is still rising.

(Figure 6-6) Atop the volcano, three tiny figures appear and cast a magic web across its crater. Can it hold?

Figure 6-5

Figure 6-6

Figure 6-7

Back inside the volcano again, the lava is still rising, but now the player has control of the game cursor. **(Figure 6-7)** Click the shovel on the wall by Rosella. Don't bother to wonder just where Rosella was keeping the item.

Rosella will dig her way to temporary safety.

INSIDER INFO: *Rosella can also dig her way out by using her hands, although this takes two clicks of the cursor instead of one. At one time, this solution meant that Edgar would end KQ7 as a corpse. Now, except for some dirt under Rosella's fingernails, the choice of solutions has no effect on the game's final outcome.*

(Figure 6-8) Back in Ooga Booga, Valanice and her rescuer begin blasting their way into the underground. Will they arrive in time? For what?

Meanwhile, back inside the volcano, Rosella emerges into a tunnel. Follow the tunnel northeast. **(Figure 6-9)** She is now in the room with the doors into the volcano control room. They're locked.

What's a princess to do?

Well, the first thing is to check her inventory.

If you've been playing along with this click-through, Rosella will be carrying the fragrant flower she picked from beneath the carnivorous plants in Ooga Booga.

If she doesn't have the flower, another one will be growing through the grate in the upper right of the screen. Of course, it's too far away for Rosella to reach.

Click the shovel on the big rock below the grate. **(Figure 6-10)** Return the shovel to inventory and click the normal cursor on the rock. Rosella will climb up and get the flower.

Go back to the door.

Rosella needs to click on the door in the same places, and in the same order, that Otar did at the end of Chapter 4. **(Figure 6-11)** If you weren't paying attention then, you probably missed the clue. There is no way to go back and check it out now, and you might prefer to *not* play that chapter over in order to get it. The correct sequence to open the door is to click the left eye, the right eye, and the center nose, in that order.

Rosella returns to the Volcano control room. King Otar is still unconscious, but the fragrant flower will revive him.

(Figure 6-12) But first, look at the machine panel Otar is crumpled against. Could that be some kind of electrical outlet next to his head? Look at the mysterious device in Rosella's

Figure 6-8

Figure 6-9

Figure 6-10

Figure 6-11

Figure 6-12

Figure 6-13

inventory and rotate it. It looks as if it needs to be plugged into something and Rosella is across the room from the only outlet in the entire game.

Click the Mysterious Device on the outlet. It will glow with charge.

(Figure 6-13) Now click the flower on the Troll King. King Otar will race across the room to the volcano control panel to shut it off.

(Figure 6-14) A cutaway shows that the magic web holds at the cone of the volcano!

Meanwhile, back inside the volcano. King Otar really does know how to operate the volcano control. Etheria is saved! The entire world, perhaps, is saved!

INSIDER INFO: *We have pointed out earlier that KQ7 was once a much different game than its final form. This is not at all unusual and happens all the time in film, music, videos, and computer games.*

However, before playing the final endgame of KQ7, it will help clarify things a bit if you have the following information. This background information, which is from the King's Quest VII design document, is stuff that Rosella and Valanice would have picked up during their adventures in a different version of the story.

EDGAR AND LOLOTTE

Figure 6-14

Edgar was born the son of Oberon and Titania, King and Queen of the Faeries. When he was just a baby, an evil faerie named Lolotte was cast from Cloudland for treachery and wicked deeds. She was so furious that she concocted a scheme to steal the baby prince from his home. Once she had him, she changed his appearance and called him her own. Oberon and Titania searched the world for their baby, but finally they had to give up and turn their attentions back to their kingdom. They thought their only son was dead.

THE FALL OF MALICIA

(How the Headless Horseman came to be)

Many years back, Malicia, who is the sister of Titania, hatched a terrible plot to overthrow Cloudland. With a band of fanatical followers, she tried to seize power from Oberon and Titania in a vicious attack on the castle. Oberon and Titania fought valiantly, and all of the guardians of Faerieland rose to defend them. All of the rebels were slain or cast from Cloudland except for Malicia, who fought like a demon and would not give up.

She was dealt a terrible blow by Count Tsepish of Ooga Booga Land. His true strike allowed Oberon and Titania to defeat Malicia, but before they could subdue her, she caused her gargoyle to slay the brave count, and she cast his head from Cloudland. No one ever knew that he had found out about Malicia's treachery and was on his way to warn Oberon and Titania. Even as she was chained by the forces of Cloudland, Malicia spit a horrible curse after the count. He rose to haunt Ooga Booga as the Headless Horseman, his bride Elspeth died of a broken heart, and his faithful hound stayed with his mansion even as it was burned to the ground by the Boogeyman, who had collaborated with Malicia all along. The three ghosts were forever cursed to occupy the same land but be cruelly kept apart for all eternity.

EDGAR AND MALICIA

After Edgar was changed back into his normal body by Genesta at the end of King's Quest IV, word quickly spread that there was a strange and noble young faerie of great power living alone on the shores of Tamir. Oberon and Titania dared not hope that it was their son, but they went to meet the young man for themselves. They were overjoyed to discover that is was their long lost boy after all. They brought him back to Cloudland amid great celebration and ceremony. They had a glittering party for him that very evening.

What Oberon and Titania didn't know was that Malicia, who had been stripped of her powers many years before, had built her power back up to a terrifying level. She kidnapped Edgar from the gardens of Cloudland in the middle of the celebration and changed him to look like the Troll King, whom she had just imprisoned in Ooga Booga land. Her evil scheme not only gained her an impostor Troll King to act as her puppet, but it effectively got rid of Oberon and Titania as well. She left false clues and rumors that lead them to think their son had been kidnapped by an evil wind. They set out to search for him immediately, and Malicia was free to enact her terrible plot.

Figure 6-15

Rosella and Otar giggle in relief. Valanice and her rescuer rush in. **(Figure 6-15)** It's a joyful reunion. And the mysterious stranger is Edgar! He has somehow survived Malicia's attack, found the Horseman's steed, obtained the robe of the Desert Spirit, discovered Valanice's existence and whereabouts, called the horse without help of the fife, flown to Valanice, and done his spell thing in Ooga Booga to get to the Troll Underground in order to return to the control room just in time to stop the eruption. Well, almost. But it wasn't from lack of trying.

Rosella and Edgar have a second happy reunion.

(Figure 6-16) Leave it to Malicia to poop a party. The evil faerie poofs in and by the time the pyrotechnics finish (and the sparks stop flying), Edgar lies dead on the floor.

You will need to be very quick here. Click on the Mysterious Device, still glowing in its socket, to place it in inventory. Click on it in inventory, then click it on Malicia. Victory! So easy, a baby could do it. Click the device on Malicia's dog, if you want to.

Get the extra life from Rosella's inventory and click it on Edgar. You only have about five seconds to do this once Cuddles the dog has either left or been zapped.

INSIDER INFO: *If Rosella doesn't restore Edgar in time, the end of the game will be different, and more somber, than what is described next. Oberon and Titania will arrive and grieve for their son. After some plot clarifications, Rosella and Valanice will be returned to Daventry upon a funereal black swan.*

Just for kicks, quit the game just before the final confrontation with Malicia and play both endings. Along the way, you might notice that Edgar and his folks pronounce Lolotte's name quite differently.

Figure 6-16

Edgar lives. Oberon and Titania arrive. Explanations are presented. Stories are told. The lovers embrace. The closing animation ends with Edgar and Rosella flying into the sunset.

The game ends.

Congratulations! You have successfully completed King's Quest VII: The Princeless Bride.

PART THREE

From the Eye between the Worlds

Since we gave up being paranoid about this several years ago, we'll lay out the facts plainly and bloodlessly. If you consider us crazy, or odd, or perpetrators of cheap fiction after reading this, it will be quite understandable. We, too, thought the same things about ourselves once.

In the latter part of the 1980s we began receiving some very curious electronic mail. The messages purported to be histories, chronicles, news clippings, and articles from a place named Daventry, a place we knew only existed in computer games.

The sender of these pieces described himself as a wandering writer of current events and an amateur wizard. His name, he claimed, was Derek Karlavaegen. One day, while nosing around the deserted home of the wizard Manannan, Derek discovered what he described as a metal head with 100 teeth and a single, great, glass eye. After much tinkering, he could make words wiggle across the eye and, after time, found words appearing there without his doing anything at all. From all we can reconstruct, it appears that Derek discovered some sort of computer in the magician's study and had somehow stumbled his way into cyberspace — our word, but a shared reality. Derek calls his strange metal head the Eye between the Worlds.

Assuming that he had found a link between his universe and ours, Derek began sending out material that he had either written, found interesting, or thought we might enjoy. He says he has no idea if anyone receives what he puts out but finds pleasure in the act. The connection, in his opinion, is one-way. We just happen to be on the other end.

After years of searching for some hoaxter and finding none; upgrading computers and changing modems; and an irregular, but continuing, flow of mail, we have been left with but one conclusion. Derek and Daventry are real.

Derek tells an intriguing tale. Once magic and the fantastic walked the earth alongside the ordinary. Elves, dragons, giants, and mermaids were as real to us as a full stomach or a good knife. But we humans started to draw away from that side of reality and began believing numbers more than faerie dust. Cities grew and people multiplied. Finally, a great gathering of all mystical, magical, and extraordinary beings — fearful of extinction, extermination or scorn — decided to make a place for themselves. A new place. They cast a great spell and *withdrew* from our world. They created their own world and named it Daventry.

Except for our myths, folklore, and legends, we have forgotten them. They have never forgotten us.

Derek claims that our two universes are so close that we can dream each other. And this is the real reason he sends us what he does. He has discovered mentions and snatches King's Quest in his searches through the aether. He was startled to find that the games, as far as he can determine, are accurate retellings of events he knows to be true in his world.

"Only a great dreamer," he writes, "can dream such dreams to tell such tales. We only dream of you as whispers of absurdity and fast flashes of frightful facts and factories, blind to the *multiverse* around you."

Although he has given no evidence of knowing her name, Derek claims Roberta Williams, the creator of what we assume are King's Quest *games* is such a great dreamer. Roberta says she just makes up the stories, but she has not denied that she dreams them. But the stories she creates, and the events Derek relates, are just too, too similar to be coincidental. We merely take Derek's information and incorporate it into our books on King's Quest, hoping others will realize that there is more to reality than we can see, measure, or classify.

What we have related above, and a great deal more, has been told in greater detail in another of our books, *The King's Quest Companion* (Osborne McGraw-Hill, 1992). If you look there, you can see just how closely Derek Karlavaegen's and Roberta Williams' versions of the happenings in Daventry match through the first six games of the series, the first 20 years or so of the reign of King Graham.

Recently, however, we received a long missive from Derek. It consisted of two parts; the first was a lengthy narration, more a romance than anything else, which Derek claims is wildly popular among the readers of "...popular gossiping and literary trifles." It is said to be an anonymous telling of a secret story concerning Queen Valanice and Princess Rosella of Daventry and the dangers they faced during an attempted kidnapping of Rosella by the king of the trolls and her subsequent rescue. The story also claims that the princess is considering marriage to a prince who has spent his entire life, with the exception of a few days, ensorcelled as something other than himself, never knowing his true nature or identity.

This, of course, reads a lot like the happenings of King's Quest VII: The Princeless Bride.

But unlike his other messages to our world, Derek cautions us about the veracity of the tale, thinking it more fancy that fact. More fiction than history as he knows it. And he concludes on an even more fascinating note, which is where we will leave you:

"...yet, while I am privileged to be close to Alexander, his parents, and sister Rosella — my pardon, King Alexander; it is a title which I still find an awkward one for my friend — I have heard nothing of such a possible marriage. Rumor or popular fabrication is possible. The mass hope for another royal wedding, manifesting itself as a true romance, is another conceivable explanation for the widespread and uncritical acceptance of the tale.

Rosella may be impetuous, but she is no fool. She would marry no man before her time, and she knows near nothing of Edgar. The queen may be warm hearted and full of kindness toward all, but when Rosella was to be sacrificed to the fire dragon, Valanice guarded her daughter's door with naked sword as her protectress. She would not be so easily swayed from her course of rescue in Etheria as the narrative asserts.

The tale could be true, all is possible, but it rings wrong for me. I have another explanation, one which suits my misgivings and, at the same time, brings our universes closer together.

Here, in Daventry, we are always recreating ourselves. The great dreamer in your world, the Other World as we call it, creates tales and fables from what is our reality, our histories. I think there is a great dreamer here now, too; one who has dreamed the fictions of your universe and is creating new realities and histories for us.

Our universes are so close together that we dream each other. We exist right over each others shoulders, if we could only turn fast enough we might see each other. We draw together; you now create your own visions of us.

And now we dream of you.

PART FOUR

The Princeless Bride

Part the First
Through the Looking Pool

"IT ALL STARTED," QUEEN VALANICE OF DAVENTRY BEGAN, "WHEN I WAS COUNSELING ROSELLA ON the advisability of making an advantageous marriage with one of those charming young princes who...."

"It all started, Mother," Rosella interrupted, "When you were boring me nearly to sleep reciting the good points of Prince Throckmorton, or whichever of those wearisome, uninteresting...."

"I don't care where it started," said King Graham, "Just stop interrupting one another and tell me everything that happened to you while you were gone, though it scarcely seemed you were gone at all, if you must know the truth."

"Time passes much more quickly in The Realm of Eldritch, dear," Valanice reminded him, patting his hand in an affectionate and familiar gesture "But I can assure you from my point of view it took long enough to get back. There I was, separated from my darling child, my only daughter...."

"And there I was," Rosella said, "imprisoned in a stone cell, transformed into a hideous troll!"

Valanice heard her husband's sigh of impatience. Graham was no stranger to adventure himself, having won both his crown and the hand and love of his queen by deeds of bravery and heroism. He had recently proven himself yet again when Valanice and their son and daughter had been kidnapped by the wizard Manannan and imprisoned far from their Castle Daventry home. He only wanted to hear their tales of the adventure, and how she and Rosella had found their way home from the land of Faerie, not all of which was as lovely and serene as the pictures in children's storybooks. Valanice looked at her daughter. "Shall I continue, Rosella?"

"Oh, all right," Rosella said with a toss of her head, "I'll let Mother begin. After all, if she hadn't jumped into the pool and gone through the door after me, I might never have come back from Eldritch at all, and poor Edgar might never have been reunited with...."

"Rosella, you were going to let your mother tell the story," King Graham gently interrupted.

"I only said that I'd let her begin" his daughter protested. "It's my story too, you know."

"Of course it is, dear," her mother assured her. "Let's tell it together. I'll recount the story of my adventures on the other side of the door to The Realm of Eldritch, and you can tell of yours. Now, as I was saying, it all began when I was telling Rosella about that nice young Prince Throckmorton."

Rosella sighed audibly, rolling her blue eyes in both resignation and impatience, but Valanice went on as though she hadn't heard.

"She wasn't listening to me of course — children never do — and when I tried to get her attention, she was very suddenly gone from my side!"

"It was a dragonet!" Rosella interjected. "It was singing the loveliest song, and it flew right past my face and through the surface of the pool and into a door. And the door was about to close!"

Valanice saw the smile forming on her husband's lips and knew he understood that his adventurous daughter was entirely incapable of passing up a chance for the excitement of a chase. She motioned Rosella to hush.

"Oh, I forgot," said Rosella. "Go ahead, Mother."

"Very well, then, I will," said Valanice. "Rosella was gone — vanished. All I could see was her comb lying on the ground. I picked it up. But when I looked into the pool we had been sitting beside, I could see her as though very far away, through a door that was very nearly closed." Her voice shook with emotion as she recounted the moment of her decision. "I gave no real thought to the wonder, or the possible danger, of what I saw; I immediately jumped in and followed her.

"Then something grabbed Rosella and snatched her away! There was a murk all around, and I couldn't see where it took her. Then the murk became a whirling wind —

hot and filled with yellow dust. When I could see again, I fell out of the sky into in a vast desert under a blazing sun. So strange were my surroundings that I thought at first I must be dreaming — that I had somehow imagined everything that had happened. But I could taste the dust in my mouth, and the smell of the earth baking beneath the sun assured me that I was quite awake. Also, while I did land on my feet, I did not land *softly.* I immediately began to look for Rosella, thinking she must have come here just ahead of me. But Rosella had not come to this desert.

"It was a dreadful place," Valanice continued, "But not entirely devoid of its own sort of beauty. The rocks had been sculpted by wind and sand into tortured shapes quite unlike any I had ever seen. There was no water evident anywhere, and many of the plants were covered with needle-sharp spines. I caught my skirt on one and kept the piece of cloth, hoping I'd be able to repair the skirt later. But, as it turned out, I had no time for such a luxury.

"I had hardly arrived and begun to take stock of my situation when I saw a strange creature — something like a large rabbit with very long ears, but on its head were horns like those of an antelope."

King Graham laughed heartily. "Surely you imagined it! There could be no such animal in all of Daventry!"

"Might I remind you, dear husband, that it was not this world in which I found myself, but another plane of existence entirely," said Valanice, wounded by Graham's obvious amusement.

"I'm very sorry, my dear. Please go on."

Valanice nodded, somewhat mollified by his apology. "The creature was laughing an insane laugh and chasing another, smaller animal nearly as strange as himself — a sort of a rat with long hind legs that leaped like a kangaroo! No, don't tell me how inconceivable that that creature is as well, for that's the very thing I was thinking when I saw him. And as if that weren't difficult enough to believe, the rat was wearing a pair of reading glasses and carrying a blue bead in its mouth! Loud and raucous yips and yells accompanied them as they raced by me and disappeared in some rocks."

"I continued looking for Rosella. After a time, I stumbled across footprints leading away into the desert. They didn't look quite like Rosella's, but I surmised that they could possibly have belonged to whomever had abducted her. I followed.

"The footsteps led to an enormous stone head — a colossus of peculiar design — the mouth of which would have been large enough to walk into, as through a doorway, had it been open. But it was not. The footsteps led up to the stone mouth and disappeared as though their owner had walked directly through the stone.

"I looked for a way to get inside the stone head, but I was unable to find one. As I explored, however, I noticed several things that intrigued me greatly, and made me wonder about their possible significance. In places, semi-precious stone had been inlaid as part of a great design. One of the inlays, just below the lower lip, seemed to be missing, perhaps taken by thieves, or perhaps only fallen victim to the relentless wind and sand. I couldn't help wondering if the missing piece still existed somewhere, and if the stone head wanted it back. I know that seems silly, but the silliest thought did not seem out of place here. I continued to look around the area near the head.

"There was a bush, of sorts — covered in sharp spines, like much of the plant life thereabouts — and on it grew little round fruits. I wondered if they might be edible. When I approached the bush to look closer at them, I saw something most alarming.

"Tracks. Footprints like those a lizard might leave, but the little jewel-green lizards in our palace gardens would never grow to such enormous size. I feared meeting the beast that had made them and quickly took my exploration in another direction.

"As I wandered deeper into the desert's sands, I glimpsed a bizarre apparition. It was a man, pale in color and surpassing strange in appearance, who seemed to come from nowhere. Not seeming to notice me, the man walked away deeper into the desert haze, but I called out to him, and finally he paused and spoke to me.

"'Leave me be,' he said in a haunting, parched voice, 'for I am driven mad by this burning, everlasting thirst.' He said he was not sure what that thirst would drive him to do. When I saw him closely, his face as pale as ash, I knew beyond a doubt that he was no living man, but a ghost. I began to tremble. He said he had died in that desert, and that I, too, would never leave it.

"Unnerved as I was, I gathered my courage, and asked him: "Sir, have you seen my daughter? An impetuous, lovely young girl with long, blonde hair, dressed in blue silk." I showed him Rosella's comb, "This is hers."

"'I have not seen her,' he told me, 'nor any living creature except yourself. These sands are as death to all that live.'

"My courage flagged then. His eyes burned so, and he seemed to shimmer in the heat. Then he drifted away, fading into the distance like the ghost he was. My heart began to pound. This was such a perilous place, where one might die of thirst or perish in a scouring sandstorm or fall prey to who knew what inimical animal or plant life and never be seen alive again. Would such be my fate — I who had been so recently happy and content in my own home with my beloved family about me? No. I would not give in. As long as there was breath in my body, I would search for Rosella, and failing to find her here, I would travel by whatever means possible to whatever strange place necessary to rescue her and bring her home again. I would learn the secrets of this wilderness and use them to continue my quest.

"TO THE EAST OF THE STONE HEAD, TALL CLIFFS LOOMED, AND THEY WERE QUITE THE STRANGEST cliffs I 'd ever seen. They were incised with weathered figures that seemed to tell a story that I might understand if only I could decipher their meaning — the story of a full well and an empty one. But I could not divine the truth of it then. And then I saw the most curious thing yet in that deadly place — a little patch of damp sand at the foot of the cliffs."

"But how is that possible?" Graham asked.

"I'm not sure," Valanice replied. "But I surmised that the land beyond the cliffs above might contain an aquifer — a great underground pool of water trapped between layers of stone — perhaps collected from the sparse desert rainfall over many years. If that were so, then it might also be possible that a tiny bit of water might find its way down through the layers and to the bottom of the cliff. Whatever the explanation, the sand was quite damp. I looked for any sign that there might be enough water nearby to quench my thirst, or to take to that poor, parched phantom wandering the sands, but there was only that tiny bit of dampness, and nothing more.

"Nearby, I had seen a dead vine with one dried-up gourd still attached. I though it might serve to hold a little water, but it was desiccated and of no apparent use. If I were here long enough, even this might look like nourishment, but I was not yet so desperate as that. As I stood from my examination of the shriveled gourd, a large opening in the cliff face caught my eye — a place to escape the burning heat of the sun, and who knew what else? Perhaps even a place to find some clue as to how I might recover Rosella and return us both safely home.

"So I explored the interior of this cave. Far from being empty, as I had secretly feared, it contained a number of interesting things. There were four pots of clay, such as might have been used for cooking or carrying water, but only one was sturdy enough to not fall to pieces as soon as I touched it. I kept that one.

"There was also a little basket with its own lid, cleverly woven of desert grasses. It contained an ancient dried kernel of corn, which at first I must confess I considered only as a possible defense against starvation. But as I turned it over in my fingers, I thought of how life can be held in suspension, waiting for the right conditions to come about. This little seed might have waited there for its opportunity for hundreds of years, preserved by the perfect dryness of the desert. I wondered if it might yet yield up its hidden life if only I could find a place to plant it.

"I thought to myself that when I returned to Daventry with Rosella — I wouldn't allow myself to think that we might not return — I would plant it here in the castle gardens."

"And did you bring it back?" Graham inquired.

"I did not, I fear. For no sooner had I thought this than I remembered the patch of damp sand outside the cave. I hurried there and made a hole in the sand with one finger, then placed the kernel inside the hole. 'I hope I'll be home again before you sprout,' I told the seed. To my astonishment, a corn seedling sprang up from the ground at once and was a full-grown plant within seconds!"

Graham guffawed in surprise. "A magical seed? I discovered one of those once. Turned into a beanstalk. There was a giant and a chest of gold at the top. Imagine you finding one, too!"

"Perhaps the seed was magical, or perhaps it was a magical place. Remember, I had already seen much that was quite out of the ordinary. At any rate, I picked the ear of corn that grew on the plant. At the very least, I could eat it later, and it would be far more nutritious than the kernel from whence it sprang. Tastier, too.

"The magical stalk of corn so interested me that I returned briefly to the little cave, intent upon finding more kernels to plant. However, a close search of the interior yielded no tangible results, and I departed, somewhat disgruntled that my efforts had been for naught.

"As I prepared to resume my search for Rosella, I noticed that the shriveled gourd had split open — whether due to the heat of the sun or the shock of the cornstalk's sudden growth I shall never know. Intrigued by this oddity, I again bent to examine the wrinkled squash, and lo and behold! Inside was a single seed, quite dry and obviously dead. As I examined the seed, it suddenly struck me that, for a short time at least, I had entirely forgotten my quest. I quickly stood, distractedly pocketing the little seed as I dusted off my skirts, and scolded myself for being so foolishly distracted. Fortified with a new resolve, I began my wanderings anew.

"South and west of the cave, I finally found a pool of water. But something was wrong; I wondered why there were no tracks of animals nearby, for surely such readily available water would be eagerly sought out by the wildlife. Then I noticed that the rim of the pool was sparkling with salt crystals. I tasted the water, and it was as salty as sea water. I spit it out, revolted at its briny taste. It would do neither the local animals nor me any good whatsoever. However, I recalled something I had once heard about the body losing salt if one perspires excessively. With this in mind, I bent over and retrieved a few of the crystals, hoping all the while that I would be home long before I found any need to use them.

"A fallen stick from some strange desert growth lay near the pool; it was the only thing I had seen since coming there that suggested a weapon or tool, although it didn't seem terribly effectual. I took it anyway, worried that it might soon become necessary to use it to fend off some hungry desert creature bent upon devouring me.

"Looming above the pool was large sandstone statue of a kneeling man. Perhaps it was some god of the people who had once lived here. On its base was another series of odd-looking pictures, very like the ones I had seen on the cliffs. One seemed to represent the pool of water, with skulls over the water. It might be a warning not to drink it. The second carving showed a crying face, with tears falling into a bowl held by a disembodied hand. The bad water was also shown falling into the bowl. There was a drop shape with a skull inside, and next to that, another hand held an ear of corn. The last carving was a bowl of water being raised to a smiling mouth. If I could decipher these drawings, I wondered, would the information I gained be of any use in my search for Rosella?

"At the thought of Rosella, I became quite melancholy. I took out her comb — the only thing of hers I possessed — and the sight of it caused me to begin sobbing uncontrollably. Some of my tears fell into the stone bowl and mingled with the brine already there. When I finally composed myself, I began to think about what sort of god this might be. Surely the most important thing in such a barren land would be water, and he was indeed holding a bowl that ought to hold something in turn. The pictures had shown water falling into a bowl. Maybe they were there to tell me — or any traveler — an important secret.

"If it was water the god wanted for his bowl, I would provide it. It might not be good for drinking, but it was unlikely this great statue was going to be drinking anything anyway.

"EVEN THE PICTURES ON THE ALTAR AND ON THE WALL SHOWED THE COMBINING OF WATER AND tears. I know it seems terribly strange, but after hearing all the tales of your adventures," she said to Graham, "and yours, my dear," she laid a hand on Rosella's sleeve, "I have come to the conclusion that strange is an inadequate word to describe the things this family has encountered during its adventures."

Graham and Rosella nodded their understanding. This might have been Valanice's first *real* adventure, at least the first in which she was not a helpless captive, but her daughter and husband were no strangers to faraway places, strangeness, and heroic deeds.

"Go on, Mother," Rosella urged. "What happened when you put the water into the bowl?"

"Well, nothing at first. Then I thought to look at the pictures again. One was of a hand holding an ear of corn. Surely it was more than coincidence that I had picked an ear of new corn only a short time before. Now I had to decipher what the pictures were telling me to do with my ear of corn. I took it out and held it in my hand, but nothing happened. Then I noticed that while one of the water god's hands held the stone bowl, the other was entirely empty. I placed the corn in it, feeling more than a little foolish, I confess. But there was no one there to see me, and if nothing happened again, I would simply take back the corn and be none the worse off.

"There was a rumbling, grinding noise, like the cracking of stone. The hand of the statue closed around the corn. When I looked into the bowl, the bad water had been transformed into sparkling, clear, sweet water, the likes of which I had feared I might never again behold. I saved the water in the little clay pot, knowing I would surely need it later, and with a final nod of thanks to the statue of the nameless deity, I continued on my search for you.

"AS CHANCE MIGHT DECREE, I SOON ENCOUNTERED THE DESERT WRAITH AGAIN. HE SEEMED SO parched that I offered him a drink of my water. His nearly transparent hands shook as he reached out to take the pot. He drank deeply of the water, and almost immediately, he seemed stronger and more substantial than before.

"'In slaking my thirst, your have broken my curse,' he said. 'You have freed me; now I may find true peace. How can I ever repay you, blessed traveler?'

"I didn't even have to think about what I would say. If Rosella were not in this place, then I must find some way to leave it and find where she had been taken.

"'Can you help me escape from this desert and find my daughter?' I asked.

"'The portal out of the desert is through the great head of stone,' he told me, 'but it has been magically sealed by an evil enchantress. Because of her, I am...as I am.'

"He glared bitterly at the sky for a moment, then leveled that burning gaze on me once more. 'However, lady, there may be something more that I can do for you. Follow me' ".

"With those words, he turned and strode toward the horizon.

"THE SPIRIT STOPPED WALKING JUST AS WE REACHED THE EDGE OF A WICKED SANDSTORM — A TINY tornado, really — which looked as if it could flay the flesh from my body. He made a motion with his hand, and the storm seemed to obey his command. It moved away from us to reveal the thing he had brought me there to find."

VALANICE PALED A LITTLE AT THE MEMORY OF WHAT SHE HAD SEEN, AND HER HUSBAND AND daughter leaned forward anxiously, waiting for her to reveal it to them.

"It was his dead body! There was a pile of bleached bones, some scraps of rags that had once been his clothing, and a leather pouch.

"'That is all that remains of Colin Farwalker, the great adventurer. That is all that remains of me,' the spirit intoned sorrowfully. 'Now, hurry. I wish to give you a gift in thanks for the service you have done me.'

"Then the spirit pointed down at his earthly remains, and the pouch opened up. Inside were a length of rope and a little vial. 'You may choose but one of these two,' he said. 'Whichever you take, may it serve you well.'

"Which might serve me best? How could I even guess? And what might befall me if I chose unwisely? I took the vial, and the rope vanished. I thanked my supernatural benefactor. This goodly man —no matter what he had been in life— had died a lonely and frightening death, but his death might yet be my salvation. He began to fade away until he was as immaterial as a dream, and then he faded from sight altogether. I silently prayed that he might find peace eternal and directed my steps in the direction of the sealed rock door.

"I moved north, still thinking of the spirit and little minding my steps. This is why, I suppose, I tripped over something in the sand. Something solid. I bent to examine it and found a brass hunting horn, tarnished and weathered. I felt certain it must have belonged to Colin. However, since he had no more use for it, I carried it along with me as I continued on my way. It was just like as your father always told you, Graham."

"Indeed," the king laughed. 'Take anything that isn't nailed down. It might come in handy sometime."

"And if it is nailed down," seconded Rosella, "look for loose nails!"

Laughter momentarily reigned. Then Valanice continued.

"Not far beyond the spirit's final resting place, I encountered an edifice nearly as astounding as the stone head. It was much like a pyramid composed of gigantic steps. There was a doorway of carved stone — quite intricate and lovely, but far different from our own architecture — and on either side of it were stone statues that seemed to guard the entrance. More of the spiny plants I had already observed grew here and there around it. I walked inside, and..."

Her voice began to shake with remembered terror, and the audience of two waited, wide-eyed and breathless, to hear what was in store for Valanice on the other side of that doorway.

"At first there was only darkness, then I heard the rasp-like scrabbling of reptilian feet from across the room. As my eyes adjusted to the murky gloom, I could make out a terrifying shape emerging from a dark hole on the far side of the room — a scorpion larger than an ox! At the end of its tail I could see a sharp, jutting stinger, which would be the end of *me* unless I could avoid it. Words can't describe my utter terror. I was certain I would not live to leave the room.

"I backed up against the wall, and the horrible creature advanced with a terrible rattling. The smell of it was horrible, like acid and vinegar." Valanice shuddered, wrinkling her nose at the memory. "I was certain I was doomed. My hands clenched helplessly. I felt the little vial that the Spirit had given to me digging into my palm. The scorpion scuttled closer and raised its stinger. With a shriek, I hurled the vial at the hideous beast."

"I realize that sounds rather silly—throwing a tiny bottle of glass at a monstrous creature like that. But I was desperate and wild with terror. The bottle broke open, and a fine powder dusted the back of the horrid creature." Valanice paused and took a sip of water from her silver goblet.

"And then what?" asked Graham, eyes wide.

"Did the scorpion cease its attack? Tell us!" Rosella insisted.

"Of course it did," said Valanice with a smile. "If it had not, we would not be having this conversation. To my utter surprise and infinite relief, the beast began to shrink! It grew smaller and smaller until it was the size of a mouse, and then it skittered away. I sagged against the wall for the longest moment, trying to catch my breath while silently thanking Colin for his gift. Whatever it had been, it had been the gift of life."

"WHEN AT LAST I COULD BREATHE NORMALLY AGAIN, I TENTATIVELY BEGAN TO EXPLORE THE PLACE I was in. It turned out to be some sort of a temple.

"There was a square, stone altar. On the wall behind it was a carving of the sun, with rays of light that writhed like snakes, and it had such a fierce, human face. I surmised that it might represent a sun god of some sort. One of his eyes was wide open, while the other was only a slit with a beam of sunlight coming through it from the other side of the wall.

"On top of the altar was a statue of a little man, or perhaps another god of the people who once lived here. He squatted on top of the altar, one hand facing up and the other down. The beam of sunlight fell right onto the palm of his hand, and then onto a carving of a corn plant.

"The altar, made entirely of a grayish sort of stone, was covered on the top and one side with carvings. Most seemed to be about water, sun, and plants. Perhaps the little man was a harvest god, I surmised.

"It was a beautiful altar, but the only spots of color were three gemstones — a red and a yellow stone on the top surface of the altar and a blue stone on the front. All three were set into shallow depressions. I could see another depression that looked like it might hold another stone in the center of a picture of the sun.

"I began to touch the carvings, hoping to understand them better with my fingers than I could with my eyes. When I touched a carving of an upside-down raindrop, I heard a click, and the three gemstones rose just a little from the surface of the altar. When I touched a gemstone, it came loose in my fingers. I thought perhaps the yellow stone was meant to go into the hollow in the sun picture, but it wouldn't fit there. The red one did, however, and when I had placed it there, the light in the room brightened noticeably. I looked up to see the sun god on the wall. Both his eyes were wide open, and the beam of light that had been coming through the eye was now very large and bright.

"There were no more empty hollows in any of the altar pictures, so when I took the bluish-green gemstone, I decided to give it to the harvest god and placed it carefully in the palm of his upraised hand. As I did, the beam of light now turned blue. What might happen if I gave him the yellow stone as well? When I put the yellow gem in the little god's lower hand, the light shining on the corn plant turned a brilliant green. Then the corn carving sank into the altar and rose back up again. Only now, its top was an arrow-shaped piece of blue stone — turquoise, as I recall. I picked it up, thinking the shape familiar.

"I knew I could not stay within the temple any longer. The need to find Rosella burned in me as thirst had burned in the ghost of poor Colin. Leaving the temple, I pushed north in the direction of the cliffs. I came to a small sign that read:

RARE CURIOSITIES

For the Curious (and the Curiouser)

"Beneath it was a tiny door. Perhaps someone lived inside who might be able to help me.

"When I knocked, a nervous little creature, whom I recognized as being the curious —or was it *curiouser*?— rat I had seen earlier, poked his head outside, shaking like a leaf.

"'Who can that be?
'I cannot see!
'I cannot flee.
'I do decree!' he squeaked."

"The little rat had been wearing spectacles when I first saw him, but now he was without, and apparently unable to see at all.

"'Is there a problem with your eyes?' I asked. He replied in verse.

"'Normally I'd trade with you,
'But since I'm blind, my day is through.
'I cannot cope!
'That awful, rotten jackalope
'Has swiped my glasses,
'And I can't even come up with a word that rhymes!
'Or in a proper meter! Hmmpf!'

"And without saying so much as good-bye, he slammed the little door."

"What a rude creature!" exclaimed Graham.

"How utterly uncivil!" Rosella agreed.

"My very thought at the time," Valanice said, nodding. "But he was the soul of good manners compared with what I encountered next, for no sooner had the kangaroo rat gone back into his burrow, but that ill-mannered jackalope creature leaped out of a hole in the ground, laughed a hideous laugh, and kicked sand in my face! Then he made a rude sound like this..." She stuck her tongue between her lips and blew explosively.

Rosella burst into giggles, but a look from Valanice silenced her. "Sorry, Mother," she mumbled, putting a hand to her lips to stifle her mirth, but her eyes twinkled with an amusement Valanice did not share.

"I was never so insulted," Valanice continued, "but I was not so upset that I didn't notice that the spectacles he was wearing were the same ones I had seen earlier on the rat."

"So that's what the ratkin was trying to tell you," said Graham. "Those were his glasses the jackalope was wearing. How droll!"

"Droll? I did not find it so," Valanice sniffed, stinging from the insult. "I determined then and there to put a stop to that little thief's antics, if there were any way possible to do so. A rather wicked thought crept into my head. The hole which the half-rabbit, half antelope had leapt from was one of a pair lead into and out of his underground home. I blew on the old hunting horn I had tripped over in the desert to clear it of sand, and, feeling quite naughty indeed, I placed the bell of it over one of the jackalope's twin holes. I filled my lungs with air and blew with all my might.

"You should have seen the result! The wretched little creature shot up from the ground with a shriek. The rat's glasses flew from his face! He slid back down into the hole as if his bones had turned to rubber. I know it was wrong, but I felt such a sense of satisfaction!

"I picked up the glasses, as well as a tuft of some fur that had come loose in his surprise."

ROSELLA AND GRAHAM CLAPPED LOUDLY AND VALANICE ACKNOWLEDGED THE APPLAUSE WITH A queenly nod.

"The rat had said he would be open to trade of some sort if he regained his glasses. I didn't have much, but it could be that *something* I had could be traded for something more useful. At any rate, it wouldn't hurt to try.

"When I knocked again at his door, the near-sighted rat answered at once and told me to go away. Before he could retreat again, I brought out his eyeglasses and placed them firmly on his nose. I wish you could have seen how happy he was!

"'Would you like to trade with me?' he squeaked.
'You never know what you might see!
'A crook, a hook, a stylish hat,
'It's *always* time to deal with the Kangaroo Rat!'

"Now, I didn't believe a deal of what I'd seen already, but that seemed beside the point. Patting my pockets for something appropriate to trade, my hand came upon the little gourd seed that I had distractedly picked up so long ago. Seeing no other use for it, I tentatively offered it to the Kangaroo Rat. He seemed delighted, though I can't imagine why.

"'For a wrinkled seed, I have a need,' he exclaimed.

'Would you accept my offer of a lovely blue bead?'

"And with that he handed me a beautiful turquoise bead. It seemed a fair trade, but from the greedy look he gave me, he obviously felt he had gotten the better of the deal.

"I didn't know what possible use a turquoise bead could be, but it reminded me of the color of Rosella's eyes. And at least I had established a friendly relationship with one of the local citizens, even if he wasn't particularly eager to make conversation once our transaction had been concluded. In fact, he gave me no time to offer another exchange. He slammed the door to his burrow and disappeared, taking the seed with him.

"WITH LITTLE REASON TO STAY WHERE I WAS, I WANDERED EAST FROM THE KANGAROO RAT'S trading post but found nothing but apparently endless desert before me. I was afraid to chance a crossing, not knowing how far it might be to the next source of fresh water, so I doubled back until I came once more to the pool of the water god.

"I couldn't help wondering who this being was and what he had seen in his centuries of watching over this place. I reached up and touched his face, then jumped back as I heard the sound of stone grinding on stone. The water god's head turned slowly around to reveal a second face — from all appearances, a sun god. Brilliant rays protruded from all around its head.

"I looked closer at the two-faced deity. For the first time, I noticed a collar beneath the head that was studded with three turquoise gems. When I touched one, a portion of the collar turned, moving the stone into a new position relative to the other two. I touched the collar again to see if the stone would move back into its original place, but it twisted around to form a completely different configuration.

"Quite curious now, I touched the collar a third time. The three stones now lined up straight. All this must be to some purpose, I thought, but what that purpose might be, I could not say. So far, the head, the collar, and the free hand had all changed position when I had touched them. Might the hand holding the bowl be capable of movement, too? I reached out and touched it, almost afraid to know.

"The hand holding the bowl turned over, and the bowl was now upside-down, letting the last of the good water drain onto the sand. I heard the sound of running water behind me, and I quickly turned to see the salt-water pool emptying itself. I hurried to the side of the emptying pool and peered over the edge. As the water retreated, stone walls were revealed, still dripping wet and covered with algae. There were steps coming out from the stones spiraling to the bottom.

"As the last of the water was sucked from the well, I saw a figure: an odd little idol kneeling on a pedestal at the very bottom. There was a sort of headdress on his head, and in imitation of the statue above, he was holding out a shallow bowl. I climbed down the steps to the bottom of the well to have a closer look.

"Inside the idol's bowl were two pieces of bright blue turquoise, like the one from the altar in the pyramid, but they were shaped differently. One of them looked much like an arrowhead missing its shaft. I thought the stone I had found in the temple would fit snugly into it, and that the two stones together might fit together into a third shape, one that seemed somehow familiar. Of course! It finally dawned on me that it was the same shape as the design on the lip of the great stone head. I had thought at the time that something might once have fit inside the design, and here might be the very pieces that were missing, fit together like the pieces of a puzzle.

"I was just about to take the blue stone, but something about the scowl on the little idol's face seemed to be warning me. It wouldn't be polite, I thought, to take the piece of stone without offering something in its place, but what did I have that he might consider fair trade? I settled on the turquoise bead I had gotten from the kangaroo rat. Perhaps it would do. I placed it in the bowl and took the stone. It was much heavier than it had appeared, but fitted perfectly like the puzzle pieces I had imagined.

"It was a puzzlement that confronted me, indeed — the puzzle of how to leave this bizarre desert and find Rosella. The spirit of Colin Farwalker had said the way out was through the stone head, and that the way had been magically closed by an enchantress. Perhaps the two pieces of stone made up the key!

"I rushed up from the well and across the sands to stand again before the gigantic head with the two stone pieces in my hands. I pressed the pieces together, and they fit perfectly, forming a crude arrowhead shape. This shape and size were a perfect match for the hollow space in the lip. I'm sure my hands trembled as I placed them, and I know my heart pounded when I heard the sound of moving stone and saw the mouth grind slowly open, revealing a tunnel into the side of the cliff.

"'At last,' I thought. 'I will be free of this place! At last, I can find Rosella and bring her home!'

"Inside was a dark corridor of stone, part cave, part tunnel. I thought I could see a light at the other end and hurried toward it, so intent on my purpose that I didn't hear the sound of claws on rock until it was right behind me. I turned and saw ....."

"What?" Rosella gasped.

"What?" Graham cried.

"An enormous, swollen lizard lumbering toward me, its mouth gaping wide, the dim cavern light glinting on a thousand razor-sharp teeth!"

Part the Second
Trolled!

"What happened?" Graham gasped.

"What happened?" Rosella echoed, eagerly leaning forward to hear the outcome of her mother's encounter with the enormous reptile.

Valanice yawned delicately behind her hand. "I declare, I'm so exhausted with telling my story, and poor Rosella has scarcely been able to get a word in edgewise. It's her adventure, too, you know."

Rosella could not believe her mother was going to stop now in the narrative of her adventure — not now of all places! "Of course I want to tell my part of the story, Mother, but not before you tell us what happened in that tunnel with that awful beast!"

"Oh, all in good time, dearest daughter," Valanice said sweetly. "I think we're all anxious to hear what *you* experienced on the other side of the garden pool."

Rosella knew there was no arguing with her mother when she used that particular honey-coated tone. It meant she expected to be given her way, and somehow that's the way it always turned out. There was nothing for her but to tell the tale of her own wondrously strange and dangerous journey.

"I WAS FALLING," ROSELLA RECALLED. "I WASN'T IN THE BEAUTIFUL land of clouds following the dragonets, but a strange and alien place where I could swim through the air as though I were a fish in water. Then something grabbed me. I remember a pulling, pushing, stretching feeling — not at all pleasant — and then a kind of a *plop* as I landed in an enormous cavern. It was more splendid than any picture book. The walls looked as though they had melted like candle-wax and had formed shapes in rock like none you can imagine.

"I heard a voice behind me, saying, 'Welcome, oh most wondrously beautiful of all princesses. Welcome to my kingdom!' It was a pleasant, friendly voice, but when I turned around — imagine my surprise — the person who was speaking to me was a troll!

"A troll?" said her father. "Was it as hideous as the tales tell?"

"At the time," confessed Rosella, "I had little to compare him to, but he seemed as hideous as any troll would need to be. He was somewhat shorter than I, very muscular and portly as seem most of the troll folk, and he had oversized, pointed ears that drooped over but were held partially upright by the clumps of coarse hair growing out of his ears. There was more of the stuff growing from his too-broad nose, on the backs of his powerful hands, and on the tops of his bootless feet. The fearsome tusks jutting upward from his lower lips completed his hideous appearance. Later I would come to judge him quite handsome in comparison to most others I encountered. But at that moment, all I could think was that I must surely be seeing things.

"To be fair, the troll seemed as shocked at *my* appearance as I was at his. For all I knew, by troll standards of beauty, I would be considered quite homely!

"'I am King Otar Fenris III, grand high ruler of the underground kingdom of Vulcanix, Overlord of the Underworld,' he proclaimed. 'You are most certainly the Princess Rosella of Daventry.'

"At least that was one thing I was certain of, although I wasn't certain of much else at the moment, and I had no idea how this odd person might think he knew me. He kept staring at me with his huge green eyes in the strangest way, and he finally said 'I wasn't quite expecting *this*.'

"I had had just about enough of this nonsense, I can assure you. But after all, he was royalty, and I supposed I ought to mind my manners, so I simply said: 'Your majesty, I was not expecting this, either. Why am I here? What's going on?' as politely as I could manage under the circumstances."

"'I wasn't expecting you to be so...*lovely*, my lady,' he said, 'You will be the most radiant bride in all the underworld. Nay, the most beautiful in all the multiverse! We are to be married in three days' time.'

"I was sure that was *not* what he meant, but I had more things on my mind at the moment than trying to second-guess a troll. I did, however, know that I would not be inclined to marry a troll no matter how well acquainted we might become. In fact, he made Prince Throckmorton seems quite attractive by comparison. I turned around, determined to leave by the way I had come, but there was a large mirror in the way. There was a troll in the mirror, and it was wearing *my dress*!

"That's when I realized what had happened. My throat constricted. I managed to squeak out two words, and that was all.

"'Oh my!'

"Then, after endless moments, 'What's happened to me? I've turned into a...a....'

"'A troll, my dearest princess,' said King Otar as though he were commenting on the color of my hair or how the color blue went with my eyes. He acted as though being a troll was the most everyday, ordinary thing in the world! Of course, for him that must have been quite true.

"'Please don't be upset, sweet princess,' he begged. 'It does so ruin your lovely green complexion. After all, you make quite a beautiful troll! Simply gorgeous.'

"As you can imagine, this was not at all what I wanted to hear. What I wanted to hear was that I was not a troll at all, but the mirror told me the awful truth.

"'But how? Why?' There seemed to be no explanation forthcoming.

"'Allow me to escort you to your sleeping chamber,' the Troll King offered. 'Rest a bit. Perhaps you'll feel better later.'

"The only thing that was going to make me feel any better at all was *not* being a troll, but I was too dejected then to argue the point. I let him lead the way and followed behind.

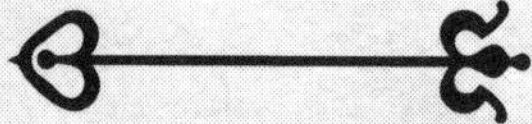

"THE TROLL CAVERN WAS HUNG WITH BANNERS AND SPEARS AND SHIELDS, AND A STONE THRONE rested in the middle. There were tunnels and alcoves, and a few trolls were about, but they paid us no attention at all. We came to a doorway. King Otar ushered me through to a chamber and closed the door behind him, saying again that a little rest would brighten my outlook.

"It was the strangest bedroom I had ever seen. There were stone walls and a stone floor, and stalactites and stalagmites had grown together into pillars that were the four posts of a bed, making it look like there were fantastic shapes and faces in the stone. It wasn't the sort of place where I would be likely to fall asleep. Oh, there was also a dressing table with a little stool and a mirror, but I didn't want to look in another mirror — not right then, anyway. I gave myself a pinch on the arm. It hurt!"

"So you weren't just imagining things?" asked her mother.

"And you were really a troll?" asked her father, horrified.

"Well, I'm not one any longer, so stop looking at me that way!" Rosella told him. "But anyway, father, yes, I was really a troll. And I knew that the most important thing I could do was find some way to escape and become human again. If I did not succeed, I might well end up the bride of the Troll King in but three days.

"As the door to my room was not locked, I set out to explore Vulcanix. Back in the great hall, I found a short, plump troll matron knitting in a carved-stone rocking chair. As soon as she saw me she threw down her knitting, leapt out of her chair, blocked my steps, and started yelling.

"'Stop right there, whoever you are! Whatever you are. Why are you in our caverns? You're a *human*, not a troll. You *smell* human. I can see right through you.' I hoped she couldn't. It was a horrid thought, and I'd had quite enough horrid thoughts for one day.

"'What were you doing with King Otar? What do you want from him?' she demanded. Of course I didn't want anything at all from King Otar, and I wanted to make this clear to this rather menacing troll woman. I tried to explain how I got there, but I wasn't that sure myself what had happened. She seemed certain I was there to somehow steal the king's throne.

"Suddenly, it was all just too much for me. I am somewhat ashamed to admit it, but I broke down and began to sob uncontrollably. As I cried, her attitude changed completely. She became quite kind and concerned.

"'I didn't mean to be so cross,' the troll said. 'But that horrible... *woman* has been snooping around again, and King Otar hasn't been acting himself lately. It's enough to make anyone suspicious. Especially me.' I wondered what woman she meant, but she was already on to the next topic.

"The troll woman introduced herself as Mathilde. She said she had been King Otar's nursemaid back when he was just a tiny little troll and had stayed to help out with the other trollkin ever since. This was all very well and good, and I listened politely. Then I grew excited when she told me that she knew how to turn me back human again!

"'Can you do it now?' I exclaimed in delight.

"'No. I must brew a special potion — a magical one — first. And you must be the one to gather its ingredients. But before I tell you what they are, promise me first that when you are changed back, you will do something for me.'

"'I will do anything that is honest and within my power,' I vowed.

"'In the world above this kingdom,' she said, 'is a dark and sinister land called Ooga Booga.' She shuddered when she said the name, as though it were something too awful to think about.

"'Our kingdoms have never been very warm to each other, but we have never been enemies. We had what you might call a *civil* relationship. Or we did until she came along.' I wanted to ask who *she* was, but thought better of interrupting.

"'Now they attack any troll who dares to show his face above ground,' she continued. 'Once you've taken the potion, and you're human again, will you go to Ooga Booga and investigate? It feels to my old bones that our kingdom is in terrible trouble.'

"I could tell Mathilde was stalwart and strong of heart, and I truly wished to help her, especially if she could return me to my true form. At once I promised her that if she could restore my human form, I'd go above and see what I could learn about the problem. I tried not to think too hard about going to some place called Ooga Booga and confronting beings who weren't afraid to attack trolls — beings that, judging from Mathilde, were terrible enough to cow even the most stout troll. One thing at a time, however. First the potion, then Ooga Booga, whatever it might turn out to be.

"My promise made Mathilde very happy. She gave me a list of ingredients for the potion: baked beetles — yuk! —, a crystal dragon scale, water of emerald, a silver spoon, and a golden bowl. This would not be easy, I was sure, but neither was being a troll.

"I bade Mathilde farewell and was setting out to find the ingredients, when I was crashed into by a little troll-girl. Her attention was on something in her hands, and she was muttering, 'Stupid old toy rat!' over and over. From her loud complaining, I learned she'd received the rat as a present. But what she'd really wanted was a battle-ax! Can you imagine?

"Then a voice from somewhere called her to lunch, so she stamped her furry little foot, stuck her lip out on both sides of her tusks, and dropped the rat to the floor. I didn't think the rat was all that terrible at all, so when the little girl left, I picked it up and went on my way. It turned out to be a wind-up toy, and I thought it looked quite dear.

"By this time, I was beginning to feel a little better about things. Mathilde had been so helpful, offering to mix up that magic potion and all, and even King Otar had been very considerate and respectful, even if he did plan to marry me. Where had *that* bright idea come from, anyway? I was beginning to revise my earlier opinion of trolls, but I still wasn't interested in remaining one. Or marrying one, either.

"I looked around the great hall. Here and there, I could see alcoves and hallways going off in various directions. One of the alcoves was giving off a sort of warm red glow that was most welcoming. I went to take a closer look and saw that a pool of bubbling mud had been set into the floor just inside the doorway. Two trolls, one very large and fleshy, the other very little and thin, were lying comfortably in the boiling muck as though it were a nothing more than a pleasantly warm bath. It looked more to me like Troll Soup, and that was not the most appetizing thought I'd had all day.

"Just as I was about to speak to the trolls, a tall, slender woman in a flowing gown of pink and black came walking from the other side of the room carrying an extremely ugly little dog. She was definitely human, which was a surprise. She was not a young woman, perhaps of an age near yours, mother, and she was quite beautiful in a haughty, arrogant sort of way. Her hair was the color of midnight, her skin was the color of new snow, and her full lips were the same shade as the dark roses of Daventry. Her eyes, too, were tinged dark red, and they were the largest I have ever seen. Their gaze cut as cold as the iced peaks of the Impossible Mountains.

"The woman's appearance seemed to frighten the trolls, for one of them let out an involuntary belch as he looked at her with nervous eyes. She glared at him in the most hateful way, called him a foul name, and strode off arrogantly. I thought the poor troll would die of terror. His companion teased him quite mercilessly about that, but I had the feeling he feared strange woman as well.

"When I asked the trolls who she was, they told me her name was Malicia and that no one around there really knew more about her. It was all quite mysterious, and they seemed afraid to say more. Malicia, I concluded, was the mysterious *she* that Mathilde had snarled about earlier. I grew impatient and left the two to their mud bath.

"THE TROLLS' KITCHEN WAS LOCATED THROUGH A DOORWAY ON THE RIGHT SIDE OF THE GREAT hall, and that's where I decided to look for the baked beetles for the potion. Even before I had quite arrived, I could smell something cooking, and it didn't smell anything like dinnertime in Castle Daventry!

"What a sight greeted me when I walked inside," Rosella recalled with amusement. "There was a chef — a large, furry troll — and he was talking to his stew, calling it pretty names and making kissing sounds over it. And drooling. From the looks of the concoction bubbling on the stove, I wouldn't have been surprised to hear it talking back. Oh, it was the most awful kitchen, with the most horrid smells that you could imagine. And the chef was bemoaning the fact that he was lacking a bat or a rat to complete the recipe! I was reasonably certain I'd never be hungry again after seeing the trolls' stew, and I hoped with all my heart that I'd be safely human and safely out of the Vulcanix Underground before dinnertime! I'm afraid the sight and the smell of it caused me to make some sort of noise of disgust, and that's when the chef noticed me.

"I tried to apologize, but he took three troll-size steps and picked me up by the back of my neck and threw me out of the kitchen.

"'Get out of my kitchen, you dreadful *peasant*, before you spoil my stew, mortify my roast, or deflate my souffle,' he shrieked. Brushing his hands of me, he went back to crooning at his disgusting concoction.

"I knew there had to be a way to get him away from the kitchen so I could look for those baked beetles. All I had were my wits and a wind-up rat. Of course! The chef was looking for a rat, so I went back to the doorway, wound up the toy, and turned it loose. It even squealed as it moved."

"How the chef's eyes lit up when he saw the rat speeding toward him.

"'Just what I need for my most wonderful of stews!' he exclaimed as he chased the rat around the kitchen, through the pantry door, and out of sight. A moment later, the rat came whizzing back into the kitchen, alone. For whatever reason, the chef had stayed behind — maybe he was searching under the counters for the furry little mechanical rodent. This was precisely the opportunity I'd been looking for. I picked up the toy and put it back in my pocket, then stepped back into the kitchen.

"IT WAS A LARGE KITCHEN, AND PROBABLY A VERY NICE ONE BY TROLL STANDARDS, BUT AS YOU might imagine, I found it disagreeable in the extreme. Still, I thought I might find something for the potion, so I gritted my teeth, wrinkled my nose, tried hard not to breathe too deeply, and began searching. I did my best to ignore the stew, which was still bubbling in a particularly unpleasant way.

"I found a baked beetle dispenser almost immediately, so I suppose it's a common spice in most troll cookery. In a cupboard were two gold-colored bowls; I wasn't sure if either was true gold, but when I looked at the bottoms of the bowls, one said 'brass,' the other '14K.' I took the latter."

"Very good, my dear," said Valanice with pleasure. "Always check for the karat stamp."

"Yes, mother. Anyway, there was no sign of a silver spoon or anything else on the list in the kitchen, so I set about to discover other parts of the Underground. Those first two items had been almost too easy — I didn't fool myself thinking that I'd just be able to walk up and take everything I needed for Mathilde's magic potion.

"As I crossed my way to the far side of the great hall, I passed the mud bath again, and this time two troll women were relaxing in the boiling muck. One of them was complaining about her insomnia. Her friend suggested that she use a wet lump of sulfur as a cure.

"'Just put it in the fireplace when you go to bed. You'll have no trouble sleeping then. Knocks me and the hubby right out,' she told the other. 'It's my secret for a perfect marriage!'

"Once again it became quite plain to me that trolls are very, very different from humans!

"I thought perhaps they might know something more about Malicia, but all they wanted to talk about was my impending wedding to King Otar, and I didn't much care for *that* subject. If that wasn't bad enough, they both burst into tears at the thought of my wedding gown! I quietly excused myself.

"As it turned out, my suspicions about the difficulty of filling Mathilde's magical shopping list were perfectly accurate. The next place I visited was the forging room. A big, strong troll with lots of overdeveloped muscles was hammering out metal tools and implements next to a blazing fire that he made even hotter with the aid of a great leather bellows. Sparks were flying everywhere, and I was worried about my dress or hair catching fire. There was a bucketful of nasty-looking, brackish water by his feet, and I gave that a pretty wide berth, as well. It reminded me too much of the chef's precious stew.

'Pardon me, sir,' I said to the forger, 'But I was wondering....'

"The forger put down his hammer and grinned at me — not the prettiest sight you've ever seen, I can assure you." Rosella made her voice deep and rough. "'Wonder no longer, sweetness,' he said. 'Instead, let Rollo de Trollo fulfill yer wildest dreams.'"

Rosella's mother and father laughed merrily at her imitation of the troll forger. Rosella joined in the laughter, but she remembered how little amusement she had found in his actions at the time.

"He tried to kiss me," she said, "but I managed to break free of his grasp and remind him that I was engaged to the king. It was a horrid thought but true and useful at the moment. He went back to his work, but not until giving me what he obviously thought was a captivating wink.

"I began to notice that over the roar of the fire I could hear a sort of tap-tapping sound. In a far corner, a mild-looking little troll was tapping at a gemstone with a hammer and chisel. He looked quite absorbed in his work, but not a bit happy about it. When I tried to talk to him, he jumped quite out of his skin in surprise.

"'I didn't mean to startle you,' I told him.

"'Oh, no, no,' he said. 'I really don't mind being interrupted, especially by someone as beautiful and charming as yourself.' I swear, he was the most polite troll I've ever met! His name was Oppi Goldworth, and he was terribly lonely — he could barely tolerate the company of most other trolls."

"He didn't like other trolls? How very odd," said Valanice.

"It was sad. He said he'd do anything to leave the underground and go to Etheria, but he had no coin, only an old, chipped hammer and a gem chisel. When we were through talking, he went back to work. Then I saw another doorway, one that didn't take me past the amorous forger, so I decided to explore in that direction for a while. Maybe when I came back this way, the dirty old troll would be out to lunch or something. I could only hope.

"This doorway led into a short corridor and back out again to a larger cavern with a most distinctive odor. The first things I saw were pits of this bubbling green guck. I was becoming more and more aware of a dreadful stench in the air with each passing second — it was rather like rotten eggs. Strangely, it didn't seem to be coming from the pots.

"There was a lantern half-buried in the dirt of what appeared to be a collapsed mine shaft — just the thing I'd need if I wandered deeper in the underground. By the time I'd taken it, I had almost gotten used to the stench, except for the way it made my eyes water. I decided to explore what looked like a deep pit in one corner of the cavern. It glowed and gave off such heat," Rosella reported. "You couldn't see to the bottom of it, and there were horrible winds howling in its depths."

"It sounds," her mother said, "like a perfect place to stay avoid."

"Oh, I agree," said Rosella. "And under other circumstances, that's what I would have done, but on the far side of the pit, I could see a pile of rocks emerging from the wall as though there had been a tunnel there. I thought I ought to explore it as a possible way out.

"There was a ledge around the pit, and I started across, mindful of my footing, when a sudden draft tried to suck me into the pit. I threw myself back against the wall and regained my footing. This was obviously going to be harder than I had anticipated! I worked my way around the ledge to the cave-in, and there was a big, gloppy, yellow wad of wet sulfur stuck up against the wall. It became obvious to me that it was the source of the dreadful smell.

"A naughty but very practical idea occurred to me: Hadn't the troll woman said she used sulfur to put herself to sleep? If the sulfur would knock *her* out, maybe it would put that conceited forger out of commission long enough for me to see if there was anything around that forge I might be able to use. At worst, the sulfur would serve as an excellent pay-back for that attempted kiss. I took it, hoping I could get rid of the smelly stuff as soon as humanly — or troll-ly — possible," said Rosella, laughing at her play on words.

"When I'd gotten safely back on the right side of the pit, I noticed another little pot full of green liquid. This one looked different somehow, and I could see that rather than a viscous welter of bubbling ooze, this one contained a beautiful, shimmering green liquid. I thought about my magical shopping list from Mathilde. Emerald water! Could this be it? I decided it couldn't be anything else and scooped some into the golden bowl.

"The forger was still hard at work when I got back to the forging cavern. He was pouring molten metal into a mold, and when I asked him about it, he explained that it was a spoon mold.

"'I poured de hot silver in dere, ya see?' Rosella said in her best troll imitation, "An' when it cools, I have me a purty spoon!'

"A silver spoon! That was just what I needed. I pulled the horrid glob of wet sulfur from my pocket and slyly tossed it into the forge. It made a terrible hiss and sizzle, and the forger leaned in to see what was making all the noise. I backed away just in time, because a big yellow cloud of sulfurous smoke came whooshing out of the fire. The unsavory forger had his face right in it!

"Did it cure his insomnia?" asked her father, smiling at his joke.

"Completely," said Rosella. "He fell over like a big tree, stuck a thumb in his mouth, and went right to sleep!

"The mold was much too hot to pick up with my hands, but I found a set of tongs on the wall so I could set the mold down in the bucket of icky water. When the water stopped boiling, I reached in with the tongs and took out the spoon, which had come free of the mold. My list of ingredients for Mathilde's magic potion was almost complete.

"I looked at the lantern I had taken from the other cavern and realized it wouldn't do much good if it wasn't lit. The fire had died down quite a bit, but I remembered how he'd heated it up before and pumped the bellows a few times until the flames rose high again. I caught a spark in my lantern so I didn't have to worry about any dark tunnels while I was searching for that crystal dragon scale.

"Back in the great hall, I looked around and spied a tunnel winding eastward.

"The tunnel led to yet another cavern room, and running through the room was a little road that led to still another tunnel on the other side. There was a terrible river of fire going through the cavern and a little stone bridge over the river. Between me and the bridge, however, was something very interesting — an old wooden structure that appeared to be some sort of elevator. There was a rickety wooden scaffold surrounding a metal bucket on chains. There were pulleys, but no rope to pull the bucket up and down, and someone had nailed up a crudely-lettered sign that read, 'Condemned,' which was probably a good thing, considering. Despite its decrepit appearance, I decided I'd be willing to try it if I had a rope — a way out of the underground and my impending marriage was not to be scoffed at.

"But I didn't have a rope, so I kept walking toward far side of the bridge. Just then I heard a slurping, splashing, *wet* sort of sound, and an enormous, wart-ridden troll scrambled up from beneath the bridge and glowered nastily at me. He was a particularly loathsome shade of off-green, and his gigantic stomach bulged out over his belt. His breath stank hideously of rotten meat and onions."

"Was he really that much more horrible than all the rest of the trolls?" her father asked.

"Truthfully, it wasn't his appearance so much as his attitude," Rosella recalled. "He refused to let me cross the bridge unless I gave him a thousand pieces of lead and a rat on a stick."

Both her parents laughed heartily.

"Needless to say, I didn't have his toll on me at the time, so I began thinking how I might get across without it.

"In a far corner of the cave, resting at the top of a slight slope, was a little cart that was missing a wheel and appeared to be stuck up to its axles in the mud. When I walked up to it and looked down the way I had come, I could see that it was a straight path to the troll bridge, then just a bit of a turn to the spot where the troll was arrogantly slouched. So I couldn't cross his precious bridge? We'd see about that.

"You see, when I'd been looking at the decorations back in the great hall, I'd noticed a small, spiked round shield hanging on the wall, and now I wondered if it might be the right size to replace the missing wheel. I went back to have another look, and it looked to be so. It was easy to reach by standing on tiptoe, and I grabbed it without anyone noticing.

"When I got back to the bridge troll's cavern, I held the shield to the cart and examined the combination. The shield was round, all right, and about the proper size, but how was I going to fasten it onto the cart well enough to make it work as a wheel? That's when I noticed that the metal spike in the center of the shield seemed quite loose. With a little effort, I was able to unscrew it. Heaving with all my strength, I pulled the cart from the mud and fit the shield to the axle. I attached the spike to hold it in place and stood back, proud of my handiwork. It looked like as good a wheel as any, and it was easily the best I had ever constructed. All I needed to do now was get the cart out of the mud.

It took me one good push to get it out of the mud and onto the road, and another hearty push got it rolling. I jumped in as the cart began rolling and barreled down the muddy rock path, picking up speed as I went down the slope and around the corner and over the bridge."

"And what of the troll?" asked her mother.

"He never knew what hit him," Rosella replied smugly. "And when I reached the other side, I hopped off and continued on my way."

"Did he die in the flames of the river?" asked Graham.

"I think not. He clearly lived quite close to them, in whatever den he occupied below the bridge, and they didn't appear to be burning him. The last I saw, he was sputtering and cursing as the current washed him down the river."

"AFTER MUCH SEARCHING, I CAME TO A DRAGON'S LAIR. I HAVE NEVER SEEN ANYTHING SO beautiful as the cave of the crystal dragon," Rosella told her parents, "unless it was the dragon herself.

"Imagine, if you can, an enormous room, as big as the entire royal palace of Daventry, composed entirely of shimmering, glittering crystal. Floors of crystal, walls of crystal, ceilings of sparkling, glistening crystal. And in the dragon's sleeping cave were precious gems — heaps and mounds and little hills of brilliant gemstones twinkling with a million rainbow lights. That was the place I entered next. Taking up much of that space was the crystal dragon herself. She seemed to have been formed from the very stuff of her surroundings. Covered in scales of radiant crystal, the slightest movement of her mighty flanks sent glitters of reflected light across the immense cavern. She was huge, large enough to crush me with a misplaced step, but somehow I wasn't afraid. How could I be afraid of something so utterly beautiful? At first I couldn't bring myself to believe that this unearthly creature was truly a dragon.

"Imagine my surprise when I saw that this beautiful creature was crying — beautiful emerald tears!" Rosella said. "I asked what had made her so sad, and she replied, 'I have lost my will to live. My spark is gone, and with it has gone all that makes this life worth living. My world has grown cold and dark. Go, leave me alone to my sorrow and emptiness, little troll.'

"I thought my heart would break for the sad crystal dragon. I considered her words. Her spark is gone. Fire? All dragons that I know of breathe fire, and steam flows from their nostrils as they exhale. But I had seen no steam nor flame from this crystal drake, and she seemed terribly cold. Then it dawned upon me — I *had* fire. 'You mean *this* kind of spark?' I asked, and held out the lantern with the glowing spark.

"'Here, here, let me have it!' she cried, and opened wide her mouth. I held up the lantern, and the spark leapt down inside her gullet. Immediately, a blazing crimson flame shot out from her mouth. The crystal dragon roared in her joy.

"'I am indebted to you,' she told me, and she reached into her pile of precious stones, drawing forth one enormous, perfect diamond. 'Take this stone as a token of my eternal gratitude, trollkin. With it, you can live as well as a princess.'

"I thought it might be rude to point out that I was already a princess — after all, the dragon had no way of knowing. 'Thank you,' I said, 'It's lovely. But might I instead ask for one of your scales?' So saying I held forth the magnificent diamond so that she might reclaim it. Waving a single claw, the dragon spoke again. 'Keep the stone, mortal. It is but a trifle, and when I return, you shall also have a scale.' She then roared again, 'But now I must fly! Now I must truly live again!' And fly she did, soaring majestically through the top of the cavern, dwindling to a shining spark in the distance. I stood looking up, awed. With no choice but to come back to the dragon's lair later, it occurred to me that I knew someone who could make much better use of the dragon's gem than I.

"Why, whoever could that be?" her father wondered.

"Do you recall the little jeweler, Oppi?" asked Rosella.

"Indeed. The one who wanted to leave the underground."

"Yes. But he had nothing but his jeweler's tools. If he had the gem, he could use it to leave and go to Etheria. The thought gave me such pleasure that I rushed straightaway to his workbench by the forge. In my excitement, I even ignored the lewd whistles and amorous winks thrown my way by that obnoxious forger, awake again and no more couth for the napping.

"When I gave the gem to Oppi, his eyes got very large, like saucers, and he gave me the biggest smile I've ever seen. 'How can I ever thank you? You've given me a chance to make my dreams come true, and for this I am indebted to you a thousand fold. I shall throw out these old, worn tools, buy new ones, start a new life!'

"A hammer and chisel might be just the thing for chipping away a crystal scale though, so I asked if I might have his old tools since he seemed to have no interest in keeping them.. 'Enjoy them, my dear, enjoy them. May they serve you as well as they have me, although I must say that I cannot imagine what you might do with them.' Thanking me yet again, he nearly flew from the room!

"I HURRIED BACK TO THE DRAGON'S CAVERN. THE CRYSTAL DRAGON HAD INDEED RETURNED, BUT she was fast asleep, exhausted after her flight. Nothing I did would rouse her, so, somewhat embarrassed, I used the chisel to chip away a small scale from her tail. She *had* said I could have the scale, after all, but I still felt bad about taking one. With a final, silent 'thank you,' I backed out of her cavern. I was so happy! This was the last ingredient I needed — Mathilde could make her potion, and I would be human again. I could leave the underground and could try to find my way back home — after fulfilling my promise to Mathilde, of course.

"I suppose I should be happy I didn't know how much longer it would be before I returned," Rosella sighed. "I would have become quite downhearted."

"Well, you're home now," said her father, "and that's all that matters to me."

"And you never would have given up, my dear," her mother assured her. "That's not the way you do things."

"I'm sure you're right, mother. I never did give up, though things got worse before they got better. Of course, before all of that, Mathilde had to make me her potion.

"WHEN I RETURNED TO THE GREAT HALL, I HANDED OVER THE GOLDEN BOWL AND MY LITTLE collection of ingredients. Mathilde put each one into the bowl and stirred the odd smelling concoction with the silver spoon. When it began frothing, she handed it to me to drink, which I did, trying not to think too hard about the baked beetles. It felt unexpectedly cool and smooth going down, and it tasted surprisingly tangy and not at all bad. As I lowered the bowl, I didn't feel as if anything had happened, but maybe the change wasn't something one could feel. I hadn't, after all, felt the change when I became a troll.

"'Am I human?' I asked Mathilde. My voice sounded strangely hollow in my ears. 'Well, not exactly, dear,' she replied, with the strangest look on her face. Then she suddenly snapped her fingers, crying out, 'Of course, of course! I had forgotten. We need a troll hair!' And with that, she yanked one from her own head, dropped it into the bowl, and stirred it again with the silver spoon, which began immediately to dissolve.

"I drank again. This time the potion was hot and pungent, and burned like a drink of liquid cinnamon. This time, there was a definite effect—a sort of shimmering and trembling from my head to my feet. Mathilde clapped her hands, and I took a little silver pellet from my mouth — all that was left of the silver spoon! I decided then and there to keep that little piece of silver as a souvenir of all my adventures in the Underground and placed it carefully in a pocket. That potion was even stronger than your tea, Mother."

Valanice sniffed.

"Just then, the Troll King walked in. I had quite forgotten about him in my excitement at becoming human again. Were we still engaged now that I wasn't a troll? I certainly hoped not.

"But the Troll King seemed to like me even better as a human! I just couldn't believe it. He was going on and on about how lovely he thought me when that woman in the flowing gown — Malicia — appeared in a sulfurous puff of smoke. She didn't look at all happy. I just stood frozen in surprise at her arrival.

'I've had more than enough of your distracting the king, you annoying little human snip!' Malicia shrieked, her beautiful face distorted by a wicked grimace. She raised up her hands like she was about to use some kind of magic on me. I stepped back nervously, and the Troll King tried to grab the woman's arms and stop her, but it was too late. There was a flash of blinding white light, the smell of ether, and the most curious wrenching feeling I have ever known. The next thing instant, I was back in my chamber — and this time, the door was firmly locked! I could hear Malicia's voice echoing in my ears, saying, 'I'll be back to dispose of you before you know it, my pretty!'

"There didn't seem to be any way out. The walls were made of solid stone, and it looked like I'd be there until Malicia came back to... Well, I didn't know what she was planning to do to me, but I was sure it would not be for my enjoyment. I had a few choice words for the portrait of the purple-eyed Troll King that hung on the stone wall, I can tell you. If he hadn't decided we were engaged..."

Rosella sighed and shook her head.

"Maybe by that time, Prince Throckmorton wasn't looking so bad, hmmm?" her mother said, eyes twinkling.

"I refuse to comment," said Rosella, crossing her arms. "Actually, I scarcely had time to think about it, because when I looked at the portrait, I could see steam coming out of the nostrils. Either Trolls painted very realistic portraits or there was an opening of some kind leading into the wall. But I couldn't reach the portrait to look behind it — it was too high.

"Despair set in, and I collapsed onto a footstool in front of my wardrobe. I sat there for several minutes, by turns frustrated and angry that escape, so close at hand, was being denied me. As I banged my fist against the cushion of the stool, an idea struck me — I was too short to move the portrait, but if I stood on a stool....

I immediately dragged my seat under the portrait and stood upon it, but it was still too low. I quickly hauled over my bedside table, and with a grunt and a heave, placed the stool atop it. The resulting structure looked tall enough, but just to be sure, I added a fat cushion to the very top of the stack. Climbing carefully to the top of the furniture pile, I was able to remove the King's portrait, which I dropped to the floor with a look of distaste. Sure enough, behind where the portrait had hung was the beginning of a low tunnel that was just large enough for me to squeeze through.

"ESCAPE AT LAST. I WRIGGLED THROUGH THE OPENING, PUTTING SEVERAL SMALL RIPS IN MY DRESS in the process. All I could think about was getting away before Malicia returned to dispose of me and figure out where I had fled when she discovered an empty bedroom. Then I saw two eyeholes in the wall, at about head level. I heard someone slamming a door on the other side, then heard the Troll King's voice, followed by Malicia's. They were talking about me, and about a volcano.

"I peeked through the eyeholes and saw a room full of technology — fantastic metal machinery. There were pipes, cog wheels, levers, and coils, and it all stank horribly of grease and oil. The king was sitting in a large seat at what looked to be controls of some sort, looking *terribly* unhappy. Malicia and her awful little dog were there, too, glaring at King Otar.

"'Listen to me, you weak-minded tool,' Malicia was scolding. 'If your fixation with that meddlesome little human snit disrupts my plans again, I'll have you skinned.

Boiled alive. Maybe both. Have you figured out how to work the volcano mechanism yet, or must I *motivate* you again? Time is wasting.'

"The king mumbled something about how he had indeed figured out the controls, but was concerned about the fate that would befall Ooga Booga and someplace called the Bountiful Woods when the volcano erupted.

"A machine to make a volcano erupt? A machine controlled by Malicia and King Otar? My brain wanted to erupt itself at the horror of which I was overhearing.

"MALICIA WASN'T IN THE LEAST CONCERNED ABOUT OOGA BOOGA OR BOUNTIFUL WOODS. Smirking evily, she said, 'What are a few villages and townships? Who cares about most of those people? Who's going to be left to miss them? They are all just unimportant pawns in the game that we play. At least the blight of Etheria will be gone and my vengeance will be complete!' Her little mutt yapped to emphasize her last point as she spun on her heel and strode from the room in a swirl of her cloak. I felt chilled to the bone. The woman was undeniably evil.

"I felt sorry for the Troll King right then. It was obvious he didn't want to go along with Malicia's plans, but he seemed so confused, as though he were trying to remember something that just wouldn't come to him. But if Malicia had her way, he would use his knowledge of dread technology, of the machines in that room, to explode a volcano, raining hot ash and molten destruction down on the surrounding lands. Something had to be done!

"I COULD SEE AN OPENING AT THE OTHER END OF THE TUNNEL. I CRAWLED TOWARD IT UNTIL I could poke my head and shoulders through, and then suddenly I was sliding down the wall and into the great hall, knocking down a shelf as I tumbled, finally landing — plop! — upon the royal throne. Thank heavens no one noticed.

"I got down as inconspicuously as possible and picked up a little ornament that had been on the shelf and fallen down with me. It was a silvery statue of a little toad-like thing with scales and large spines running down its back, something like those on a dragon. It was sort of cute, actually. It made me smile, and not too many things had been able to do that lately.

"I could hear voices again — this time it sounded like Malicia and Mathilde arguing about the King. Mathilde was saying 'Don't you dare hurt him, you wrinkled old hussy!' and Malicia was commanding her to mind her own business, '...or you'll spend all of eternity regretting the day you were born! Or was it *hatched*?'

"Mathilde was accusing Malicia of doing something to King Otar to make him different. Malicia wouldn't admit anything to her, but I got the feeling that whatever it was, it was only the beginning of her plans for the people of the underground, and the whole world thereabouts — what she called the Realm of Eldritch. A moment later, Mathilde came stomping out of the doorway. A ferocious blast of ill magic hurtled down the tunnel, and she barely dodged it with a loud squawk.

"Poor Mathilde. Her shoulders seemed to sag. She walked slowly to her rocking chair and sat down, slumped over her knitting like a woman condemned. Feeling nearly as bad as she, I warned Mathilde she should be careful in confronting Malicia. Mathilde told me that she was convinced Malicia had done something to King Otar, something that had changed him in some way. She sat, slumped and dejected, her normal fire gone, seeming to have lost all hope. To cheer her, I took the funny little toad-thing from my pocket, hoping that the sight of it might make her feel better. I didn't realize how well it would work!

"'Otar's dragon toad!' she exclaimed, suddenly enthusiastic. 'This was the King's magical guardian when he was just a wee one. When little Otar got into a scrape, it would run home and tell me where he was! I had thought it lost long ago!'

"It certainly didn't look very lively, but Mathilde explained the dragon toad was alive but had been dormant for years. She pulled a handful of powder from her pocket, and sprinkled it over the toad, which began to shimmer and open one of its eyes. Mathilde asked it where King Otar was, and the toad replied in a low, unlikely, but sonorous voice, 'Imprisoned deep in the land of Ooga Booga.' It's vital energy apparently exhausted, the little toad creature then sank back into slumber without elaborating further on the King's predicament.

"'Ooga Booga? But that means the king who's been in cahoots with Malicia is not Otar, he's an impostor! I knew it! I knew the *real* Otar would never do anything with that frigid strumpet!' Mathilde exclaimed. I figured that more bad news couldn't hurt at this point, so I related what little I knew of Malicia's plan to unleash the volcano.

"'If Malicia can ignite the volcano, the entire Realm of Eldritch will be destroyed, flooded in lava or drowned in ash!' Mathilde's face became pale as death. I had no reason to disbelieve her. From beneath her apron, she brought forth what she claimed to be a magical rope and begged me to use it to travel up to Ooga Booga to find and save the real King Otar.

"Just then, I glimpsed a flash of movement — Malicia coming back. Quickly I ducked behind a prominent rock, praying silently that I had not been noticed. She was peering about looking for me, and she might have found me too, but as she neared the rock I hid behind, a bat flew out of the kitchen — probably one of the ingredients escaping the stew — and swooped past Malicia's head.

"You should have heard her squeal! 'Plague-carrying, mange-ridden, nasty, smelly *vermin*!' Rosella cried in her most revolting voice, 'Someday I'll come up with a way annihilate every bat, rat, and snake in existence!' I got the distinct impression she was unhappy. At any rate, despite her continuing threats to vermin kind, she quickly left through the door to the forging room. This might be my only chance to get away.

"I hurried towards the cavern that contained the decrepit mining elevator, but no sooner did I reach its entrance than Malicia appeared out of thin air — again! I was getting a little tired of that trick of hers, although I must admit it was quite impressive. If only I knew then how much more tired I'd become of it before this was all over!

"Frantically, I dived behind another rock and hid. As Malicia stepped past me, still muttering about rats, I took the little mechanical rat that I still carried, rapidly wound it up, then turned it loose in her general direction. I nearly laughed aloud when the rat ran right up her skirt! She screamed *very* loudly, kept on screaming, and disappeared more quickly than I would have thought possible. As I dashed for the elevator, I could hold back my laughter no longer.

"With Mathilde's rope, I was able to fix the elevator, or rather the rope was able to — all I had to do was unravel it, so I guess it was magical after all. I got into the little metal bucket and began pulling on the rope, raising myself up to the ceiling that led to the dark kingdom of Ooga Booga. I was almost to the top of the cavern when I heard an awful cracking and crumbling around me.

"The whole elevator shaft was beginning to fall apart around me!"

Part the Third
I Wood if I Could

"OH, MY GOODNESS!" VALANICE EXCLAIMED. "WERE YOU HURT?"

"She doesn't look as though she was," Graham assured her. "What happened then, Rosella? Tell us!"

Rosella smiled sweetly at Valanice. "You were absolutely right, Mother. This recounting of one's adventures is tiring in the extreme. I fear I can speak no more until I've rested." She placed one hand delicately against her forehead and sighed.

Valanice put her hands on her hips and raised one eyebrow.

Rosella broke into giggles in spite of, or perhaps because of, the silly pose she was holding and the mock-serious look on Valanice's face. "Your turn, Mother," she said when she had recovered. "I've talked long enough. Now tell us what happened when you were face to face with the giant lizard."

Valanice knew when it was pointless to argue with Rosella any longer, and even Graham seemed to agree with their daughter. "Tell us, dear wife," he said, eyes twinkling with humor, "were you eaten by the beast?"

"I very nearly was," she told him in all seriousness. "It certainly looked hungry enough, and I knew I had nothing to offer that it might prefer to me as a meal. I was still very near the entrance — the mouth of the stone head — so I took a chance and ran back toward the light. Once safely outside, I realized my knees were absolutely weak with fright. But this was the only way out of the desert, and I had to get out to find Rosella. And that meant I had to find a way past that scaly monstrosity.

"I noticed that the bushes growing near the stone head looked much like pieces of plant matter I had seen on the floor of the cave — some of which had appeared half chewed. Perhaps this prickly plant was a staple of the reptile's diet. He might even prefer it to Filet of Queen of Daventry, if luck were with me!

"I used my stick to knock one of the thorny red fruits from the cactus bush, then picked it up carefully and returned to the tunnel, hoping my guess about this fellow's dietary habits proved correct. In moments he was back and eyeing me ravenously, tongue flicking in and out of his toothy maw. I tossed him the fruit, and he snatched it up with a quick twitch of his neck, then retreated back into his hole in the wall. You can't imagine my relief! Now I could continue on my way, leaving behind the endless desert and the blazing sun. How pleasant it was when I reached the other end of the tunnel and stepped out into a lovely, deep wood.

"The trees were ablaze with fall color," Valanice recalled. "There were flowers perfuming the air with their fragrance, and buzzing hummingbirds were everywhere. It was quite the loveliest place I'd ever seen — next to Daventry, of course. There was a river just ahead with barely a trickle of water running through it, and on either side of it were giant marble statues. The one on the near bank was of a maiden with a water jug that she appeared to be tipping into the river, while on the far bank was another maiden holding a cornucopia as though to spill its contents out onto the ground. But both the pitcher and the cornucopia were empty.

"It looked as though an arched stone bridge had once spanned the river, but it was shattered. Only the bases of it remained, jutting majestically from the river banks. I tested the mud of the river bed and found it dangerously soft and deep — no doubt it could suck me down in a moment if I were to be so foolish as to venture out in it. I was stranded, it seemed, on this side, and I began meandering westward into the trees.

"The woods were even lovelier further along, if that were possible. There was a beautiful clearing with an ancient, majestic oak, surrounded on all sides by tall trees displaying their fall finery. Someone had pounded a large iron spike into the trunk of the oak, and sap was running down from the wound like blood. A stag lay at the base of the tree, showing no fear at my approach and wearing an expression of deep sorrow on his noble face. As I watched, a tear slowly trickled down his furry muzzle. He stood slowly, turned his handsome head towards me, and spoke in a clear, human voice.

"'Turn ye back, my lady,' he warned. 'These magical woods are under the pall of a horrible curse, and none are safe here now. Turn back while you still can.'

"I told him I appreciated his concern, but that my mission was so important that I had to continue on, no matter what perils lay in wait. He then told me that the oak tree had once been his wife, Ceres — Mother Nature and the Lady of Spring herself. He was Attis, Lord of the Hunt, but an evil enchantment had turned him into a stag, and he had been unable to save his lady from her fate. 'Only the faerie nobles of the high court of Etheria have such power,' he said, 'but for one of them to have done this is unthinkable. I fear that my lady may perish of that wicked wound, but I can do nothing to save her as I have nothing to work with but these clumsy hooves.'

I tried to help, but try as I might, I wasn't strong enough to remove the spike. I asked Lord Attis what would happen if Ceres were to perish of her wound, and he replied, 'I believe that these ancient woods will perish along with her — as will I.

"I turned to leave, but he called after me to wait," Valanice said, remembering the stag's next words. "He told me that to the west lay the were-woods, where I must not go unless I wished to risk being devoured by creatures too horrid to think upon. I thanked him again for the warning, but I knew I had no choice but to continue my search. 'Is there nothing that can break the enchantment over you and your wife?' I asked.

"'Perhaps,' he replied, 'the Rock Spirit will know something. You would have to awaken him from an eons-deep slumber, though, and I can no longer recall the ritual necessary to revive him. I am becoming a stag in truth, and the forest sings to my blood.' My heart ached for Attis. I promised I would help if I could find a way. Then I remembered I had not asked him about Rosella."

I showed him the golden comb, and he said, 'I have not seen her, nor have any in this forest, but the birds that bring me news from afar say she is to be married to King Otar, troll lord of the Vulcanix Underground.'

"My darling daughter was to be married to a *troll*? I knew I must waste no time rescuing her; after all, Prince Throckmorton was a *much* better choice. Attis told me the only known portal to the Underground was west, beyond the dreaded were-woods. He also spoke of a merchant in the town of Falderal who sold a salve that could grant one safe passage through the were woods. Falderal lay to the northwest, and so I knew that was the way I must go.

"I began north and soon encountered a bend in the muddy river bed. It was plain to see that way was closed to me until I could find a way across the soft, dangerous mud. I turned west, hoping to find a crossing further upriver.

"The woods to the west were darker, more menacing than the forest behind me. I walked a few steps farther, but I imagined I could see pairs of glowing eyes staring at me from the dark places under the twisted trees and contorted bushes. Staring hungrily. I decided it would be better if I didn't go back in there until I had the protection Lord Attis had spoken of. Instead, I went north.

"In time, I again came to the banks of the river. The mud was as treacherous here as it had been at the bridge, but there were stepping stones jutting from the river bed that I was able to jump across. It required care and patience but, my long skirt notwithstanding, I made it across. A path that led between two trees, and stretched across it was the largest and most frightening spider's web I had ever seen. In its center a tiny hummingbird fluttered, crying out for help.

"A bloated red spider was walking across the web toward the hummingbird, dwarfing it in size. I tried to free the bird before the spider could harm it, but the bird screamed a warning about the spider's lethal venom.'

The spider glared at me. 'Back off!' he growled in a nasty, chattering tone. 'You let that poor little bird go!' I ordered the spider, but he was evidently not accustomed to obeying whomever came along and tried to deprive him of lunch. 'Get away if you value your life, tidbit!' it snarled, this time clicking its fangs for emphasis."

"Weren't you afraid of the spider?" Rosella interrupted.

"After all, the bird said it was poisonous," Graham remarked.

"I *was* afraid of the spider," Valanice assured them, "but I couldn't just walk away and let it kill the hummingbird, either. You may remember I had brought a little basket with a lid from the desert, and now I knew the perfect use for it. I clapped the basket down on the spider and slammed down the lid! Oh, you should have heard him curse, the nasty little devil! Such language! Then I tossed the basket into a nearby bush and, with a little care, I was able to extricate the hummingbird from the sticky strands. 'There you are, my feathered friend,' I told her. 'Safe and sound.'

"'Thank you for my life, kindest of travelers,' piped the hummingbird. 'If I can do you some good in the future, I promise that I will.' And with that, she flew away. It was a sweet thing to say, but how unlikely it seemed that such a tiny creature could aid me in my quest. Still, I thought it would be nice to see her again."

"And did you, mother?" asked Rosella.

"Patience, my dearest daughter, patience," said Valanice, knowing full well that of all Rosella's many virtues, patience was not the most prominent.

"I continued on my way down the path and soon came to a city wall that seemed to run as far as I could see to the left and right. There was an enormous, gaudy red gate set in the center of it, with a gigantic gilt knocker hanging on it. As I approached the gate, a sliding panel near its top slid open, and a pair of small, suspicious brown eyes blinked down at me. A huge, booming, yet whiny voice called: 'Halt! Who goes there?' I identified myself, and the voice said, 'By decree of the powers that be, you may only enter the great city of Falderal if you bring unto me a golden-haired fruit snake!'

"That's ridiculous," said Graham. "There's no such thing!"

"That's exactly what I told the gate guard, and he said that if I was going to let a little thing like *that* stop me, I didn't *deserve* to enter his city! Well, I wasn't about to give up so easily. I banged the knocker against the gate again.

"'Have you brought me that golden haired fruit snake yet, human?' the guard asked. 'No, of course I haven't! There isn't one, you silly creature!' I replied. He slammed the door panel shut again.

I was about to knock one more time when my attention was caught by the sight of a little door set unobtrusively in the wall just to the right of the gate. No sooner had I reached for the handle than the gate panel slid open with a bang.

"'Entry through that portal is expressly forbidden! You can't go through there!' the guard screamed, 'There's an enormous, drooling, purple cockroach waiting on the other side! You just wait and see!'

"Even with all the strange things I had seen so far, I thought I could risk that. Trailed by the gatekeepers frustrated exclamations, I stepped through the door into the oddest little city you could imagine.

"There was a plaza with oddly shaped buildings, the lot of them constructed from what appeared to be gigantic slabs of basalt and painted in overly bright pastel colors. The trees, too, seemed unnaturally slick and polished, and a meandering cobblestone street haphazardly connected all of it together. A little white dog with bulging eyes was walking on his hind legs, wearing a lavender waistcoat, and carrying a walking cane. He trotted toward me, lisping in a high-pitched, yapping voice.

'Thtop in the name of the powers that be! I, Archduke Fifi le Yipyap of Falderal, do tho order it! Thtop!'"

Valanice's family was more than a little amused at her imitation of the archduke, but she swore to its accuracy. "'You are a thtranger here,' he insisted. 'You have no buthineth being in beautiful Falderal! Why, I thould have you imprithoned for illegal thide-door entry! Explain yourthelf ere I call for the guardth!'

"I really couldn't bring myself to take this ridiculous little beast seriously, but every time I tried to walk around him, he stepped in front of me and barked again. Perhaps it would be better to reason with him after all. I begged his indulgence and told him I was on an errand of great importance. He was not inclined to believe me until I showed him Rosella's golden comb and told him the sad story of my search for her.

"To my utter surprise, the archduke's eyes began to fill with tears. 'Tho tragic, tho tragic! I cannot in good conscious try to thtop you from carrying out thuch a noble mithion, madam!,' he wailed. 'Enjoy your thtay in Falderal. If you go to the Faux Thop, my lady, remember to take it with a grain of thalt. Farewell, and good fortune in thy motht noble of quethts!' Then he blew his nose wetly into an embroidered hanky and turned away, sobbing.

"As if all this weren't curious enough, a little yellow fowl wearing a great sunbonnet came dashing down the street, squawking at the top of her lungs, 'The sky is falling! The sky is falling!'

'Pay her no mind, my good lady,' the archduke said. 'She'th really very thilly, alwayth thcreaming about dithathters and whatnot.'

"My immediate task was to find the merchant Lord Attis had spoken of — the one who could provide me with the ability to cross the were-woods unharmed. I strolled east down the street and almost immediately saw an odd little cart packed with jars and bottles, baskets and boxes. The chicken I'd seen only a moment before was standing in front of the cart, still squawking about the sky. I walked closer to hear what she was saying.

"'Why won't anyone believe me? Why?! You'll all regret it eventually, you will! When you're all crushed under the weight of the heavens, then you'll wish you'd listened!' The chicken was wailing to a green, scaly snake-man who was coiled behind the counter of the cart. The snake seemed to be trying to sell her something, but she didn't appear interested. In fact, the little chick was only growing angrier and more agitated, and a moment later, she was screeching again as she ran down the street.

"I approached the cart with a certain amount of trepidation. This person was not only a snake, but evidently some kind of salesman, and I'm automatically wary of salesmen.

"'I was told of a merchant who sells an item that can get me through the were-woods safe and unharmed,' I said to him. 'Would that perhaps be you?' Oozing charm from every scale, the salesman stretched his long neck from the cart and stuck his face so close to mine that I could smell his rather sour breath.

'That would be me indeed, dear lady,' he hissed. 'I have the ssstuff you desssire; a magical sssalve of great power and potency, almossst completely unavailable in this remote area. However, I am willing to sssell it, and for a mere sssmidgen of itsss true worth to one asss charming asss you. However, I will only take one *very* ssspecial item in exchange for this sssalve. This item isss a magic ssstatuette; a lovely depiction, though of little worth, of a nymph gazing into a foressst pond.'

"'You don't say. Just where can I find this magical statuette?' I asked.

"'The archduke hasss it.'

"You can imagine my reaction to *that*," Valanice said to Graham and Rosella. "How could I take something that belonged to the archduke, as though I were some common criminal? But the snake-oil salesman went on to explain that the statue was said to belong to Titania, Queen of the Faeries, though no one knew for sure. He had been hired to reaquire it for her. It seemed a weak story, but I could only hope he was right, because I had to have the statuette to obtain the salve, and I had to have the salve to cross the were-woods, and I had to...."

"Yes, yes, my darling. We understand," said Graham, patting her hand. "What happened next?"

"I questioned him further about the statuette and its powers. He told me that if one placed an object belonging to another person on the statuette, that person's location would be revealed, swirling in the nymph's pool. I could only imagine why he would want it, but I suddenly knew how very valuable it could be to *me*.

"AS IT HAPPENED, WHEN I WENT TO THE ARCHDUKE'S COMBINATION mansion and town hall, musing on the ethics of my possible theft, I found a sign posted on the door. It read:

Town hall closed by the Imperial Decree of The Powers That Be!

Come back a Little Later for the archduke's Super-Secret Birthday Party and Masquerade Ball!

"A PARTY SEEMED A PERFECT OPPORTUNITY TO GAIN ENTRANCE, AND A MASQUERADE BALL WOULD provide wonderful concealment, but it also meant I needed a mask. Where in this strange little town would I find one, and how would I pay? I had no money, and not all merchants were so noble as to accept barter. Well, the party wouldn't start for a while — there was time to explore Falderal.

"The first establishment I entered was a China Shop. Inside were hundreds of pieces of the loveliest and most fragile china, and behind a glass counter filled with wonderful, delicate knickknacks was a hulking black bull crying softly and dabbing at his eyes with a dainty lace handkerchief.

'Welcome to my shop, dear lady,' he said in a soft voice that seemed wholly out of place coming from his massive frame. "I am Fernando Bullforth, proprietor. I would normally wish you a good day, my lady, but today is not a good day. Oh, no. It is a day of sorrow and tragedy, for some cruel and heartless soul has stolen my Treasure.'

"'How awful,' I said. 'Surely the thief could not have gotten far lugging a trove of silver and jewels.'

"'My Treasure is not of metal and gems, my fair lady,' he replied, 'Treasure is my precious china bird.' He went on to tell me how he had loved his little bird more than all the stars in the sky. 'She is my only true friend. And now she's gone, stolen by ruthless thugs and villains,' he sobbed and dabbed at his eyes some more.

"The only bird I had seen was a mockingbird who had his nest in a tree near the fountain pool. He was wont to hurl insults at whomsoever walked by, so I was certain he could be no relation to Fernando's friend.

"'I, too, have suffered a loss. My daughter was taken from me,' I told him. 'She is a pretty girl with long golden hair and mischievous blue eyes, dressed in blue silk. Have you heard word of her?'

"Fernando brightened a little. 'I have just read of the upcoming marriage of King Otar of Vulcanix and a blonde-haired, mystery princess. Could she be your daughter? Although I must say that you look little like most trolls,' Fernando said. He seemed to enjoy the subject of society.

"Now it's true that I'd been encouraging you to marry, Rosella, but this was the second time I'd heard the rumor that you were engaged to a troll. I feared more than ever that it might be true."

"I hope you knew it wasn't an engagement of my choosing," said Rosella indignantly.

"It seemed unlikely that it was," Valanice assured her. "After all, you had seemingly been snatched away before my very eyes and taken away — kidnapped. My only thought was to save you."

Rosella's head hung, and her cheeks flushed with guilt. Valanice smiled, just a little.

"AS I WAS LEAVING, I HAPPENED TO NOTICE A LOVELY MASK HANGING ON ONE OF THE WALLS OF the shop. I inquired as to its price. 'The price is 100 gold coins,' the bull said, 'but I'll sell it to you for 80. I just don't care about wealth any more, now that Treasure is gone.' And he started crying yet again. I could have joined him — 80 pieces of gold was still 80 more than I had.

"As I walked away from the China Shop, a curious thing happened," Valanice told her husband and daughter. "I saw the chicken again — the one who'd been so perturbed about the sky. She was running down the street once more, screeching about the usual thing, but this time she ran up to me, grabbed me by the front of my dress, and screamed *right* into my face: 'Did you hear me, Lady? Did you?! I said the sky is falling! Listen to me, damnit!'

"I didn't know exactly what to say, so I asked her how she knew it was so.

"I know the sky is falling because we've been placed under a foul curse by an evil faerie sorceress!" the chicken shouted at me. "The whole thing's gonna flatten us at any minute! Run! Run! Women and children first!"

"Here we go again with an evil magic-wielder casting curses. I wondered if it were the same one who had sealed the stone head in the desert and cursed Attis and Ceres back in the forest. I had no chance to question the foul little fowl further, for she ran off again, still screaming. It was all most curious, but I had no idea how much *more* curious it was to become.

As I wandered about Falderal, I returned to the cart where the snake-oil salesman plied his trade, but this time saw something I had failed to notice before — a bird cage crudely concealed beneath a coarse woolen blanket. Taking care not to be seen, I approached and pulled back the cover. A beautiful, delicate, white china bird was cowering inside. Treasure?

"I opened the cage door, but the bird backed away. I spoke softly to her, and when I mentioned the name Fernando, she brightened considerably 'Will you please take me back to him? Please?' she asked. Then she hopped onto my finger, and together we quietly returned to the China Shop. The snake-oil salesman seemed more interested in counting coin than in queenly pilfering."

"Mother!" gasped Rosella.

"Wife!" gasped Graham.

"Well, I did need some practice for my grand theft. And the pale bird did need to be returned to its rightful home."

"FERNANDO HADN'T MOVED FROM HIS PLACE BEHIND THE COUNTER, AND HE STILL SIGHED AND dabbed at his tear-filled eyes. 'I know someone who can make you feel better, Fernando,' and I held up my hand to show the bird perched on my finger. The bull clapped his hooves and cried out in joy, 'Treasure! My darling, you have returned!'

"The bird fluttered around her friend's head, chirping and trilling. She landed on his shoulder and pressed her feathered cheek to his. 'I cannot thank you enough, good lady,' Fernando said. 'I know you admired this mask. Please, allow me to present it to you with my compliments and gratitude.'

"I thanked Fernando. It was perfect for a masquerade ball. I hastened back to the archduke's and knocked upon the great front doors. A short little badger wearing a breastplate and carrying a halberd greeted me with a welcoming smile. He was not unlike — actually, not at all unlike — the obnoxious guard at the town gate, except this little badger was polite. Bowing low, he motioned for me to enter. This was certainly a warmer reception than at the gate! I strode past him with my very best regal manner and entered the ballroom.

"To say the Town Hall was decorated for a party would be the most outrageous of understatements," Valanice told her family, then proceeded to describe the profusion of flags, streamers, and bright balloons that crowded the room. "An immense cake took up most of the dining table, and the gaudily costumed citizens of Falderal, all seemingly of the kingdom of animals, yet quite civilized, were dancing to a waltz conducted by the somewhat inebriated archduke himself. It was terribly bright and terribly crowded and terribly noisy, but that was the way everyone seemed to like it. For my own part, I wanted only to leave the ballroom as quickly as possible and search for the magical statue of the nymph.

"No one was paying me the least bit of attention, and so I was able to poke around a bit under and behind things. Some hanging birthday flags at the back of the room concealed a narrow door. I slipped through.

"On the other side was a roomful of stairways — but not any ordinary stairs. These stumbled off in every possible direction. Some even hung upside-down, and when I walked on them, I was upside-down! It was most unnerving. Beyond the stairs, I could see a pair of rounded doors. Perhaps what I sought was behind one of them, but it was impossible to tell which stairway would lead me there. It was discouraging, I can tell you.

"After many frustrating attempts to make sense of those stairs, I found the end of a stairway and the door I sought. But when I opened the door, a monstrous white powder puff thrust itself through the doorway and covered me in dusting powder! Then the door slammed in my face!

"Undoubtedly the door to the powder room," chortled Graham. Valanice rushed on as if he had never spoken.

"I hoped everyone didn't have to go through *that* every time they tried to go inside. The second time I tried the knob, though, I got inside without further incident, or dusting.

"The room itself was monstrously overdecorated, with an overly large fountain, gold-framed mirrors, and cherubs all over the wallpaper. There was even a chubby, gold-plated cherub on the vanity table, poised on one fleshy foot, with its little mouth open in an 'O'. On its base I could see an inscription of some sort, unreadable for tarnish. Well, that ugly thing certainly couldn't be mistaken for a nymph.

"The mirrors lining the walls were quite odd. As I passed each one, I saw my reflection, but it was oddly distorted — short and squat on one, impossibly tall and thin in another. It was amusing, but not very useful. One mirror, however, showed a perfectly normal me, except for the fact that I was upside-down. 'That's odd,' I thought as I reached out to touch the mirror. That's when my reflection grabbed my hand and pulled me through to the other side!"

"And what was on the other side, Mother?" Rosella asked excitedly.

"A very normal room," replied Valanice, "or at least," she recalled with a laugh, "a normal room for the town of Falderal. It was as silly and overdone as everything else I had seen, and it was decorated with enough fancy scrollwork to outfit an entire royal palace! A large desk occupied most of the space, and there was a poorly done portrait of the archduke himself on the wall. It looked to be the archduke's office. I began to search it as thoroughly — and quickly — as possible.

"I began, logically enough, with the archduke's desk. There was a drawer in the side, and when I opened it, the golden statuette of the nymph was inside. I turned it in my hand, then placed Rosella's golden comb on it as the snake-oil salesman had said.

"'Please show me where my daughter is!' I said.

"The nymph on the statuette was gazing into a pond, and now that pond began to shimmer and change. A picture was forming, but at first I couldn't tell what it was. Then the nymph looked up at me and spoke: 'Your daughter is in dire peril in the dark land called Ooga Booga,' she said. Now I could see the image quite clearly: Rosella dangling in some kind of large bucket, high above the ground, and it was collapsing around her! In fright, I picked up the statuette and ran through the office room's door as fast as my feet would carry me, ignoring the meaningless stairs and the less meaningful party in my haste.

"AT LAST I FOUND MY WAY OUT OF THE TOWN HALL. I WAS HURRYING DOWN THE MAIN STREET, intent upon giving the snake-oil salesman the statue, obtaining the magical salve and continuing on my journey to rescue Rosella, when I heard a familiar commotion.

'The sky is falling! The sky is falling!' It was that silly chicken again, but I couldn't be bothered to spare her any thought. All my thoughts were on how to find my child.

"Suddenly a shadow fell over the pond, and it grew larger and larger by the second. Then a huge..." Valanice interrupted herself. "You really must believe me when I assure you it was a wheel of green cheese that fell into the pond. It splashed the mockingbird and sent him squawking away from his nest and into the sky. It splashed me and everything around, too.

"'Bagaaawk! I *told* you so!' The chicken was still screeching. She reached into the pond with her stubby wings, as if to rescue the cheese. 'Please, that cheese is ruined now," I advised her. 'Certainly you can buy yourself another wheel of green cheese somewhere in town.'

"'Green cheese?' the chicken shrieked. 'Green cheese?! That's not *green cheese*! That's the *moon*! *The sky has fallen*!!!' And she flapped away, screeching incoherently at the top of her lungs.

"THE MOON?" ECHOED ROSELLA.

"Made of green cheese? Is that possible?" asked Graham.

"All things are possible, and apparently more so in Falderal," Valanice told them.

"I LOOKED INTO THE SKY, BUT THERE WAS NO MOON IN SIGHT, AND I WAS CERTAIN IT HAD BEEN there before. True, it looked like cheese, but it did seem a bit tiny for being the moon. Still, things seldom are as they appear. Could the chicken possibly have been right all along? It was all too confusing, and the last thing I needed was more confusion.

"The mockingbird still hadn't returned to his nest, and I couldn't help but wonder what might be in it. If it were eggs, he wouldn't have been so quick to fly away. I peered inside and saw what appeared to be a coin made of wood. Heedless of the advice I have heard many times, I took it. I couldn't imagine what use the mockingbird would have for it, and in a town as topsy-turvy as this one, this unreal currency might just be as genuine as any.

"And where better to test my theory than the shop nearby? Its sign read:

FAUX SHOP
fakeries, falsehoods,
and genuine counterfeit imitations
Friends and foes alike welcome!

WHAT A PERFECTLY PERFECT PLACE TO SPEND A WOODEN NICKEL! I OPENED THE DOOR, WALKED through — and discovered the shop to be nothing more than a facade. I walked back around to the front, quite irritated. Then I remembered something.

'Be sure to take the Faux Shop with a grain of salt,' the archduke had told me. Well, I still had some salt with me from pool in the desert. On impulse, I swallowed it. Ugh! The Faux shop suddenly shimmered for a moment. I reached for the door, opened it, and discovered that an entire shop had appeared on the other side!

"The shop was crowded from top to bottom with the strangest goods. There were some lovely plants in one corner, but on closer inspection, I was dismayed to see that they were cheap wood, not real at all. There were glass eyeballs, wooden legs and stuffed, wind-up animals strewn throughout the shop. In fact, everything I could see was fake! An odd little turtle busied himself behind one of the counters.

"I learned that the turtle was named Ersatz de Faux, owner of the shop. He was proud of his large selection of totally artificial merchandise, proudly claiming that he was himself a mock turtle. It seemed fitting, somehow.

"'What can I buy with this?' I asked, showing him the wooden nickel. 'Why, for the price of one wooden nickel, you can buy this fabulous tome of ancient, Eldritch lore!' he exclaimed, 'The Wit and Wisdom of Falderal!' Something about the idea of any kind of wit or wisdom being associated with this queer little town struck me as infinitely amusing. And I would be paying for it with a wooden nickel. How droll. I gave the nickel to Ersatz de Faux, and he handed me the book.

"I wasn't quite ready to give up the pleasures of examining this odd boutique, though, and continued looking through more of Ersatz's merchandise. I couldn't help noticing three plucked chickens hanging by their feet from the ceiling. They were so realistic that I reached out and touched one to confirm that it was, in fact, a synthetic bird, not a real one. It smiled at me and waggled its eyebrows. Even live chickens don't do that!

"'This is the finest and stretchiest rubber chicken I've ever seen,' the turtle said. 'If you wish to purchase it, I will require something rare, odd, and special in exchange.' I wasn't sure I had anything very special to offer, especially something fake, but then I noticed the empty rack behind the counter. The sign read 'masks,' but all the pegs were empty.

"'Everyone wanted a false face so that they could attend the archduke's birthday party," Ersatz explained after noticing my gaze. 'I don't have a single one left, I'm afraid.'

"Well, I did, and I had no further use for it. I showed the mask to the turtle in a silent offer of barter.

"'In exchange for such a fine mask, I'll give you the rubber chicken that you showed so much interest in,' he said happily. The chicken grinned, showing me its teeth! Teeth? I gasped, then remembered my manners. 'Thank you, Ersatz,' I replied.

"I couldn't think of any possible use for such an unusual item, but he offered it in such goodwill that I was unwilling to refuse it and risk hurting his feelings. I looked the chicken over very carefully, making sure he could see how much I admired it. That's when I saw what appeared to be a genuine feather on his, er... posterior. I didn't think I ought to tell Ersatz about *that*, so I plucked out the feather. To my surprise, the faux fowl squawked angrily and glared at me! Embarrassed, I put the feather in my pocket and bid the mock turtle good-day. As I left the shop and passed the fountain, I noticed that the moon was now bobbing in the pool."

GRAHAM LAUGHED. "I'VE SEEN MANY AMAZING THINGS IN MY TRAVELS," HE SAID, "BUT SURELY this town of Falderal is the only town in all existence where such a perfectly silly thing could happen!"

"I'm sure I saw things as odd in Ooga Booga," Rosella said, "and they were a lot scarier, besides."

VALANICE COULD TELL ROSELLA WAS BECOMING ANXIOUS TO TELL MORE OF HER ADVENTURES, BUT SHE was not quite through talking yet, and Rosella *had* promised not to interrupt. She gave her

NO POSTAGE
NECESSARY
IF MAILED
IN THE
UNITED STATES

BUSINESS REPLY MAIL

FIRST CLASS MAIL PERMIT NO. 1225 BOULDER, CO

POSTAGE WILL BE PAID BY ADDRESSEE

SUBSCRIPTION DEPARTMENT
P.O. BOX 59710
BOULDER, CO 80323-9710

daughter a stern, motherly look, and Rosella mellowed a bit.

"Please go on, mother," she said. Valanice thought that she almost sounded as though she meant it, too.

"I wished there were something I could do about the moon — evenings would never be quite the same without it — but I couldn't imagine what. Something to hook it and bring it to the side of the pool where it could be lifted out, would be useful, but I had seen nothing in the Faux Shop — or the rest of Falderal — that would be of any help. Besides, I had other business to attend to — I still felt obligated to find a way to help Attis and Ceres before I continued with my own quest."

"MOTHER! YOU WERE SEARCHING FOR ME! WHY HELP THEM?" ROSELLA CRIED.

"Because they seemed such kind folk that I could never have lived with myself had I just abandoned them without making the slightest attempt to assist them. And I knew I would be searching for you at the same time."

"I LEFT FALDERAL WITHOUT BEING HARASSED — BADGERED — BY THAT ASININE GUARD AND walked back to where I had freed the little hummingbird.

"This time I did not cross the river but ventured east until I found the Rock Spirit that Lord Attis had spoken of. Oh, at first I did not realize it was an entity; indeed, I paused to lean against it and rest. That was when I noticed the strange cast of the stone. It had the shape of a great, craggy face, complete with mossy eyebrows and mustache. The sides of this rock-head vibrated slightly, as if the entire thing were slowly breathing. At any rate, it was he who knew the way to heal the woods of their curse, and I felt that if there was something I could do for Lord Attis and Lady Ceres, and everything that lived here, then I must do it. I had not lost my determination to find Rosella, of course, but I felt there was something greater going on — something which could affect the lives of thousands of creatures.

"To awaken the spirit, I removed the chicken feather from my pocket, placed it under its nose, and proceeded to tickle him. The Rock Spirit snorted once, almost blowing the feather from my grasp, then began to snore. I tickled him again. He sneezed, and blew the feather right out of my hand. 'What foolish mortal dares to awaken me from my eons-deep slumber?' he demanded in a voice like granite slabs grinding slowly together.

"I told the spirit of the terrible fate that had befallen the woods — about the river ceasing to flow, about Attis transformed into a stag and Ceres into an oak. 'You must start the River of Life flowing again, or all shall perish,' he said. 'Pour the sacred drink into the River Maiden's pitcher. Replenish the cornucopia with the sacred food of the Gods. Only then shall all be made whole again.' His eyes began to grind closed as he fell asleep again, and try as I might, I could not awaken him again. Musing over just what the sacred nectar and the food of the gods was, I returned to Attis and his imprisoned love.

"The oak that was Lady Ceres still stood, though sap still oozed fitfully from the cruel spike wound in her trunk. There seemed nothing I could do there.

"I continued on from the oak to the River Maiden statue the Rock Spirit had mentioned. I knew that I must find sacred drink to refill her vessel, but where? And how? I didn't even know what the Rock Spirit had meant by 'sacred drink,' and I'd had no chance to ask him. 'What *did* gods drink?' I wondered.

"The phrase 'nectar and ambrosia' recurred to me from a childhood story that my mother had told me once when I was very small. Nectar was sacred drink, and ambrosia was sacred food. And nectar came from flowers. Of course! I looked all around me, but the only flowers I could see grew high on a cliff, and I could find no way to climb up to them.

"I heard a low-pitched buzzing sound over my shoulder, and when I turned to look, a tiny, lavender hummingbird hovered there, looking at me with one bright eye. It was the same bird I had freed from the spider's web.

"'Do you desire some of the sacred nectar?' she asked.

"'I do!' I told her. She asked me for a vessel, and I took out the little pot I had carried from the desert. 'Hold it below the flowers, so that you will not loose a drop,' the bird told me, and I held the pot as close as I could to the bright-colored blossoms.

"The hummingbird flew up to the flowers and tipped one over. A trickle of nectar fell from the flower and into the pot. I thanked the hummingbird, and she kissed my cheek gently before flying away. So the tiny creature *had* been able to help me!

"Carrying the pot of nectar carefully, I climbed up onto the River Maiden statue until I could reach the pitcher and emptied the contents of the pot into it. To my amazement, the nectar turned from a trickle to a stream, and the stream poured out of the pitcher and into a river. Soon the space between the banks was filled with beautiful, clear water, and the River of Life began again to flow. As this happened, a rainbow formed between the broken ends of the ancient bridge, seeming to become a part of the shattered span. While I stared in wonder as these magical changes occurred, the stag I had spoken to earlier came walking out of the woods toward me.

"'Lord Attis,' I called to him. 'The River of Life is flowing again! Perhaps a drink from its waters will give you the strength to shake off the evil curse that is upon you.'

"The stag walked quickly to the river's edge and drank deeply of the clear water, and as I watched, Attis was transformed from a stag into a tall, surpassingly handsome man clothed entirely in green and black, with black hair and beard.

"'I am myself again', he said in a wondering tone. 'Though I wish to thank you properly for this deed, I have no time. Ceres stands dying and I must try to save her!

"When we reached the great oak, Lord Attis took the iron stake in both hands and, with a great heave, pulled it out and flung it aside. The flow of sap from the would ceased for a moment, then resumed as a flow of red, red blood! Ceres did not regain her true form. Instead, her branches drooped even more, and she appeared near death.

"'The curse is of a power greater than my own," said Attis in an angry voice. 'But I will not let her die. I cannot stop, even if it costs me my life. And I must offer you, too, such aid as I can.'

Attis told me he had learned of a terrible monster that dwelled in the murky waters of the swamp outside of Ooga Booga. He said he could help me evade the monster, but first he had to try to save his beloved Ceres. A vibrant green glow enveloped him, and he slipped into a trance with his hands on the trunk of the tree.

"I knew Attis wouldn't be able to help me more just then. I would return soon, before I journeyed to Ooga Booga, and learn how to evade the swamp monster. Meanwhile, I would put my time to good use. There had not been anything in the Falderal Faux Shop that would help me get the moon out of the fountain pool, but I knew another place, not too far away, where a rather odd assortment of treasures was to be found.

"South of the River of Life was the entrance to the great stone head — the portal back to the burning desert wastes. I soon found myself back in the tunnel where I had seen the giant lizard, but there was no sign of him now. Perhaps the thorns on the prickly pear I fed him were giving him a case of indigestion. In any event, I hurried through the tunnel and out the open mouth of the colossus, then proceeded east to the burrow of the kangaroo rat.

"The rat opened his door at my knock, stared up at me, and recited his rhyme. By now I had deduced that the little fellow only traded for things that rhymed with one another, and I hoped to trade something I didn't need for an object that might help me to rescue the moon — perhaps a hook. Looking through my possessions, I noticed the book the mock turtle had traded me for the wooden nickel. This might be just perfect! I offered it to the him.

"'AHA! You wish to trade to me a book,

'In return, I'll give to you a pawn and a rook.'"

"I frowned in disapproval.

"'Well, I can see by your irkish look,

"'You'd rather have a shepherd's crook!' and with that, he ducked into his burrow. I couldn't believe my luck. In a moment he was back with a long, straight rod that ended in a sort of hook. This would do wonderfully! The kangaroo rat tipped his hat, then slammed the door.

"This time my walk back to Nonsense Land was simpler and less fraught with peril. As I walked through the woods, I saw Attis still deep in his healing trance. I hurried silently past and didn't stop until I came to the Falderal town gate, where I banged the knocker against the gate. 'Go away, you gate crasher,' the badger guard shouted down at me. 'You have no respect for the authority of The Powers that Be!' I supposed he was right, especially considering I was going to enter the town through the same little door he'd forbidden me to open once before.

"'No!,' he shouted. 'You're *still* not allowed through there! There's a gigantic carnivorous cactus waiting on the other side!' I laughed and walked through anyway. 'Oh, and big, fat, hairy *rats*!' muttered the guard. I almost felt sorry for the pompous little fellow. Almost, but not quite.

"As I had expected, the moon was still lying in the fountain pool. Using the crook, I fished around in the pond, trying to get a firm grip on it. After a moment, I was able to pull it toward me and get my free hand around it. Being made of cheese, however, the moon was very slippery and was about to slip from my hand and back into the pool. I let go of the crook and grabbed the moon with both hands. The crook fell into the pool, but now I had the moon, safe and sound.

"I heard a noise behind me and turned to see the badger guard and the archduke marching toward me. They didn't look particularly friendly.

'I *thaw* what you jutht did, you wicked, wicked creature!' the archduke sputtered. 'You jutht thtole the *moon*! We've caught you red-handed, you, you...common criminal!'

"'You are now placed under arrest for all of those reasons that his great highness, Archduke Yipyap has stated,' said the badger, 'plus the heinous and wicked crimes of littering and illegal side-door entry into the sovereign town of Falderal.'

"The archduke pointed his furry white paw in my direction and cried 'Guards, theize her!'

Part the Fourth
The Boogeyman Will Get You!

"AND DID THE GUARD ARREST YOU?" GRAHAM ASKED, SHOCKED.

"He did indeed," said Valanice, "but you must wait to hear it until Rosella has had a chance to tell more of *her* tale. She's been waiting patiently — well, nearly — all this time, haven't you, dear?"

"Well, let's see," said Rosella, looking up. "Where was I when *my* story ended?"

"You were in a crumbling elevator shaft," said her father. "And you were in danger of falling to your death in the cavern below." He was very interested in hearing what came next.

"So I was," said Rosella, nodding. "The elevator was falling to pieces, and at any moment I would be plunged a great distance to the hard, jagged stone floor."

"Well, what happened?" cried both her parents in unison.

Rosella laughed. "Would you believe me if I told you I fell to the floor and was smashed flat?"

"No," said her father.

Her mother raised an eyebrow in a gesture Rosella knew all too well. She tapped one royal foot impatiently.

"Oh, all right," Rosella admitted. "I didn't fall. I thought I must be about to, but when I looked up, a *very* strange-looking man, large and hunched and lumped, was holding out a shovel to me. So I grabbed it. He pulled me up out of the elevator shaft, and a moment later, the whole thing went crashing to the cavern floor in a thousand pieces. If I left this place, it wasn't likely to be the way I had come. Just the same, I heaved a sigh of relief at finding myself on solid ground again. 'Thank you, kind sir,' I said to the man. He simply nodded wearily and went back to his work.

"It appeared that I was in some kind of a cemetery. I could see strangely twisted gravestones and what looked like a tomb. The strange-looking man who had rescued me was digging what seemed to be a grave using an impossibly small shovel.

"'Drats, but I'm never gonna get this done at this rate,' he muttered. 'Stupid, useless little shovel!' He seemed quite irritated. I wasn't sure whether I should interrupt him. 'Thank you again, kind sir,' I trilled loudly, still trying for his attention.

"He eyed me wearily, then hopped out of the grave and strode up to me, holding a measuring tape. He did a quick measurement of my height, and said, 'Okay, miss, I got your measurements. I'll get to work on diggin' your grave tomorrow. Sorry about the delay, but there's been a real backlog of orders lately — people are just dyin' to get in here.'

"'Thank you anyway, but I don't think that I'll need a grave any time soon', I said, 'But please, could you tell me if this is the land of Ooga Booga?' He told me that it was.

"'Pardon my saying so,' I went on, 'but shouldn't you be using a larger shovel for your work?' The one you have now seems far too small.' 'You're absolutely right,' he replied. 'I just don't have the right tools anymore. Here, come an' take a look at this.' He trundled over to the tomb and threw open the doors, revealing a bizarre contraption that had a pair of arms in front and rotating paws and teeth. It seemed perfect for digging. I had to admit I was impressed at the design, even though the whole thing was a little scary, like the gravedigger himself. I noticed there was an empty rodent wheel in the center of the machine,

"'This baby is a fully automatic, mostly automated, steam-driven, rat-powered grave digging machine,' the gravedigger told me. 'Made it myself. It worked great until those derned kids broke in and swiped my rat!'

"'Why don't you just get another rat?' I asked. A great sadness came over his coarse features. 'Iggy's special,' he said. 'Iggy's the strongest, smartest, best trained rat I've ever known, and I don't think another one could come close to replacing him. Nope.' He wiped his eyes with the back of his grimy hand. I was touched.

'I'm sorry. He must have been very important to you,' I said. 'He was, miss. He was,' said the gravedigger, his voice just a little unsteady. He didn't seem interested in any further conversation, and I had work to do. I had promised Mathilde, the Troll King's nursemaid, that I would find out what happened to the *real* King Otar. I supposed it was time to get out there and meet some people who might be inclined to help me.

"From the graveyard, I walked to the south and west until I came to a spooky old house covered in vines and surrounded by an iron fence that was topped with sharp points. As haunted as it appeared at first glance, I could see someone moving about inside. There was a name on the mailbox — Dr. Mort Cadaver. *That* made me more than a little nervous.

"The house was very old, ill-kept, and more than a little frightening. There was a black cat sitting on the porch, though she looked harmless enough. Someone had hung strips of some sort of flimsy white paper all over a dead tree in the yard, and pictures — not very good ones — had been drawn on the walls. I could see drawings of a skull, a bat, and a spider. A tremendously ugly little child with ghastly green skin was drawing on the wall. A very short little old man in a badly wrinkled black waistcoat opened the door and shouted at the child, 'Get out of here, you little menace! Get away, I say!' He sounded scared to death. The child shouted 'Boo!' and the little man and his little cat jumped back into the house. It certainly wasn't the sort of place I like to visit.

"I opened the gate, which made a horrible, shrieking kind of noise, and went up to the house. The little man opened the door a crack and looked up at me. 'Um, hello sir,' I said. 'I don't think we've met. I'm Rosella of Daventry. Would you mind if I ask you some questions?' 'Certainly, Miss Rosella, I'll be glad to offer any assistance that I may,' he said most civily, and he invited me in. His parlor was cluttered with so many things I could scarcely see them all. There was laboratory equipment, a sewing machine, dozens of books and bottles and jars — even a silk-lined coffin! 'My name is Cadaver, Dr. Mort Cadaver. I am the chief medical practitioner, coroner, and undertaker of Ooga Booga,' he told me. 'How may I be of service?'

"His skin was waxen and his eyes were sunken, but he seemed like a good fellow at heart, despite his almost corpse-like appearance. For some unfathomable reason, I trusted him. I told Dr. Cadaver I was looking for the Troll King, who might be held captive somewhere in Ooga Booga.

"'I would presume that the enchantress Malicia is at fault, miss Rosella. She is ever up to no good,' he said. He told me that Malicia had been responsible for the destruction of a Count Tsepish, who had once been the ruler and defender of Ooga Booga. Since then, the Boogeyman had taken over, and the ghoul kids (one being the hideous little green fellow I had seen earlier) were out of control. 'I fear to even venture out of doors!' he exclaimed.

"I didn't even want to think about what the Boogeyman might be, so I made conversation. 'If you're having trouble with kids, why don't you do something to stop them?' I asked. 'Threaten to tell their parents that they're misbehaving.'

"'I'm just the coroner and doctor,' he replied. 'I catalogue the dead, take care of the living, and perform the occasional operation. Why, just last week I gave my spine to a woman who had broken hers falling off a cliff. Now I haven't the backbone to stand up to a bunny rabbit, let alone a ghoul.'

"He had no spine at all?" asked Valanice, horrified.

"None at all," said Rosella, "which is why he was so short and his coat was so wrinkled. He had been much taller before. I asked him if he could get his old spine back, but he wouldn't hear of it. 'In medicine, the patient's welfare must always come first,' he said gallantly. But I could tell that he badly wanted another one none the less.

"Then I asked him about the children who were terrifying him so. He said they'd been children for the past 130 years! And he warned me to stay away from the Boogeyman, a tall, stick-like figure who had become completely evil and vicious under Malicia's influence.

"'If you see him, run! If you think you see him, run! To be safe, just run anytime you're outside,' he told me. For one brief instant, I was filled with an inexplicable, nameless terror, a crawling, creeping dread the likes of which I had never known. I decided the doctor's advice was probably the best course of action.

"The good doctor seemed rather busy, so I left him to his work and walked east until I came to the strangest house I had ever seen. It was in the shape of a great, grimacing orange jack-o-lantern sitting up in the twisted branches of a dead tree. There was some sort of web or net connecting the house to a big hole in the ground, and there was a pulley elevator with a metal bucket, something like the one in the Underground, but smaller — and hopefully more stable.

"There were two very odd-looking children on a deck in front of the treehouse, and they were playing with a rat. Playing *catch* with a rat, actually, and the rat didn't look at all happy about it. I recognized one of them as the little vandal from Dr. Cadaver's house. As they tossed it back and forth, they chanted a rhyme:

"'When e're the branch shaped like a snake
is pointing up, for heaven's sake,
run away! Run away!
Neep, neep! Neep, neep!
Go and hide! Go and hide.
The bogeyman will be inside!
When e're the branch is pointing down,
the Boogeyman has gone to town.
And we'll stomp and play all over town!'

"It was a very strange rhyme.

"'Hello, kids!' I called up to them. 'Hiya, lady!' said one child, and he held the rat up by its tail. 'Would you like to have your head shrunk or your kidneys punched?' the other one wanted to know. 'No, but thank you for the offer,' I told them, and I tried hard to sound very friendly and cheerful. 'That's a great rat you've got to play with.'

"'This is the most bestest rat in Ooga Booga, lady! We swiped it from the gravedigger' the first child said. By this time, he was swinging the rat over his head by the tail. I asked if they'd like to sell him, but they weren't interested. They said they might be willing to trade for a really spooky pet. Something with big teeth and bad manners.

"'What do you kids do for fun around here anyway? Besides torment Dr. Cadaver and your rat,' I asked them. 'Aw, we always run around an' jump in open graves,' the first child said. 'You always find a grave surprise in them.'

'Yeah, and we talk to the Woman in Black, too' the second child added. I made up my mind then and there not to do either of those things since these little monsters thought they were fun. I had never encountered kids so unrepentantly rotten. I felt terribly sorry for the rat, and I wanted to see him returned to the poor gravedigger where he'd be loved and cared for, but how on earth was I going to find a weird pet to trade the little beasts?

"I was pretty curious about what was in that treehouse, but I didn't feel exactly safe going in when the kids were there. I went away for a little while, and when I came back, they were nowhere in sight. The elevator was down, and I used it to raise myself up to the treehouse. Inside was several times more weird than outside, if you can believe that. There was a row of shrunken heads on a shelf, and a mummy was propped up in the corner. Even the jack-in-the-box didn't look much like your everyday toy, and I had absolutely *no* desire to turn the handle.

"I noticed what looked like a backbone stuck in a knothole in the floor, and someone had been playing ring toss on it with slipped disks. I looked around quickly for anything else that might be of use, not wanting to be caught here when those awful kids came back. I knew I wanted a backbone for Dr. Cadaver, so I pulled it free. It looked to be about the right size. I was sure that he'd be quite pleased to get it.

"I looked on top of a pile of bizarre toys and saw a bag of some kind. I looked inside and shuddered. I didn't see it quite clearly, but I'm sure there was a foot in there!"

"How horrid!" cried Valanice.

"Indeed. I set it back down, but after a moment, I reluctantly picked it up. I told myself, 'I suppose a girl never knows when she'll need a foot-in-a-bag, especially in a place called Ooga Booga!' I didn't see anything else I wanted, so I let myself back down and hurried back to Dr. Cadaver's house.

"When I arrived, the doctor was seeing a patient in his parlor," Rosella recalled, "and what a patient he was! Dr. Cadaver called him Mr. Bugbear, and the strange, squat little fellow fit right in with all the other truly strange things I had seen in such a short time..

"Mr. Bugbear had a broken heart — literally! He looked very unhappy about it, as you might imagine, but Dr. Cadaver fixed it up as good as new with some staples and glue. When he put it back, the little fellow was all smiles again. It was easy to see why his patients — even the heartless ones — loved such a kind-hearted man, and I was happy to be able to do something nice for him."

"'Doctor, I wonder if you can find a use for this?,' I said, holding the backbone for him to see. Dr. Cadaver admired the backbone for a moment, then stood up, opened his mouth *very* wide, and swallowed the spine like a sword swallower. His body stretched upward, and he became quite tall and thin. 'Thank you, Miss Rosella,' he said. 'I was fast becoming tired of being such a spineless old fool.' He looked about at the items crowding the shelves in the room and found a black box that shook and twitched and made distasteful little noises. He gave it to me.

"'Here. It doesn't come close to evening my debt to you, but here is a little companion to make your travels in this dark land a little less lonely. I made him myself.' I opened the top of the box to peek inside. I immediately wished I hadn't. I thanked the doctor again and hurried back to the treehouse. I had just the thing now to trade those ghoulish kids for the gravedigger's rat.

"'Hey, kids! I found something to trade you for your rat! It's the creepiest pet you'll ever see!' I yelled up to them. The kids didn't believe me, so I lifted the lid and showed them the pet, being careful not to look again myself. 'Drop it on the lift!' cried one kid. 'Why dontcha bring it up yourself?' said the other kid, and they both laughed in a particularly awful way.

"There was no way I was going up to that treehouse while they were in it! I put the box on the elevator, and they pulled the bucket up. A few moments later, the rat leapt from the window and landed in my arms. I was horrified for a moment — it was, after all, a rat — but then the dear little creature kissed my cheek. My heart melted. 'It'll be okay, little fella,' I said. 'Let's get out of here!'

I found the gravedigger still scratching pitifully away at the half-dug grave with his tiny shovel. I walked up to him and held out the rat. 'Excuse me, sir, but look who I found!' The gravedigger turned around, and when he saw his rat, his somber face broke into a huge grin. 'Iggy! You found my Iggy!' The rat squeaked in delight and leapt into the gravedigger's arms.

"The gravedigger was so grateful, he promised to dig me a grave anywhere, anytime. He handed me an antique horn that he pulled from a large pocket like a rabbit from a cap.

"'I'll hear this horn whenever you blow it, and when I do, me an' Iggy'll come along and dig you a nice, deep grave.' Then he put the rat inside the wheel of the grave-digging machine. The rat started to run, and the machine started up with a rattle and a roar. The two of them were tearing up dirt right and left, happy as could be. I picked up the gravedigger's shovel before leaving — if a girl can find an excuse for a foot-in-a-bag, imagine what I might do with a shovel!

"The next time I walked by the treehouse, the ghoul kids appeared to be having some sort of funeral. They were standing in front of a little coffin, all dressed in black, and there were terrible yowling noises coming from inside the coffin.

"'Ashes to ashes, dust to dust,' one of them intoned, 'We are gathered together for the somber purpose of burying our kitty. Alive!'

"'We need a shovel to bury her properly!' the other kid cried maliciously. 'Come on, let's go grab one from that stupid old gravedigger!' squealed the first. 'It's not like kitty's going anywhere!' They laughed evilly and ran off. They were trying to bury a that poor little kitty alive!

"I tried to open the coffin, but it was sealed shut. The hammer and chisel that Oppi had given me worked well, though, and when the lid sprang open, a little black cat jumped out. 'Kitty, kitty, are you all right?' I asked.

"'I think so,' the cat said. She walked closer to me and meowed.

"'I heard you ask my friend the coroner about the Troll King,' she said. 'He is imprisoned in the lair of the Boogeyman, inside the fastness of the deadfall. However, before you seek him out, I wish to give you something in return for saving my life.' She touched my hand with her paw and gave me a pulsating golden ball of light. It hummed against my skin and felt warm like a living creature.

"'This is one of my nine lives. I feel that I owe it to you; a life for a life.' I protested that I could never accept so valuable a gift. 'You must,' she whispered urgently, then ran away.

"I walked west, past the doctor's house, and soon encountered another cemetery. It seemed to me that most of the real estate in Ooga Booga was devoted to cemeteries. I would have found that odd anywhere else, but somehow it seemed rather fitting there. Oh, and the inscriptions on the gravestones were so amusing. Let me see if I can remember one of them:

"'The debonair Archduke von Drake
Was always a bit of a rake.
He chased a maiden through the grass,
But when he caught up with the lass,
She kicked his bum into the lake.'"

VALANICE AND GRAHAM LAUGHED. ROSELLA GRINNED. "OF COURSE, SOME OF THEM WERE OF darker tone, as seemed to benefit the grim nature of that land. For example, one read:

"'Mr. Kurtz, he dead.'

"And immediately under that was inscribed:

"'The horror! The horror!'

"Then I noticed a particularly large and elaborate crypt. A woman dressed from head to toe in black stood in front of it, and she was weeping so grievously that I was sure that her heart must be broken! There were dead flowers everywhere on the ground in front of the tomb, as though someone had been bringing them here and leaving them for a very long time. I felt sorry for the woman, but I didn't think it would be right to disturb her in her grief, so I went on my way.

I had turned south, and in a short time, I came to the deadfall the cat had told me about. One tree stood here, dead and dry but not yet fallen, and behind it was an immense pile of warped, sun-bleached sticks. Or were they bones? As I looked again, it seemed almost impossible to tell. One gnarled branch on the tree looked amazingly like a snake, which led me to remember the rhyme those awful kids were singing when I had first seen them. How did it go? I tried to remember, knowing it might be important.

"'When e're the branch shaped like a snake
is pointing up, for heaven's sake,
run away!'

"Run away? But why? If only I could remember! Run away...."

"'run away!
go and hide!
the Boogeyman will be inside!'

"Yes, that was it! If the branch pointed up, the Boogeyman would be at home, and Dr. Cadaver had told me to *always* run from the Boogeyman. Well, the branch was pointing down now.

"'When e're the branch is pointing down,
the Boogeyman has gone to town.'

"That was how the rest of the rhyme went, I was sure. With any luck, that meant that the Boogeyman — whoever or whatever he was — was away. Now I had to get down beneath the deadfall, where the cat said King Otar was being held prisoner. It looked like I would have to dig, but I had nothing but the gravedigger's tiny shovel to dig with, and the ground was thickly laced with stones and tree roots. Then I remembered that I knew someone who had just the thing I needed! I took out the gravedigger's horn and blew on it.

"A moment later, the gravedigger came riding up on his amazing machine. 'Dig there,' I said pointing to the edge of the deadfall.

"The gravedigger gave me such a fearful look. 'You don't want to be buried there, do you, miss?' he asked. I handed him back his horn. 'Yes, I'm afraid that I do.' 'All right,' he sighed. 'It's your funeral. Stand back.'

"I moved as far away as I could from the machine. The gravedigger started the engine, and the machine started digging wildly. In only a few minutes, he had finished the grave and, with a fearful glance backwards, drove hastily away.

"I tried to climb down carefully into the hole, but the steep side crumbled and sent me falling under the ground and deadfall. When I opened my eyes, I was in a small, dark space under the dead tree. There were roots protruding from the ceiling and the walls. It was like being buried alive.

"I tried climbing back up the way I had fallen down, but the way was too steep. I had to find another way out, though it seemed obvious such a way didn't exist. I examined my surroundings as carefully as possible in hopes a way out would present itself.

"A big coffin took up much of the space in the grave, and it was wrapped in heavy chains, which were held together with a lock. Wanting to think of anything but feeling trapped in this close, unpleasant place, I took a closer look at the lock. Like everything else in Ooga Booga, it was weird. It looked like a lock, but instead of a key, it had a dial with pictures of spiders and snakes and other creepy things. They looked familiar.

"I thought about this while I looked at the pictures. Here was a picture of a skull. Where had I seen one like it? Suddenly I remembered. The pictures on the side of the doctor's house! What were they? One was a skull. Of that I was sure, or nearly sure. I turned the dial to the skull and thought harder. What was the next picture? A cat? A rat? No, a bat! I turned the dial to the bat and pictured the doctor's house in my mind. When I was certain of my memory, I turned the dial to the spider. The lock fell open in my hand. I felt as though I had accomplished something, even though it was a way out of the grave I needed, not a way into a coffin.

"I quickly pulled the chains apart and opened the coffin, scarcely daring to think what might be inside. It was the Troll King! Despite being in a coffin, he was more alive than anyone I'd met since I came here. He looked as surprised to see me as I was to see him.

"'Are you really King Otar,' I asked, 'of the Vulcanix Underground?'

'Indeed I am!' said the troll. "And who am I to thank for releasing me from this coffin?' But before we could get any farther into introductions, an alarm hooted nearby. Malicia suddenly appeared, somehow managing to look both annoyed and triumphant at the same time.

"'I do so hope that the two of you get along well,' Malicia sneered, 'since you're both going to rot together in the Land of the Dead for all eternity!' I stumbled backwards, desperate to get away from her, and fell into the coffin! The door slammed. I could hear the chains winding around the outside of the coffin, and I could hear the earth falling in on top of them, and from far above, I could hear the scrabbling of dry branches — or bones!

"It was dark," Rosella recalled, shuddering at the memory. "Terribly, horribly dark. A flash lit the darkness, quick as lightning, and was gone. The next flash remained, and I could see a little ball of light hovering over the Troll King's hand. I took a deep breath and found my composure. We were able to introduce ourselves without any further interruptions, and I told him the story of how I had found myself in his kingdom, and how I had come here looking for him.

"'You are as brave as any troll, princess, and I wish to thank you for all that you've done. However, I am afraid that your efforts will amount to naught, and for this I wish to apologize.'

"'Don't worry, King Otar, we'll find a way out. We have to.' The truth is, I wasn't at all certain that we could, but I didn't want to make him feel any worse than he already did.

"We suddenly were assaulted by a deep, awful rumbling sound, like the door opening into a massive crypt. We could hear pounding, scratching noises, like someone — or some*thing* — was trying to claw its way into the coffin, which had begun to shake and tip under the beating. 'I hope you are prepared to sacrifice your life, dear princess,' the king shouted over the noise, 'for unless you have a plan, I fear that we are doomed.'

"I did have one idea. I took out the dragon toad I had brought from the Underground and offered it to King Otar. 'Can this help us? Mathilde said it was your magical guardian.'

"'My dragon toad! Such luck! The magical gem that will bring him to life is set in my armband!' King Otar pulled at the jewel, but it would not come free. I brought out my hammer and chisel and tapped at the stone until it came loose from its setting.

"Then King Otar set the stone into a hole on the dragon toad's head. The toad began to shimmer, and his eyes opened up. The King put the toad down on the earth floor. 'Save us!' he commanded. 'Dig! Dig!' The dragon toad began to burrow into the soil. He quickly made a tunnel and vanished into it. King Otar followed him down the hole, and I didn't hesitate to follow.

"WE CAME OUT INTO YET ANOTHER GRAVEYARD THAT WAS CLOAKED IN FOG. KING OTAR GAVE THE dragon toad a message for Mathilde. 'We are coming! If Malicia enters the Underground, do not try to fight her, but stall her for as long as possible! Keep faith, for we come with haste!' Then the king told me we were still in mortal danger and must disguise ourselves. He handed me a strange metal wand and told me to point it at him, so I did. There was a strange sound, and some sort of beam came out of one end of the wand and struck the king. Otar disappeared, and where he had been standing was a miniature scarab beetle! 'Your Majesty, what happened? What have I done?' I wailed.

"'Fear not, princess,' the beetle said in Otar's husky voice. 'I have merely changed my form so that I may travel safely and unnoticed through this nightmare realm. We must also disguise you as a....' Just then there was an ear-splitting shriek from the direction of the deadfall. It was Malicia. She had discovered our escape, and she wasn't very happy about it.

There was another flash of magical light, and I saw a black veil — more a cloak, really — hanging in a nearby tree. 'Quickly! Hide yourself before she comes!' said the king. I scooped up both the magic wand and the beetle King, then took the veil from the tree and put it on. 'You now look just like the Lady Tsepish,' piped the beetle.

We hurried north to Dr. Cadaver's house and banged on his door.

"'Ah, Lady Tsepish,' the doctor said when he saw me. "Have you lost your mind again? I can replace it for you, of course, but really! Three minds a week is a terrible waste.'

"When he saw it was me, he pulled me into the house, slammed the door and bolted it. 'Miss Rosella! Malicia and her Boogeyman are hunting for you even as we speak! You must leave Ooga Booga quickly, before they find you.'

"'I'd like nothing better than to get out of here,' I assured him, 'but I don't know how to go about it. You see, the entrance to the underground that I arrived from has collapsed, and I know of no other way to leave this land.'

"'That does present something of a problem then, Miss Rosella,' said the doctor. He told me we'd have to leave through the main gate, but Malicia had put a nasty swamp monster on guard there. Rummaging through some bottles on his shelves, he found a little bottle with an atomizer on top. 'Take this. It's a defoliant that will absolutely kill any plant life that it touches. Go now, and may luck speed you in your travels. It has been an honor to know you, Miss Rosella.' I kissed the doctor my thanks and hurried away.

"Southeast of his house, I found the gate that leads from Ooga Booga into the woods, by way of the swamp. I didn't like the sound of the 'swamp' part, but I pushed open the gate and stepped through. The gate slammed shut behind me, clanging ominously like a funeral bell. I turned at the sound, and when I turned back, a gigantic moist green thing was shambling toward me, dripping swamp muck, reeking of mold and loam. It was hideous!"

"BELIEVE ME, I KNOW," SAID HER MOTHER.

"You do?"

"In good time, dear. Don't stop now."

"AS QUICKLY AS I COULD, I BROUGHT OUT THE BOTTLE OF DEFOLIANT AND SPRAYED IT ALL OVER that awful green monstrosity. The potion stank something awful, but it made the swamp thing disintegrate right in front of my eyes until all that was left was this tiny little gob of goo that oozed back into the vastness of the swamp. My knees — and stomach — were shaking, but I had to go on.

"I continued east until I came to a forbidding gray stone house, almost like a small castle, with turrets and towers, and even a stone gargoyle guarding the front door. It wasn't a pretty house, but a rather unfriendly looking one, and I had no desire to get any closer to it."

I began to walk past, but King Otar spoke to me from my pocket. 'Be cautious, princess,' he said, 'for this is the dwelling place of Malicia. Your disguise is good, but we must tread cautiously near this evil.' The king told me we must go inside and get a device she had stolen from him — a device that might possibly be used to defeat her. She had taken it from Otar when she first captured him, but he had convinced her it was some form of alchemy tool. After that, we could try to get to the town of Falderal, where there was a secret entrance to the Underground. In fact, the entrance was so secret, even he had no idea where it was hidden.

"I wondered why we couldn't just take this device and end Malicia's reign of terror then and there, but evidently it had to be powered by a socket — whatever that was — in the wall of the fearful mechanical room I had seen in the Underground. King Otar was very vague on what the device would actually do.

"Going into Malicia's house was not exactly my idea of a good thing, but the king insisted and urged me to hurry. The house was dark, so Malicia probably wasn't home, but she could return at any time. I moved around to the back of the house, seeking a less obvious way inside than the front door.

"There was a huge, twisted vine growing up the back of the house, and a tangle of its old, dead roots covered much of the exterior. As I poked around in the roots, still being careful not to walk on the swampy ground, I saw a small hole underneath. Pulling a few of the roots away from the hole, I saw that it went right under the house. This was my way in, or would be if the hole were larger — right now it was too small for me to squeeze through, and digging with my hands did little good.

"I cleaned my hands on the front of my already ruined dress and thought about how one went about enlarging a hole. The shovel I had stuffed in my girdle provided the easy answer.

"That shovel made it *much* easier to enlarge the hole enough to climb through. I hung my black veil on a root, took a deep breath, and crawled in. A loose floorboard came up easily when I pushed on it, and I found my head and shoulders poking up into the room. Then I heard what I'd been hoping very hard I wouldn't.

'Ah, home again, Cuddle-Poo,' trilled Malicia's voice. 'Back home to our dreary little shack in this dreary little swamp. How glad I'll be when all of Eldritch has ceased to exist! Then I can begin anew and construct a dwelling more suited to my greatness.' I heard the little dog yapping, probably in agreement.

"Malicia! Rats! I ducked back under the floor, and the loose board settled down above my head. I looked up. Directly above me was a large knothole, and if I looked through it, I could see some of the room. Then all I could was something black and wet — a dog's nose! Malicia's ratty little dog was sniffing through the knothole, and in another moment he would probably let Malicia know I was here. I thought all was lost — then I thought of the hideous smell of the defoliant. I quickly sprayed some of the defoliant through the hole, right into the little mutt's nose. The dog began sneezing and snorting and rubbing its nose with its paws.

"Malicia started cooing over the awful little thing in the most disgusting way. The dog looked pitiful, but of course it couldn't tell her what was wrong. She scooped it up in her arms and took it away. I heard her say 'Would Cuddles feel better if we found him a nice, juicy arm bone? How about some stupid peasant to bite?' Then I heard the front door open and shut, and I figured if I was going in, I'd better hurry. I pushed up the floorboards and opened a way inside.

"What can I say about Malicia's house? It was simply full of those little personal touches that tell you about the personality of whoever lives there. Her furniture looked like something out of my childhood nightmares, decorated with skulls and spiders and carvings of twisted, evil things. There was even a table with all sorts of alchemy equipment set up on it — jars of potions, a meat cleaver, and less recognizable items. I had no doubt Malicia felt right at home here, but I couldn't wait to find King Otar's device and clear out.

"King Otar told me that the thing we were looking for was made of brass, with some sort of crystal lenses. It was from Etheria — that was the land of clouds I had glimpsed through the garden pond in Daventry — and it had the power to destroy Malicia, though she didn't know that. He had no idea where I ought to look for it, of course.

"I looked all over the house. The device wasn't on or under the bed, and it wasn't anywhere on the floor or under the rug, as far as I could tell. I remember there was a tall lamp with lots of crystals hanging from the shade, and the crystals made a sound almost like a song when I brushed against them. One of the crystals fell off, so I picked it up and put it back on the lamp. I already felt like a burglar — there was no point in wrecking her house while I was about it, even if she did deserve it.

"The next place I looked was the chest of drawers by Malicia's bed. The first and second drawers were of no particular interest, but they contained a number of interesting and odd items of Malicia's undergarments, and a fantastic-looking metal object. 'That is the object we require, princess!' exclaimed the king, terribly excited.

"I put the device into my pocket and put Malicia's things back in the drawer. As I did, a woolen stocking fell out of her clothing and onto the floor. It certainly didn't look like the rest of Malicia's things, and there wasn't a mate for it. I stuffed it securely up one sleeve, closed the underwear drawer, pulled up the loose floorboard, and crawled back into the tunnel under the house and out into Malicia's back yard. The black veil was still hanging on the root where I had left it, and thinking it might be better to stay disguised, I quickly put it back on. The undergrowth was too thick to walk any farther east, so I walked back in the direction I had come.

"I'd gone nearly as far as the gate to Ooga Booga when I heard a voice right beside me, saying, 'Hey, hey, my sweet, why don't you just come on over so that we can get a bite, er, a *look* at you?!' The voice came from a curious plant that had what looked like teeth lining the edges of three green pods, one of which was open like a mouth and talking to me, in honeyed tones. 'Just because we're vegetable matter doesn't mean that we don't know what we, er, what *you* want. Besides, we can help you out, sweetmeat,' the toothy pod assured me. Then two more pods opened their mouths and chimed in. 'Yeah! Come a little closer so we can help ourselves, er, help *you*!'

"The plants *were* quite helpful, telling me that if I wanted to get through the were-woods I'd better carry some silver, as were-folk were frightened of it. Just the same, I didn't trust them. They continued to try to get me to come closer, and no matter how innocent they tried to look, they appeared hungry! I was afraid of what might happen if I got too close.

"Growing near the toothy plant was a lovely, fragrant orange flower. I could smell it from where I was standing, and I really wanted to pick it and be on my way, but I was afraid to reach for it with all those big green plant fangs so near.

"I stopped and thought for a moment: If a plant would eat *me*, what else might it eat? That's when I remembered the grisly memento I had taken from the treehouse, and I brought it out. All three heads started drooling at the sight of the foot, which only confirmed my suspicions. Throwing it to them, they began to fight over the morsel. I plucked the sweet-smelling flower, then backed away quickly before the plants could finish their appetizer and be ready for a main course!

"There was no way else to go, so I was forced back along the path through the swamp, past Malicia's house, hoping to find my way back to the Underground in time to keep Malicia from setting off the volcano.

"The swamp eventually ended, and there was a forest, but it wasn't much more comforting than the swamp had been. I thought I could see glowing eyes staring out at me from the shadows of the hideously twisted trees. No sooner had I taken a few steps down the shadowy path that led through those woods than an enormous, unnatural looking, hairy man-bear stepped out from between the trees. He was roaring and waving his paws. He must have been at least eight feet tall, and his claws and fangs looked like sharpened daggers. Its breath was heavy with the rancid stench of carrion!

"I was too terrified to move, but I remembered what the plant had said about the were-woods and silver. I pulled the silver pellet from my pocket and held it out before me. The bear hesitated — then took another step forward, growling low in it's throat. I pulled back my arm to throw it at him when I was struck with a wonderful idea. I pulled out Malicia's woolen stocking, put the pellet into it and spun my new sling over my head with all my might in what I hoped was the general direction of the bear. The pellet hit the bear squarely on the snout! To my immense relief, the bear yelped and ran off into the woods. I took off at a run, so frightened I didn't even stop when something snagged the black veil and pulled it from my face.

"When the forest began to seem more normal, I stopped running; there was no sign of pursuit, and I was awfully short of breath, anyway. It was funny, but I had almost grown used to the grim darkness of Ooga Booga, and this lovely green landscape seemed a little strange to me. I was pretty sure I'd get over it, though.

"A little further on, I saw a magnificent oak tree in a clearing. As I approached, a man stepped out from behind it. He was dressed in green and black, and he exuded an aura of power that made his noble countenance seem all the more handsome. But he also looked tired and sad, and in spite of my surprise at his sudden appearance, I felt terribly sorry for him. 'Good day, sir,' I greeted him. 'I am Princess Rosella of Daventry.'

"'Good day, my lady,' he answered gravely. 'I am Lord Attis, protector of the Bountiful Woods. Recently I have met with your mother, lady, and she wanders this land seeking you.'

"NOW, MOTHER," SAID ROSELLA, "YOU CAN IMAGINE HOW SHOCKED I WAS TO HEAR THAT YOU were in this strange place, too! I hadn't know until that very moment that you had followed me. I asked Attis if you were well, and he replied that you had left for Ooga Booga!"

"We must just have missed one another," said Valanice. "How much quicker our trials would have ended had our paths had crossed sooner. But that's not how things happened, is it?"

"That's never how things happen in *this* family!" said Graham.

All three laughed at that. "But do go on, Rosella," said her mother. "Since we did not meet, we had further experiences in the Realm of Eldritch, and your story is not yet through."

"WELL," SAID ROSELLA, "I TALKED TO ATTIS AT SOME LENGTH AND FINALLY KNEW I MUST continue my own quest to stop Malicia. When I mentioned her name, Attis recognized it immediately. He said she was the sister of Titania, Queen of Etheria, and that she'd been banished long ago for trying to usurp the throne. He believed it was she who had cursed his woods. He spoke of her enormous power and her boundless evil, and I shuddered to think of what I might yet have to face. When I asked him about your whereabouts, mother, he said, "I know not where she is now, but seek the town Falderal to the north. They may have word of her.'

"I bid Lord Attis good-bye and continued on my way. In time, I came to a fence with a tall gate. No sooner had I walked up to it than a shrill, demanding voice barked, "Halt! Who goes there?" An officious badger looked down at me, wearing a scowl on his pointed, furry face.

Valanice smiled. "You met that dreadful little fellow too!"

"Indeed!

"'My name is Rosella of Daventry, good watchman!' I called out. 'Is this the town of Falderal?'

"'Yes, this is Falderal,' the badger replied, 'but it has been decreed by the powers that be that you may not gain entry into our town unless you bring us a half-melted head of iceberg lettuce!' The guard was offended when I burst into giggles, and things just went downhill from there until finally he refused to let me in under any circumstances. I might have been upset by this, but just like you, Mother, I spied the little door in the wall and decided to try that.

'Stop! Halt! Desist!', shouted the badger. 'There's a horde of foaming field mice waiting right on the other side!' I opened the door, and as I suspected, not one foaming field mouse — let alone a horde — was in evidence. What I *did* see was the town of Falderal, much as you described it, and a white dog in a lavender waistcoat who was running around in circles, chasing his tail. When he noticed me, he stopped running, came over, and greeted me.

'Be welcome to the lovely town of Falderal!' he exclaimed. 'My name ith Archduke Fifi le Yipyap, Madame. Might I be tho honored ath to learn yourth?'

"'I am Rosella, princess of Daventry,' I replied. 'Have you perchance seen my mother, Queen Valanice? She's a tall woman, middle aged, with brown hair and garbed in green.'

"Imagine, if you can, my shock when he told me you had been arrested!"

"Well, I wasn't arrested for very long," said Valanice.

"That's what the archduke said. And then he went back to chasing his tail. Personally, I didn't believe a word of it.

"I noticed an impressive-looking white building with columns in front. Perhaps someone here would be able to tell me how to get to the Vulcanix Underground, or even explain the unbelievable story I'd heard from that little dog of an archduke. I opened the door and walked in.

"The place was an absolute mess! It looked as though someone had thrown a party, and the cleanup committee had suddenly left town. There were half-inflated balloons, wilted streamers, and ever so many cake crumbs. There was no one in sight to answer my questions, so I decided I'd look around on my own. Maybe I could find someone more credible than 'Archduke Fifi' to speak to.

"I found a door behind a curtain at the back of the hall, and on the other side, the strange staircases you described. After a few false starts, I found a door. Yes, it was the powder room door, and as soon as I opened it, I was covered in powder!"

"And what did you think of the decorating scheme?" asked her mother.

"It was every bit as horrid as you described it," Rosella assured her mother. But I found something there that you did not. It was on the cherub."

"Oh, that awful, garish little cherub!" moaned Valanice.

"It *was* awful. And it must have been some sort revolted fascination that forced me to look closer, but when I did, I could see letters carved on its base. The tarnish made it impossible to read, but I used Malicia's woolen stocking to scrub at the writing until it became clear. Let me see if I can remember the inscription.

"No. I cannot. But it did state, quite clearly, that if one were to make an offering to it, the offering should be one of fruit. And it referred to an opening of some sort. A secret passageway, perhaps?

"I searched my pockets, but I had no fruit. I looked around frantically, for surely the cherub's rhyme referred to the very thing I was looking for; the opening to the Underground. All I could see that even *resembled* fruit were the golden grapes on the columns. Artificial grapes for an artificial cherub. I had seen much stranger things in Ooga Booga!

"One of the grapes was quite loose, but I couldn't budge it with my fingers. My hammer and chisel yet again proved just the thing, and when I had the grape in my hand, I placed it in the cherub's mouth and stood back. A huge bolt slammed across the powder room door and I was shut inside. That wasn't at *all* what I'd hoped might happen — I was trapped!

"Then the cherub spit out the grape, which bounced around the fountain and finally landed inside. I heard a grinding noise, and the fountain began to open up, but before the opening was large enough to squeeze through, the fountain ground to a halt. I tried with all my strength to enlarge the opening, but the fountain wouldn't budge. I just wasn't strong enough, and there was no one here to help.

"OH, BUT THERE WAS!" SAID HER FATHER.

"Yes, and I remembered him just in time," Rosella said. "I took the scarab beetle out of my pocket, pointed the magic transformation wand at him, and changed him back to his normal size and shape. 'Your Majesty, the door to the Underground won't open! Perhaps with your strength, the portal might be forced!' I urged.

King Otar pushed and pulled with his mighty green arms and opened the fountain with little trouble. 'We must move quickly, princess! Malicia may already be activating the volcano mechanism!' he shouted, and leaped without hesitation into the hole. I followed and landed roughly into an underground tunnel. The Troll King was already hurrying away. I followed him down the tunnel to a huge metal door cast in the shape of a trollish face and studded with levers and the like.

'We must hurry! There may still be time to keep Malicia and the impostor from the mechanism!' said the king as he began manipulating the features on the metal face. Left eye lever, right eye lever, pull down on the center switch. I watched carefully, in case I should ever need to repeat the steps when Otar wasn't about. When he was finished, the door gave a strange hiss and swung open. I recognized the room beyond as the room of strange, dreaded mechanical devices I had seen through the holes in the steam tunnel.

"The false Otar was standing at the control panel, and when he saw the *real* Otar, he shrieked in freight and pulled on a switch. The real king threw himself at the counterfeit, but it was too late. 'You utter fool! What have you done?' Otar cried. No sooner had he said it than everything went black.

"The cavern began to rumble and shake as though the very earth were quaking itself to pieces!"

Part the Fifth
Alone in the Clouds

"OH, MY GOODNESS!" EXCLAIMED VALANICE.

"Exactly my words at the time," said her daughter, "Or very nearly. But really, Mother, I think we should hear the rest of *your* story now. You were trying to save the moon and they arrested you?!"

"Well, yes," Valanice said, "but you haven't told us what happened when the false Troll King started the volcano. That *is* what happened, isn't it?"

"I'll be glad to tell you just as soon as you tell us what happened to you after you fished the moon out of the pond and the archduke arrested you," said Rosella sweetly. "So go right ahead."

"I WAS TAKEN TO THE TOWN HALL," SHE SAID WITH A SIGH, "AND TRIED IN THE ROOM WHERE only a little while before, I'd been attending the archduke's birthday party. The archduke himself was there, wearing a ridiculous little periwig, and there were a jury of those badgers and other silly creatures. Even the hysterical chicken was there, though she was somewhat calmer now.

"In very short order, I had been convicted of moon theft, illegal side-door entry, defying the powers that be, littering, and several other things. No one could agree on a punishment for these heinous crimes until the chicken suggested that I be made to put the moon back into the sky. This seemed to make everyone happy.

"The archduke gave me until sunset to replace the moon or be fed to a 300-pound killer tomato."

"Were there such bizarre beasts in Falderal?" Graham inquired.

"I sincerely doubted it, but I knew these silly creatures would dream up some equally ridiculous punishment if they couldn't find one. Meanwhile, if you recall, there was some unfinished business to attend to — I needed to take the magical nymph statuette to the snake-oil salesman, who in return would give me the salve I needed to get through the were-woods and find Rosella.

"First, though, I could not resist the urge to look into the nymph's pool one more time and see you, my dear, lost daughter." Rosella blushed at the sentiment.

"I placed the comb on the little statue and was at first relieved, then horrified, to see your situation had changed. The nymph could not see you — you were in utter darkness. I was chilled to the bone. I *must* get the were-salve and rescue you from Ooga Booga.

I hurried to the snake-oil salesman's cart. He snatched the statuette from my hand and replaced it with a tarnished silver jar.

"'Here'sss the ssstuff that you wanted, lady,'" Valanice hissed in imitation of the snake, sending her family into peals of laughter. "'Sssmear it on your body when you want to ussse it, but be sssure to mix it with a bit of animal hair firssst.'

"Animal hair? I was wondering which citizen of Falderal might be willing to give some up when I though of the tuft of jackalope fur I had picked up in the desert. That should work as well as any.

"I gave the matter of the moon a lot of consideration. How does one go about putting the moon back in the sky, anyway? I could throw it up in the air, but somehow I doubted I could throw it far enough and hard enough to do the job. Finally, I had a ridiculous idea that might possibly do it. I swear to you, being in Falderal affects your thinking!

"I approached the tree near the pond, on which two of the branches formed a Y-shape, rather like a slingshot. I held out the rubber chicken I had acquired at the Faux Shop, and he obligingly grasped the branch in both feet. So far, so good. I handed him the moon, and he clutched it in both his stubby little wings. Ersatz had said that this was the stretchiest rubber chicken in Falderal. He was quite correct.

"I pulled back on the rubber chicken until he was extended as far as I dared stretch him, then let go. The moon hurtled up into the sky and stuck there. The rubber chicken let go of the tree branch and ran off down the street, squawking loudly, and I headed back to the Town Hall to clear my good name with the local government.

"Just as I approached the Town Hall, the archduke came hurrying out and granted me a full pardon. Then he said that the volcano was smoking, and that he was off to hide in the basement in case of an eruption. That was the last I saw of him.

"I supposed I must be free to go now, and so I left Falderal the way I had come, by the little door in the wall. I entered the woods, and walked to the beautiful maidens of stone.

"The cornucopia in the arms of the large statue on this side of the river was still empty, and I wondered where I would ever find sacred food to put into it, for I was sure that only then would the forest be completely healed. I hoped that I would find some somewhere on my quest.

"I crossed the rainbow bridge and turned toward the Were-Woods. As I went, the forest began to turn darker and more forbidding — trees twisted into unnatural forms, and the raucous, waiting silence increased tangibly. The wooden sign in the distance still warned me away, but I knew I had no choice in the matter — I had to deny my fear, trust my fate to the snake-oil salesman's salve, and hope for the best. I mixed my tuft of jackalope fur into the salve and rubbed some of it into my skin.

"And then, the oddest thing happened to me," Valanice told her audience, who leaned forward eagerly to hear. "I began to feel very strange. A sort of warm, tingling glow spread over me, and as my body transformed itself in some magical way, I was seized with an uncontrollable urge to laugh maniacally! I ran into the woods more quickly than I would have thought possible when I had had only two feet. I think I saw a large animal standing by the side of the road, but I was by him so fast it was difficult to tell what sort of animal it was — I was moving so fast, everything around me had been reduced to a blur.

"When I finally came to a stop and transformed back into my own form, I saw that I was at the rear of an ominous-looking gray stone house. It was Malicia's house, of course, but I didn't know that then. It was overhung by tall, dark trees dripping long trailers of slimy gray-green moss. There was a cold, unwelcoming light in the window coming from a lamp hung with long, narrow crystals. The overall result was that I had *no* desire to go around front and knock on the door.

"Suddenly, the moss on the trees began to form itself into a creature of slime and decay that slithered down to confront me, bellowing in a thick voice and dripping with putrid muck."

"The swamp monster!" cried Rosella. "And you didn't have any defoliant!"

"No, but I had help from a very special place," said Valanice. "I was terrified, of course, but before I could draw a breath to scream, Lord Attis appeared between me and the moss monster and held out his hand toward it. A beam of bright green light shot out from his hand and struck the monster, who gave a high-pitched squeal and exploded. Attis smiled at me, and before I could thank him, he had faded away in a shimmer of green. I knew it was his way of thanking me for starting the River of Life.

"I walked quickly past the front of Malicia's house, not liking the look of the lifelike gargoyle perched there, and west toward a gate in a fence. As I passed a clump of tall, green plants, one of them spoke to me.

"Those awful plants!" Rosella exclaimed.

"They tried their best to convince me they were only being friendly," Valanice remembered, "but like you, Rosella, I didn't believe it for a minute. I walked past them and through the gate, and I found myself in quite the most frightening place I had ever seen — it could not be anywhere else but the dark land of Ooga Booga. I ventured nervously past gravestones and what I would later learn was the house of the coroner. I rounded a corner, and there was a deadfall of sticks — or bones? — in my path, and a small, glossy black cat who seemed to have been waiting for me.

"'Mrrrow! Might you be the human called Valanice of Daventry?' she inquired. I suppose I should have been surprised, but by that time, nothing much was startling to me. I replied that I was. 'I owe a debt of life to your daughter Rosella,' purred the cat. 'I feel that I must tell you that she has left this dark land and is now deep in the heart of the Vulcanix Underground, at the roots of the great volcano. Soon the volcano will erupt, and then all will be lost — the land, the people, everything will choke to death on dust and fire."

"I begged her to tell me what I could do. 'I know not what you can do, but if I may advise you: Seek help from the Faerie Court of Etheria," counseled the cat. 'Their power is great, and they may be able to affect even so great an event as the eruption. Count Tsepish, the former Lord of Ooga Booga, could once have taken you thither, but in death, he has lost his head and become accursed. He was a good man, and if you can help him, he will certainly aid you, for the survival of the entire Realm of Eldritch is in your hands.' Then the cat turned and walked away, disappearing before I could ask her to elaborate further.

"The cat had not told me where to find Count Tsepish, and now it looked as though I would have to wander further in this frightening place to locate him and find my way to Etheria. I skirted the awful pile of dead wood, and ventured north until I came to a burned-out house. As I wandered through the ruins, I heard a dog growling, and I thought I saw a shadow creeping along the wall near me. A shadow with glowing red eyes! I turned to look, and the shadow became a large black dog, which leapt from the wall and came toward me, barking and growling savagely.

"I spoke sweetly to the beast, thinking to make friends with it, but the creature kept up his ominous snarling. I quickly backed away from the house, quaking just a bit from the encounter.

"East of the ruined house, I saw a treehouse in the shape of a huge, grotesque pumpkin. There was a large net of some kind reaching from the treehouse down to the ground. As I approached, a very strange-looking little child emerged from the doorway and threw an egg at me. Then another child joined the first, and they both made a rude noise in my general direction. I wanted no further dealings with them, so I walked back the way I had come, but I decided I shouldn't fear them — they were children, albeit unruly. I walked back to the treehouse, and those awful children were gone.

"I was curious as to what might be inside that grotesque pumpkin treehouse, so I looked for a way to get inside. A rope elevator hanging from the tree above seemed the best way. I climbed into the bucket and pulled myself up to the top of the tree. The top of the treehouse was hideous, as you already know, Rosella, but if there was anything I had learned on this involuntary adventure, it was that no matter in what strange circumstances or surroundings one found oneself, there was almost always something that could come in handy later. I would look around as quickly as I could.

I thought the mummy particularly odd, only partly because it was wearing a wig and holding a leg-bone in one hand. Its own, perhaps? I didn't even care to speculate. I reached for the bone and pulled, but to my utter surprise, the mummy pulled back. I was startled and frightened, but angry, too. I pulled again, harder, and the bone came loose in my hand, along with little bits of the mummy's hand. I had already thought of someone who might like this bone a great deal.

"When I had let myself down from the tree, I walked back to the ruined house. The black dog was still waiting there, growling, and I tossed the bone in his direction. The dog eyed the bone suspiciously, then lay down to chew it.

"'You're not a bad dog at all, are you?,' I said, watching him enjoy his treat. He raised his massive, noble head and looked at me with what can only be described as canine amusement. 'Nor are you such a bad human,' he replied. 'In fact, you are the first person to be kind to me since my master and mistress died. No one else was willing to face me down, even though my bark is in truth worse than my bite.'

"The dog spoke to you?" asked Graham.

"At that point, it seemed the least miraculous thing I'd encountered that day," Valanice laughed. "I asked the dog what had happened to his people, and he replied that Malicia was to blame."

"Why am I not surprised?" Rosella sighed. "Was there ever any grief in the Realm of Eldritch that Malicia *wasn't* at the bottom of?"

"Not any that I knew of personally," Valanice agreed ruefully. "At any rate, the dog told me that his master was cursed to ride the heavens in search of his head, which had been cut off by one of Malicia's gargoyles, and that his mistress had died of grief and was now a sinister phantom. Malicia had sent the Boogeyman to burn down their home, and the poor dog had been unable to defend it.

"Was his master Count Tsepish?" asked Rosella.

"He was indeed. And I asked the dog if I might help by attempting to recover his head."

"'That would be a very noble deed if you can accomplish it,' he replied, 'but in the end, I do not know. We can only hope that it will turn out for the best.' He then offered me his master's medal, which he wore about his neck, to help me in my search. I took the medal gratefully, uncertain just what I should do with it.

"'Might your mistress be capable of helping us aid your master?' I asked him. 'When she still drew breath, she was the most beautiful woman in all of Eldritch,' he sighed, 'and she loved my master more than life itself. Now she is the most bitter phantom in the entire land, her undeath fueled by rage and grief. Now she hates the living with every ounce of her considerable willpower. You would do well to avoid her.'

"I walked south from the ruins of the count's house and came to a large tomb where a woman garbed totally in black was weeping piteously. A shadow passed overhead, and I looked up to see a horseman riding by in the sky above me, a chilling, ghostly wind marking his passing. This would be odd enough in and of itself, but there was more: This horseman had no head. This, then, was the poor soul whose skull I must find and return to him so that I could be shown the way to Etheria.

"I could not tell which tomb might belong to the count, so I wandered among the gravestones, reading epitaphs. None seemed to refer to the late, beloved leader of Ooga Booga. Perhaps it was the crypt where the woman in black wept, but because of the way she obscured the front of the tomb, I could not read the inscription, and I hesitated to disturb the poor soul in her grief.

"After a time, the horseman returned, riding along the ground this time. I was uncertain how he might react to me, so I stayed out of his path. At last, I decided that the woman in black must be the sorrowful widow of the count. But hadn't the dog said she died of grief? Perhaps he only believed her to be dead. With some trepidation, I approached the woman and showed her the medal the faithful dog had given me. 'Good woman, please take this medallion. It once belonged to your husband.,' I said.

"The woman took the medal and, sobbing and wailing, glided away. She was several feet above the ground and left a bitterly cold wind in her wake. So the dog was right after all," said Valanice with a shudder. "Now that she was gone, I could read the inscription on the tomb: 'Count Vladimir Tsepish; Lord Protector of Ooga Booga, High Paladin of the Land.'

"There was a keyhole set into the tomb door, but I had no key. As I was wondering how I would get inside to search for the headless horseman's skull, I heard the sounds of an awful commotion coming from the direction of the treehouse. I heard the piteous wails of a cat, so, fearing the worst, I hurried to see if I could save it from those horrid children. One of them was chasing after my feline friend with a string of paper tubes that sparkled with fire, but she was easily eluding him and seemed to be in no danger. Some of the paper tubes fell off the string behind the children and exploded! As they ran past, one of the lit tubes fell off the string and onto the ground just in front of me, sputtering sparks. This might be just the thing to try on that old keyhole, if only I could act quickly enough, before the thing exploded! I quickly —and fearfully — snatched it up and hurried back to the count's crypt.

"I reached the tomb, and jammed the little sparkling tube into the keyhole — a perfect fit! Then I stepped back and plugged my ears. The tube exploded with a sharp, hollow boom, the lock was blown open, and the door swung outward with a haunting metallic wail. I felt quite strange about violating a tomb in this manner — or at all, for that matter — but I felt certain that if the count could have his head back, he would forgive me my transgression.

"In the center of the crypt was a large stone sarcophagus with a carving of a dog draped mournfully over the lid — I recognized him to be a depiction of the count's devoted companion. I knew I had no choice but to open the coffin and examine its contents. Heaving with all my might, I was able to shove the lid aside.

"At the bottom of the sarcophagus was dust and a skull — the headless horseman's lost head. Shuddering, I averted my eyes and removed it. I walked outside to the spot in the road where I had seen the horseman touch down and awaited his return. He appeared presently, charging along like demons were at his back, bearing down on me with alarming speed. I held the skull over my head and fervently hoped he wouldn't trample me. He might have been a ghost, but from that angle, he looked as solid as anything I'd ever seen! He reigned in his horse, stopping just short of me. He then reached down and took the skull from my hands. Trembling, the headless horseman placed it on his shoulders. A ghostly face appeared over the skull — a handsome face, and not unkind — and the horseman looked down at me and smiled. He thanked me for lifting the curse.

"There followed a tender reunion between the count and his dear wife, the details of which I will spare you as being of far too personal a nature. Suffice it to say that their happiness at being once more together moved me to tears of joy. Even the black dog was reunited with his beloved master and mistress. Then the count asked if there was any favor he might do me in return. I replied without hesitation that I must find my way to Etheria.

"'It is the least I can do for one who has helped us to find happiness and eternal peace,' he told me, and he gave me the use of his beautiful black horse — Necromancer — and a fife with which to call him anywhere on the ground, though he would not be able to hear me if I summoned him from Etheria. He helped me onto the horse, and we flew off into the clouds, leaving the count, his lady, and their loyal dog behind.

"There followed the most fantastic ride I could ever have imagined," Valanice reported, clapping her hands with remembered joy. "We galloped through the sky and into an alien world suspended in the air. Looking down made me terribly dizzy, so I concentrated on the view ahead.

"The first thing I saw was a sky island suspended over four colorful rainbows, which arched out of sight toward the ground below. The ghost horse slowed and stopped, kneeling low to allow me to dismount, then flew away. I gazed in wonder at the fabulous landscape of floating islands and suspended stones that the earth seemed to have no hold upon.

"Walking east from the place where I landed, I came to a meadow full of bright flowers. In the distance, I could see a palace floating high in the sky. Tiny creatures, which I first took to be dragonflies, buzzed around me, singing bits of beautiful melody. Upon closer inspection, I could see that they were miniature dragons, each a different color. I tried to tempt one closer, but they would stay near only a moment before flitting off again.

"It was a dragonet that first lured me through the door to Eldritch," Rosella remembered. "Now you understand, Mother, why I had to follow it. At least, I hope you do."

Valanice patted her daughter's hand. "Of course I understand, Rosella. Still, not every young woman would have dived into a pond to fall through a door into another world simply so she could get a closer look at a miniature dragon. Still, that's the kind of daughter I have, and I assure you I would not want any other.

Rosella blushed. "What else did you see there, Mother?" she asked.

"Well, to the north of the meadow was a beautiful garden, and in the center of a cluster of sweet-smelling roses was a silver colored sphere that reflected its surroundings in miniature, like a mirror on another world. There was a kind of harp beneath it, with delicate golden threads stretched between the bottom and top. It was decorated with carvings of the dragonets. I plucked one of the strings and heard a musical note, very clear and sweet. I tried another string, and it gave a different note. I was quite curious and perplexed.

"I couldn't go any further in that direction, and as lovely as the garden was, it seemed to hold no clue to my quest. I went back through the dragonet meadow and turned east until I came to the base of a mountain. A path led upwards, then divided into two. I chose the path that led up to a plateau and a twisted tree.

"I heard a sound like blowing wind, and then a horse rushed by. This was no ordinary horse," Valanice assured her listeners, "but it would be difficult to describe him. He seemed to me to be made of the wind itself. I heard no hoofbeats, and his passing blew me onto the path below. By the time I picked myself up again, he was gone.

"I walked back up the path to the tree, hoping no other creatures of the wind were prowling about. A strange substance grew above the tree that intrigued me a great deal — it smelled delicious! I tried touching it from the ground, but it was just out of my reach. I hadn't climbed a tree since I was quite a little girl, but I supposed I hadn't forgotten how. I grasped the trunk and pulled myself up until I could reach the odd fruit, then broke off a bit and carefully climbed back down.

"The fruit smelled sweet and lovely, but it wasn't like anything I'd ever seen before, and I wasn't sure it was good to eat. The dragonets would certainly know if it were edible, I thought, and I decided to carry it to the meadow to see whether or not they ate it.

"When I returned to the meadow, I held out my hand with a bit of the fruit on it, and to my delight, a dragonet landed lightly on my hand and began to eat. As it ate, it hummed a tune — the same simple little song over and over. Then it cleaned its face like a cat and flew away.

That song — those golden strings — could they be important? I walked back toward the garden with the gazing ball, humming the dragonet's melody. I intended to play the melody on the strings of the gazing ball's pedestal to see what effect this might produce. I knelt by the pedestal and tried out the strings until I knew which ones produced which notes, then duplicated the sweet little tune the dragonet had hummed.

"Nothing happened until I touched the silvery globe. My hand, then my arm, then my whole body was pulled inside just as if I were made of taffy!"

"Dear me!" said Graham. "What was inside the ball?"

"A whole different world. It seemed to be a plain of velvety blackness, with no ground below and no sky above. I was suspended in the air! Three women sat in front of me around a strange and magical thing that looked like a loom. They were spinning, measuring, and cutting golden thread, and they paid no attention to me as they went about their work silently and gravely. 'Pray tell me, good people, who are you?' I asked them, and my voice sounded unnaturally loud echoing in that endless void.

"'We are the Fates,' one of them replied matter-of-factly, and they introduced themselves: 'I am Clotho. My weaving spins the fates of women and men.' 'My name is

Lachesis. It is I who take measure of the fates of women and men.' 'You may call me Atropos. I am responsible for severing the fates of women and men.' This last now cut a thread with her scissors, as if to illustrate. 'And you, mortal. Tell us what you want of us.' I was quite overwhelmed, but I managed to find my voice.

"'It is imperative that I see Lord Oberon and Lady Titania at once. I bring important news from the land below," I told them. 'We are sorry, but that is impossible,' one of the Fates said. 'The king and queen have gone in search of their lost son, and none know where they can now be found. If your case is truly urgent, seek out Mab, the Lady of Dreams. The way to Mab is difficult, for she resides on an island of dreams and nightmares, an island called Dreamland that cannot be reached in waking reality. This is all that we can tell you at this time.' Then the woman with the scissors —Atropos— waved her hand, and I found myself in the garden once more, wondering how I could reach this island of dreams.

"I walked back to the place I had first touched down upon the strange soil of Etheria. How I wished now for the count's horse to carry me to someone who could tell me how to reach the Lady of Dreams! But the horse would not hear me call from here, or so Count Tsepish had told me. I would have to find another way down.

"I looked closer at the four rainbows. One of them, in deep blues and purples, reminded me of that strange land of Ooga Booga. Perhaps it was a path of some sort. Perhaps someone there could help me to find the island of dreams, for I felt much too anxious to sleep. I stepped onto the path, and an instant later, I was sliding down with breathtaking speed and the dreadful sensation that I was leaving my stomach behind. An instant after that, I was thumping down onto the ground of Ooga Booga.

I wandered through that dark land and soon found myself facing a very old, very dilapidated house surrounded by an ancient, decrepit iron fence. I opened the rusted gate, which shrieked at me almost like a human voice in pain. The name on the mailbox read: Dr. Mort Cadaver. It occurred to me that a doctor might be able to give me a sleeping potion."

"My Dr. Cadaver?" Rosella cried. "Isn't he just the *dearest* man?"

"He is indeed," said Valanice with a smile. "And a most helpful one, too, although I must admit I wasn't too sure about his methods. When I had introduced myself, he invited me into his parlor. It was, as you know, odd.

"'My name is Cadaver,' he said kindly. 'Doctor Mort Cadaver. How may I be of assistance to you, madam?'

"'I need to find the Lady Mab in Dreamland. Her island cannot be reached through the waking reality, and I have no idea how to get to her,' I explained, and the good doctor invited me to take a nap in his coffin. 'This coffin is lined with pure Dream Silk', he assured me. 'Normally, it assures the dear departed an eternal rest, but in your case, it will just put you into a deep slumber.'

"'You expect me to fall asleep in a coffin?' This was not a thought that appealed to me, but the doctor insisted. 'Oh, don't worry, it's very comfortable — I often nap there myself. I'll make sure that you're not disturbed or buried, and I can wake you quickly if you encounter anything unpleasant in Dreamland.' I was torn, but I really had no choice. I had to trust the Doctor. I climbed into the coffin and lay down. Doctor Cadaver pulled a silk shroud over my face. 'Sleep well, madam!' he said. I found myself slipping quickly into the dark abyss of sleep. Now I would find the Dreamland and Lady Mab. I was getting one step closer to finding Rosella and going home.

"I felt that I was half-walking, half-floating through a hazy landscape somewhere between sleep and waking. An ominous shadow hovered above me, blocking — no, *sucking in* — the light, and a horrible monstrous *thing* appeared out of nowhere, reaching for me. It was indescribable; it seemed a sea-bottom horror, with tentacled protrusions that seemed to almost shift around its lunging, amorphous form. I tried to run, but the ground seemed to pull at my feet as if it had a malign intelligence and purpose, slowing me to a crawl. This was the island of dream and *nightmares*, I realized, and the creature was all of my childhood nightmares rolled into one awful form.

"I looked over my shoulder at the rapidly approaching horror, tripped, and fell down, down, down through swirling mists and clouds of gray for what seemed like an eternity. I was screaming noiselessly until I landed with a silent splash in a fantastic green-blue sea. I swam above the water without even trying until I came to a tiny island upon which was a large temple. I glided out of the water and onto the beach, and — lo and behold! — my garments were not even damp!

The temple looked larger on the inside. The air was thick with colored mists that rolled above a marble floor and among tall marble columns, obscuring the details and true dimensions of the structure. I found myself floating toward the back of the temple, deeper into the swirling mists. A solid block of ice came tumbling toward me. A green-skinned, black-haired woman was encased in the ice, frozen solid, her mouth open in a soundless, eternal scream. I screamed again, and the room twisted horribly and faded out of one reality and into another. I was back in Doctor Cadaver's parlor.

"As I sat up, the silken shroud fell from my face. The doctor was hovering over me with a worried expression pasted across his drawn features. 'Are you all right, madam?' he asked. 'I heard you scream and was about to wake you when you came to. What happened?'

"'I journeyed deep into the land of dreams, Doctor," I said. 'The Lady Mab has been frozen into a gigantic block of ice, and horrible *things* are stalking that land!' Dr. Cadaver shook his head with a pained, worried look. 'It appears that things have become worse than you believed', he said. I thanked the good fellow for all of his help and hurried back outside.

"I was desperate. Whatever could I do? The Fates had told me where to find Mab — perhaps they knew where to find the one who would be capable of unfreezing her. It was my only hope. I blew on Count Tsepish's fife, and his horse appeared. I quickly mounted it and flew away to Etheria. I hurried to the gazing ball in the garden, plucked the dragonet's song out on the golden strings, and touched the reflective sphere. Immediately I found myself back inside that strange nothing-world inhabited by the Fates.

"'Mab has been frozen into a block of ice, cold and lifeless!' I exclaimed frantically. The Fates turned and silently regarded me. Lachesis said, 'Ice? But all ice must melt under the warmth of spring. Ask the Lady of Spring what is to be done.'

"'She, the Lady of Spring, is who melts the frosts of winter' added Clotho.

"'She resides in the forest, and her power keeps it whole,' said Atropos. She waved her hand and Iwas again pulled back through the ball and into the beautiful garden.

"I decided the Fates must have been speaking of Ceres, but she was accursed, turned into a great, dying oak. How could I undo the evil that had been done to her? I had poured the sacred drink into the river maiden's pitcher and started the River of Life, but the healing of the forest had not been complete, and Ceres was still a tree, still dying.

"What else had the Rock Spirit said? Ah, yes, put sacred food in the cornucopia of the other statue maiden. But what was sacred food? I thought that it was called ambrosia, but there my knowledge ended. But wait! I had seen a sort of food growing above the twisted tree at the base of the mountain — the odd fruit I had given to the dragonet. Could *that* be ambrosia? It seemed impossible, but the impossible seemed to have a way of happening in the Realm of Eldritch. There was only one way to know for certain.

"After I had picked another handful of the fruit, I went back to the rainbows. One had led to Ooga Booga — might another one take me to the enchanted forest? Maybe it was the one in shades of such deep and restful green —that seemed appropriate for such a deep and peaceful wood. I stepped onto it and sat down.

"Moments later I found myself in the forest, at the clearing of the statue maidens. I hurried to the cornucopia and placed the strange fruit inside. The pitcher glowed momentarily, and then fruits, vegetables and grains instantly overflowed from the cornucopia, tumbling in profusion onto the ground. I had guessed right! The impossible had again happened! I reached out and took a dark red, juicy pomegranate. It was real, and so were the other magical foods. Had my act saved Lady Ceres? I hurried to see if a transformation had occurred.

The great oak still stood in its clearing, its branches a little less green, a little more wilted At its base was good Lord Attis playing a sorrowful melody on his pipes.

"'I have traveled to Etheria seeking help, Lord Attis,' I informed him, 'But the king and queen were gone and Mab has been frozen into a block of ice by some horrible enchantment!'

"Attis stopped playing and looked up at me. He looked tired and drawn, hopeless. Slowly he began to speak. 'Were my beloved Ceres still able to speak, she might have been able to tell you. She is — was — the Lady of Spring, responsible for melting the snows and ice of winter. If only she were still human, she might be able to help.' His voice trailed off, and he slumped forward tiredly. I showed him the pomegranate, and told him of replenishing the cornucopia.

A sudden hope lit in his eyes. 'In ancient lore, the pomegranate was thought to symbolize regeneration, rebirth,' said Attis. If that was so, then perhaps it had not been an accident that I had chosen it. I carefully placed the pomegranate in the outstretched branch of the oak, and held my breath. It worked! This began a magical transformation that, when it ended, had changed the dying oak tree back into the lovely Lady of Spring.

Attis and Ceres embraced one another happily, but each had work to do that could not wait. Attis said he must try to stop the eruption of the volcano, and Ceres had to complete the healing of the forest. She thanked me most graciously and went to her work. I followed.

"'I have traveled through Dreamland and seen the Lady Mab,' I said to Ceres, 'but she has been frozen into a block of ice by some evil magic. Do you know of anything that could be done to cure her?' Ceres thought for a moment before answering. 'You must fill a crystal shaft with pure sunlight and use this to thaw the ice that surrounds her,' she said. 'However, you cannot take material objects into Dreamland with you when you are asleep. Thus, you must find a way to travel into the land of dreams while awake.' 'Can you tell me how to do this?' I asked. 'No, I cannot,' replied Ceres. 'However, there is little that the Fates do not know. Perhaps if you ask them, you will receive an answer.' Bidding me farewell, she turned back to healing the stricken things of the Bountiful Woods.

"A crystal filled with sunlight. How in the world did one *fill* a crystal, and where would I find one to begin with? I seemed to remember having seen some... Of course! The lamp in the window of that ominous gray stone house on the outskirts of Ooga

Booga! I would have to go back there and find a way to get one. But first I would fly to Etheria for more ambrosia. It had proved useful twice now, and I had a feeling I shouldn't go on any extended trips without it.

"I called the horse and off we flew to Etheria. It took me only a few minutes to get another handful of the ambrosia, and I was on my way down the purple rainbow and to the house in the swamp. The lamp with the hanging crystals was still in the window, but this time it was turned off. I hoped that meant that whoever — whatever — lived there was not at home.

"I felt a little strange about going into a stranger's house and taking a crystal from the lamp, but it was for a good cause. Going in by the front door still seemed unwise, so I searched for another way, and soon found it at the rear of the house — the hole you had made, Rosella, though I did not know then that you were responsible.

"When I came to the end of the passage, I could see floorboards over my head. I pushed on one of the boards and was able to poke my head up and look around. Then I heard a door open and a woman's voice, so I quickly ducked back under the floor.

"'Tonight, vengeance shall finally be ours!,' the woman was saying to someone. 'Tonight, the volcano will erupt and blow that thrice-cursed Etheria right out of the sky, and the rest of this puny realm of Eldritch will shrivel and burn to black ashes!' I suppressed a frightened gasp. Now I knew it was Malicia's house I had come to! And Malicia was so deranged that she was planning to destroy everyone and everything. I had to leave here as soon as I had the crystal and warn someone — anyone. If only she would leave so I could get inside the house!

"Suddenly, a ratty little dog started sniffing and pawing at the knothole right over my head, sticking his vile little nose right down into my face. I knew he'd alert Malicia to my presence, and that was a complication I didn't need. What could I do to distract him? Then it came to me. All dogs love a treat! I reached into my pocket, took out the chunk of ambrosia, and pushed it through the knothole. The dog snatched it happily and began chewing. Malicia strode over to see what he was eating, but the little mutt swallowed it just in time.

"'Come here Cuddles, you naughty creature!', she cried. 'How many times must I scold you for eating those rat droppings? No matter. Come, let us go and watch all of Eldritch suffer in the heat of my wrath!' At that point, she swept the horrid little creature up in her arms and left the house.

"I waited breathlessly until I was sure they weren't coming back, then pushed up the loose board again and climbed out into the living room. It was a particularly ugly, forbidding house, and I found nothing there of interest except the crystal lamp. I unhooked one of the crystals, then climbed back down through the floorboards and outside.

"Now all that remained for Mab's cure was to fill the crystal with sunlight. There was no sun in Ooga Booga, so this was clearly not the place to look. I summoned the horse once more and went to the sun-drenched plains of Etheria to hold the crystal up to the sun. Although it reflected off the surface, it didn't seem to hold any of the light inside. Perhaps there was another way, or perhaps what was needed was a special *kind* of sunlight. I remembered the shaft of sunlight in the desert temple that had had such a magical effect upon the pictures carved into the altar. Maybe that was the kind of sunlight I needed.

"I examined the rainbows once more. One of them seemed to be made of the yellows and reds of the desert. I gathered up my skirts and slid down, and sure enough, I landed in back in the burning wasteland.

"I entered the temple and walked directly to the little harvest god's altar. I held the crystal in the beam of piercing sunlight that came from the eye of the sun god. Instead of reflecting the light this time, the crystal seemed to drink it up until it glowed with its own inner brilliance.

"When I had summoned the horse and reached the land of clouds again, I went directly to the gazing ball and performed again the steps that would take me inside. I hoped Ceres was right — that the Three Fates would know the answer I sought.

"'I have spoken to Ceres, the Lady of the Forest,' I told them. 'She says that I must enter the Dreamland while still awake, but she knows not how I might do this. Please, I beseech you, tell me how I my enter Dreamland while still awake.'

"'To enter the Dreamland, you must ride on the wings of a dream,' said Lachesis.

"'There is only one who can help you to do such a thing,' added Clotho.

"'Our nephew,' said Atropos, 'the weaver of dreams.'

"Lachesis handed me a curious object. It looked like a small net of some kind. 'You may need this in your quest, for our nephew often surrounds himself with dark terrors that are best not spoken of.' Then Atropos waved her hand, and I was back in the garden. The Fates had not told me where to find this Dream Weaver, but by now I was no stranger to exploring new places. In a short time my wanderings had taken me to the base of the windy mountain once again, to the place where the one path became two. One of the paths led up to a cave in the side of the mountain, and I thought that looked as good a place to investigate as any.

"As I approached the cave, an indescribably horrific figure emerged from its mouth. This was certainly one of the dark things the Fates had warned me about — it was every bit as terrifying as the one in my dream, but more so because this one was real. I wanted with all my heart to run, but I found myself rooted to the spot with heart-stopping terror. Bringing out the little net, I held it in front of my face in the vague and panicked hope that it would protect me from that gliding, amorphous horror. The creature struck out, and I felt a moment of hopeless fear before the attacking creature was pulled into the net like so much smoke. I was still shaking when I entered the cave.

"How to describe what I saw there?" Valanice mused. "In a place where unusual things were utterly commonplace, this was still a sight to give one pause. A vast loom took up most of the space in the cave, and attached to this loom by hundreds of tiny colored threads was a curious being — the weaver of dreams, I took him to be — who did not appear to notice me. As I watched, something — a dream? — detached itself from the loom and fluttered upward through a hole in the ceiling of the cave."

"I called out to him, but the Dream Weaver didn't respond. I touched him lightly on the shoulder, then stepped back in surprise as he turned his face to me, for his eyes were every color of the rainbow, changing from one color to another in dizzying, almost hypnotic, succession.

"'What is it that you desire?' he asked in a whispery, unnatural voice. 'I require your assistance, Weaver,' I said, not willing to show him how afraid I was. 'Assist you? I help no one,' he replied coldly. 'Leave here, ere I call up another nightmare to flay your flesh and drag your soul screaming into the eternal darkness.' I showed him the dream catcher and told him what had happened to his *last* nightmare, still trying to hide how frightened I was. He seemed remotely amused. 'A pity that I do not have a second nightmare, but they destroy one another on sight. A true pity.'

By this time, my fear had changed to anger, and I had had enough of his distant amusement. What I needed was help, and right away. 'Lord Oberon and Lady Titania are gone in search of their son, and none can find them,' I told him, rather angrily, 'and Mab has been changed into a block of ice! I have to enter the land of dreams while awake to save her, and you are the last person who can help me, but judging from what I've seen of your personality, I think I can do without your assistance!' I turned to leave. His head at last turned toward me. 'Mab accursed?' Now, it seemed, I had his attention. 'She must be freed! You must go quickly, but wait a moment. I wish to give you something.'

"That was more like it. I watched as he set to weaving a tapestry on his loom as effortlessly as a child might make a cat's cradle. It floated up from the loom and hovered in the air.

"'This will allow you to enter the Dreamland still clothed in your flesh, but be warned! As you can enter in the flesh, so, too, can your flesh be harmed. You could die, for Dreamland is not a friendly place. Now go!' The tapestry of dreams whisked itself to my side. I watched for a few moments as the Dream Weaver set back to work. Now his weaving had a more ominous tone and darker hues. There would be nightmares in the world tonight, I was sure.

"At the bottom of the mountain, I dropped the tapestry and stepped on. There was a strange, inner lurch, and then I was back in that place of swirling mists I had seen in my dreams. The tapestry landed, then flew away as soon as I had stepped off. I hoped there was an easy way back to the world of waking reality, but whether there was or not, I resolved to do what I had to do here.

"Without warning, another nightmare fiend appeared, no less horrible than the others, lunging viciously and ravenously at me. I held up the net that had caught the first nightmare on the mountainside and hoped it would snare this one, too. To my utter amazement, the first nightmare poured itself out of the net and attacked the second, tentacles flailing. They fought furiously for a moment, then the newcomer ran off with the first monster following in pursuit. I breathed a heartfelt sigh of relief and walked away, finally noticing that I was not floating as I had on my previous visit, but walking as if on solid ground.

"The ground didn't stay solid for long, but gave way again to nothingness. I fell off the edge of reality and into the same awful, long fall I remembered from my dream. I splashed down in the same ocean, this time a genuinely wet one! And I would drown just as genuinely, I realized, if I didn't start swimming! I could see no sign of land, so I picked a direction and swam for all I was worth. Soon, I saw the island and the temple ahead.

"It was just as awful awake as asleep. The dark mists still flowed over the floor, and Mab still floated, helpless, in her block of ice. I took out the glowing crystal and reverentially touched it to the frozen surface. Sunlight flowed from the crystal into the Lady of Dreams, and she began to slowly come alive. The very air in the temple seemed to change, and the dark mists became light and lovely, glittering as if with the light of the sun. When it was done, the crystal shattered into a million pieces, which dissolved themselves into vapor.

"Mab, a formidable yet lovely woman, seemed to come out of a deep sleep. 'Who are you?' she asked when she noticed me. I told her who I was, what Malicia had done, and that Oberon and Titania were missing. Her eyes turned to steel.

"'So. That is why she cursed me. The evil hag wishes to destroy us all! We must stop her. I will go forth and try to stop the volcano's eruption, and you must harness the wind and use it to find Oberon and Titania, for without their power and assistance, I cannot contain even a fraction of the eruption for long.' She handed me what looked like a horse's bridle.

"'Harness the wind? Why? How do I do such a thing?' I was confused, and my questions showed it. 'You must capture and harness the wind Scirocco,' she continued relentlessly, 'then ride him to the summit of the Mountain of Winds. There you will find King Levanter, Lord of the Winds, and he will certainly assist you in your search.'

"'Now we both must go about our separate missions,' Mab said. 'May good fortune and good dreams follow you'. She then waved her hand, and I found myself once more at the base of the Mountain of Winds. I climbed up to the plateau and waited.

"I had not long to wait before the horse of wind galloped past again. This time I had hidden myself behind a tree, and when Scirocco came past, I threw the bridle over his head. He bucked wildly, then flew straight up, carrying me along as I clung desperately to the reins. I was not on his back but flying out behind him like a flag!"

Rosella covered her mouth, stifling a giggle. Valanice glared. "Soon we came to the top — a plateau of wind-sculpted rocks and twisted trees and plant life.

"I heard a terrible roar, and a big, dark, brawny man—or should I say wind—flew up with terrifying speed and attacked us. Sirocco bucked, and I was thrown from his back and onto the ground as he flew away. The man, who was as ghostly and strange in appearance as the wind horse, laughed horribly and came toward me.

"'Borasco! Stop this foolishness at once, I say!' came a woman's voice. 'You are not to eat people, understand?' A woman appeared, dressed in flowing red veils that spun around her in the wind she seemed to bring with her. She scowled at the monster.

"'Mom!' he whined. 'I wasn't going to eat her, honest! I just wanted to scare her a little!'

"'Hah! That's just what you said the last time I caught you, you big bully!' she said, smacking him about the head and shoulders.

"Just then, a regal-looking man of wind came sweeping down on them like a hurricane. "What is the meaning of all this commotion? His eyes fixed on me. 'You, human! Tell me the meaning of this intrusion lest I grow wroth!" he commanded.

"I was in no mood for delay. 'Your Majesty, might I first know the name of the one who commands me to speak?' I asked him. He regarded me with what I assume was amusement. 'You are audacious, mortal. Very well. I am Levanter, King of the Winds. Now, who might *you* be?'

"'I am Queen Valanice of the land of Daventry, your majesty', I replied. 'Please, we must find a way to contact Oberon and Titania! The enchantress Malicia plans to cause the volcano to erupt, and if that comes to pass, all of Eldritch will be doomed!'

"Levanter looked at me for a moment, then took a deep breath and called in a huge, booming, inhuman voice, 'Come to me winds! Your King commands it!' The woman and the brawny young man sped to his side. A moment later Sirocco flew in, and from another direction a pale and wispy young woman came, bringing a gentle breeze. 'Borasco! Gharbi! Sirocco! Zephyr! Go forth and find the Lord and Lady of Etheria, wherever they might be!'

"Each wind took off in a different direction, making my hair and clothes fly with their passage. I waited, for how long I could not tell. At length, one of the winds — Zephyr — returned, leading a beautiful man and woman in a magnificent flying chariot, which landed atop the plateau of the Mountain of Winds.

Without preamble, the pair of them turned to me, transfixing me in place with the strength of their gazes. 'Are you certain that Malicia has ignited the volcano, human?' the man said.

"'Look for yourself, Lord Oberon,' I said, pointing to the cone of the smoking volcano. 'By the blood of all the Gods!' Oberon exclaimed, going a little pale.

"'We extend to you our deepest thanks, mortal,' said Titania. 'Without your warning, we would never have had a chance. Now we have one, though it is indeed slim. To Oberon she said: 'Come, my husband. We must try to halt the evil that Malicia has wrought.'

"The chariot rose majestically into the sky. I rushed to the edge of the mountain and called after the chariot, 'Wait! My daughter! I must save my daughter!' but no one seemed to hear. The chariot flew away, out of sight.

"I was left standing on the mountain top," said Valanice, "not knowing if they would ever be back, or whether I would ever be reunited with my dear family." She couldn't help sniffling, just a little, as she recalled the sorrow and anxiety of that awful moment.

Part the Sixth
The Eyes Have It

"Perhaps you had better let your mother recover a bit and go on with your story, Rosella," her father suggested.

"If that's all right with you, Mother," said Rosella.

"Oh, perfectly all right, my dear," her mother replied. "I'll be all right in a moment, I'm sure." She blew her nose delicately into a lace-trimmed handkerchief.

"All right then," Rosella began, "Where was I?"

"The real Troll King and the false Troll King were fighting in the volcano control room," said Graham. "What happened then?"

"It was suddenly very dark, as I may have mentioned. All I could see were two pairs of eyes, one set green and one set purple, flashing as the two trolls fought. One of them shouted at me, 'Princess! Change the wand! Change the impostor to his true form!' About that time the lights came back on, but even then I couldn't tell one king from the other. Change the wand? What? How? I drew out the magic wand and began twisting it. I felt something turn at the tip of the wand, but I had no time to worry whether I had 'changed' the wand or just broken it. I looked back to the wild melee in front of me and knew I had to transform one of the two struggling trolls. But what if I used the transformation device on the wrong one?"

"There was only one difference between them — the eyes. I tried to think. What color were the eyes of my troll suitor, the one who saw me as a bride? Green! Time was running out! I pointed the wand at the troll with the emerald eyes, and he was instantly transformed. He changed into Edgar!"

"Edgar," said her father. "That was an unexpected surprise, wasn't it?"

"Much like the moon falling from the sky." Rosella replied.

"BUT THAT WAS ONLY THE FIRST SURPRISE. LET ME TELL YOU THE REST. I WAS CERTAIN I MUST BE imagining things. What did trolls have to do with Edgar, my friend and rescuer from far off Tamir? I blinked, but he didn't go away. 'Edgar?' I said, astonished. 'Is that you? What in the name of the world are you doing here?'

"King Otar seemed equally astonished when he heard Edgar's name. 'What!?' he gasped. 'Oberon and Titania's missing son?' My jaw dropped. I had always thought Edgar to be the son of the wicked faerie Lolotte!

"Edgar appeared as confused by all this as anyone. 'What? Rosella? What are *you* doing here? And where is 'here'?' he asked as he groggily looked from side to side. Edgar looked like someone who had just awakened from a long, deep dream. Before I could begin to explain, that is if I *could* have explained, Malicia herself burst into the room and saw me. Screaming angrily, she loosed a bolt of magical energy in my direction, but King Otar flung himself between the blast and my body. The bolt struck him, and he was flung against the wall, knocked unconscious.

"Before either of us I could act, Malicia turned to Edgar with a venomous look. With not a word, just a wave of her hand, she conjured a fearsome wind that lifted Edgar like a straw doll and blew him out the tunnel door! Then she looked at me, her eyes still like those of a hungry snake —cold and vicious.

'Ah, Rosella,' she crooned. 'So we meet again. And this time I will guarantee that you do not escape me, my pretty!' She gestured wildly at me. There was a flash and the odor of brimstone, and then I wasn't in the control room any longer. There were walls of heated rock everywhere I looked, and a terrible heat from beneath, coupled with a fiery red glow. I had been transported inside the very heart of the volcano!

"I was perched on a narrow ledge above a rapidly rising pool of molten lava. I was so frightened, I almost fell in, but I managed to grab onto the hot, jagged rock of the wall behind me and keep my footing. As I hung on for my life, my hand encountered a little niche in the wall where I could stand further from the edge. Before I could feel any safer, however, the lava began rising! There was no doubt I would soon be immersed in it! From beyond the walls, I could hear the sound of Malicia. She was laughing.

"I knew I had to find a way out, but it felt like I was in a prison of solid rock. From somewhere deep within me, I found a bit of courage that I wasn't sure was still left. I *might* die even if I tried to escape, but I would *surely* die if I didn't. I clawed frantically at the scorchingly hot wall behind me, hoping to find any opening at all that might take me away from my certain death. Finally, I felt some of the rock give way under my hand. I had made a hole!

"I dug at the hole with my hands, but it was taking much too long, and the burning pain was almost more than I could bear. In my near panic, I had almost forgotten the shovel I had been carrying with me all this time! I attacked the wall with it. It was softer than I had feared, and I quickly had an opening large enough to slip through. I wasted no time in getting through to the tunnel on the other side. I spent no time congratulating myself. How could I? Lava would be flowing through my escape hole soon.

"The tunnel branched into two, and I knew I had taken the correct branch when I saw the mechanical troll face door at its end. As quickly as I could, I repeated the steps I had seen King Otar perform to open the door. In moments, I was back inside the room. The Troll King was still unconscious on the floor.

"I grabbed the device I had taken from Malicia's house. 'It must be inserted into a socket for it to regain its power,' King Otar had told me. What was a 'socket'? I discovered that it had a pair of prongs on its back, as if it were meant to be attached to something. I looked about anxiously — there were so many strange-looking mechanical devices, so much *technology* in the room. A moving pointer labeled 'Volcano Pressure Gauge' was wildly swinging.

I noticed an opening just to the side of Otar's unconscious form that looked as if it might fit the prongs on the device. I pushed them into it. At once, the globe began to glow. I hoped it wouldn't take too long to fill with charge, if that was indeed what it was doing, because I feared Malicia might return at any moment.

I attempted to wake King Otar. I shook him and spoke loudly into his great ear, but nothing seemed to have any effect. 'What I need are smelling salts,' I thought. I remembered the sweet-smelling flower I had picked in the swamp outside the gate to Ooga Booga. There was something the lady trolls in the Underground had said...

"It worked! As soon as I waved the flower under King Otar's nose, he came awake with a loud snort, frowning at the smell of the flower. Then he jumped urgently to his feet and ran to the volcano controls. He turned dials and flipped switches while the earth rumbled and shook. When he had done everything he think to do to the controls, the rumbling got worse, and the shaking became a full-fledged earthquake. The king looked at me, and I could see in his eyes that all hope was gone.

"'Embrace eternity, princess,' he said, 'for Malicia has destroyed us all.'"

"I knew we were going to die," Rosella said, "and I would never see my family again.

"BUT THE FATES WERE KIND. NO SOONER HAD I THOUGHT IT THAN THE SHAKING STOPPED AND THE gauge ceased its wild swings. And that's when you ran in, Mother, although I had no idea how you'd gotten there."

"I HAD BEEN STANDING AT THE TOP OF THE MOUNTAIN OF WINDS," VALANICE REMEMBERED, "when a cloaked figure had appeared riding Necromancer, the ghostly steed that had first brought me to Etheria. He offered me his hand, a strong one, and without fear nor thought, I got on the horse behind him. I somehow *knew* that if I did, he would take me to you."

"And he did," said Rosella, "but how?"

"We came through Ooga Booga, through the place where the elevator had once emerged from the Underground. The cloaked man raised his hands, and with a blast of fiery magic, reopened the hole down into the ground. He took my hands as we jumped into the abyss. Cushioned by his magic, we landed unharmed. From there, we dashed through a series of hellishly shaking, crumbling caverns that led here. Once, the very ground opened up right in front of us as if it were a great maw anticipating a feast! But Edgar — for that's who the horseman was — saved me and brought me to you."

"And I begged you to forgive me," rushed Rosella. "I told you about the door in the pool, and King Otar, and Edgar...."

"I couldn't believe what you were saying," Valanice remembered. "Edgar? It was all too unbelievable. But you pushed back his hood, and there he stood. Although I had never seen him before, your shouts left no doubt as to who he was. And how happy you looked to see him, Rosella."

KING GRAHAM RAISED AN EYEBROW AT THIS, BUT HIS DAUGHTER IGNORED HIM, AND WENT ON with her story.

"Right then, Malicia rushed back into the room, and the heat of her anger made the fires of the volcano seem as ice in comparison. She lunged at me, but Edgar stepped between us, glaring.

"'Do not touch her, witch!,' he said.

"'The first time we met, I enslaved your mind and body, but now your usefulness is over,' Malicia hissed in return. Prepare to die, worm!'

"Edgar only shook his head, never taking his eyes from her face. 'Then kill me if you can, you withered hag!'

"Malicia raised her hands to destroy him, but a blast of magic came from his hands first, and she staggered back. He deflected her next bolt and blasted her again. She bent over in pain, and Edgar lowered his hands. But it was a base and lowly trick! As soon as Edgar's guard was down, Malicia spun around and blasted him with a deadly burst of magical force. He dropped suddenly, limply, onto the floor — perfectly, horribly still, like a puppet with cut strings. I felt as if my heart were crushed in my chest. For a split second I was paralyzed, but you were there, mother, and I couldn't let her harm you, too.

"I looked to the wall where I had plugged in King Otar's device. It glowed brightly, and I saw my chance to defeat the evil faerie if only I could but reach it. I dashed for the wall and came away with the device. Malicia turned to face me, black death in her eyes, energy crackling at her fingertips, and I raised the device and pointed it at her, snarling in defiance. A pulse shot out of it and enveloped the witch in a ball of bright light. What had I done? King Otar had said the device would destroy Malicia, but all I had really wanted to do was to keep her away from you, mother.

"The magical energy ball shrank, and then it vanished altogether. There on the floor lay a tiny baby, right on the spot where Malicia had been standing. Malicia's obnoxious little dog ran up and sniffed it, obviously confused.

"I gave this a moment's thought. It had worked once — why not twice? I pointed the blasting device at the dog. The dog disappeared and was replaced by an adorable little furry puppy. It tottered over to Malicia — now a baby — and licked her cheek. Lowering the mysterious device and staring incredulously at what I had just done, I whispered, 'I got you my pretty. And your little dog, too.'

"EDGAR WAS STILL LYING ON THE FLOOR, UNMOVING AND VERY PALE. HOW UNFAIR THAT HE should lose his life, while because of him, I still had mine. I knelt by his side and stroked his cold brow. My eyes filled with tears, my heart with heavy anguish. And then I remembered! I had a life to spare — the black cat's! Would it work on Edgar? I warmed the glowing life between my hands and touched it to Edgar's forehead. His eyes fluttered open, and he smiled at me."

She sighed. "*That's* when King Oberon and Queen Titania came in."

"They'd been trying to help Lady Mab control the volcano," said Valanice. "I think they must have sensed something when Malicia killed Edgar, and they came to him there."

"They were so happy to see him alive and well," Rosella remembered with a smile, "but they were a bit confused how Edgar and I knew one another, and we were *all* confused about how Edgar had been put in King Otar's place. I was also startled to hear that he had played such an important part in saving us all."

"And the most startling thing of all," Valanice added, "was that Edgar had been the son of the king and queen of Faerie all along!"

"Edgar explained it all as best he could," Rosella told her father. "He had been stolen as a baby by Lolotte. You remember her, father."

Graham smiled. "Not nearly as well as you do, I'm sure."

"Then he told about how we had first met, and all that."

"'All that' being how you rescued him and how he had never forgotten you?" her father chided her.

"Yes, all that," said Rosella. "Well, then he went home, only what we didn't know was that 'home' was the kingdom of Etheria. Then Queen Titania — that's Edgar's mother, you understand — told how happy they were to have him back. They held a ball in his honor, and he vanished again that very night! They set out to find him, never guessing until today that it was all a part of Malicia's evil plot!

"Queen Titania looked over at the baby on the floor. The baby reached her arms up to her. Titania hesitated, then picked her up. 'Sister, something evil went wrong with you. Let us now make a new beginning', she said to the child. 'This time, you will grow to love that which is good, and will frolic in the light instead of reveling in darkness.'

"Through this, Edgar was looking at me strangely, acting as though he were ashamed of something.

'I must apologize to you, Princess Rosella,' he said when we were alone. 'It was *I* who cast the spell that lured you into Eldritch. I am responsible for your troubles here. Can you find it in your heart to forgive me? I beg this of you!'"

Rosella sighed. "What a silly young man. How could I *not* forgive him? I pressed his hands in mine and asked if he would show me the sights of his realm. It *was* what I jumped into the pool for in the first place."

"And did you get your tour of Etheria?" her father asked, his eyebrows raised in an expression Rosella knew quite well.

"Yes, and it was even more beautiful than I could have imagined. I think it's quite the loveliest place I've ever been."

"Hmmm," said Graham thoughtfully. "And do you suppose you might be going back there sometime soon for a visit?"

Valanice laughed. "I suspect she just might at that. And I wouldn't be at all surprised to see young Prince Edgar visiting Daventry fairly frequently in the near future."

Rosella knew she was blushing, but she didn't particularly care. Edgar had, in fact, asked her permission to come courting, and though she wouldn't have believed it herself when this whole adventure began, she was looking forward to it with a great deal of pleasant anticipation.

The shadows were deepening in the garden, and the air had grown cool. One by one, the castle windows were illuminated with the golden glow of candles as day gave way to evening. The time of story-telling had ended in a glow.

"Come, my dearest wife and daughter," said King Graham, rising to his feet and holding out a hand to each of them, "It's time we went inside, I think. You had quite a lot of amazing experiences in the world on the other side of that magical portal, but now the adventures are over."

Valanice nodded and turned her head to give Rosella a wink King Graham could not see. Valanice and Rosella looked at one another and smiled. "Yes, father," Rosella agreed. "*That* adventure is over."

"For the moment," Valanice said.

PART FIVE

Where's Where?

Mapping — accurate mapping — is an essential skill for all computer adventure game players. Game designers take pride in making the worlds they create confusing to navigate. In fact, they get paid real money, sometimes lots of it, to make this so. They have fun doing it. They *expect* people to make maps.

While many people enjoy the process of making their own maps, many others would rather not be bothered. Other folks find the task confusing, frustrating, or daunting. And, of course, a lot of people want to know what's beyond the next doorway before they get there. We don't consider this cheating at all; we hate driving (and hiking) in unfamiliar territory without some sort of a guide.

The Boy Scouts are right about one thing, at least. Be prepared.

While the layout of the world in King's Quest 7: The Princeless Bride is not terribly perplexing, it is filled with a lot of places to visit and a few to avoid. The maps we have included in this chapter make getting around a lot easier — and a lot less deadly — for Rosella and Valanice.

We're using a traditional type of adventure game map known as a "box map." Using them couldn't be simpler, although if you've never used (or seen) one before, it might appear the opposite. The maps are made up of a number of square boxes connected by lines. (OK - there are sometimes a few circles or other shapes, but just think of those the same way you do the boxes.) Each of the boxes represents a location in the game that can appear on the screen.

All you need to remember really is one simple concept: *Forget geography*. Box maps show the relationship between different screen locations on your computer.

This means that the map location below labeled Start is connected to

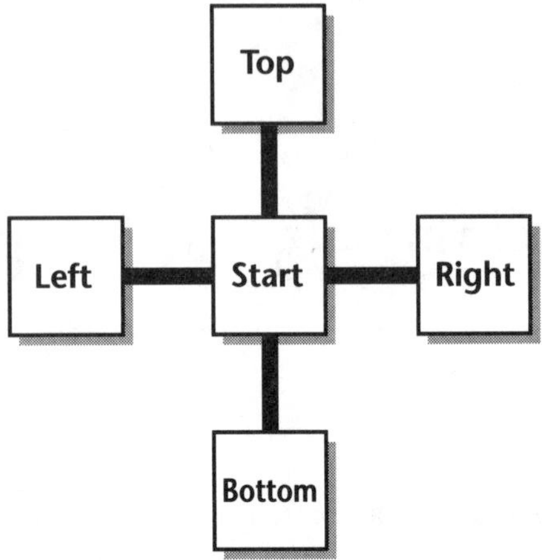

locations that can be reached by moving toward the top, bottom, left, and right of the screen. It's also clear that you would leave from the bottom of the screen when you're in the location labeled top to get back to Start.

King's Quest VII also contains several wide rooms that you can scroll through smoothly or, with the Scrolling Off option chosen, treat as discrete rooms. We've chosen to map this rooms as if Scrolling On is enabled. These cases look like this:

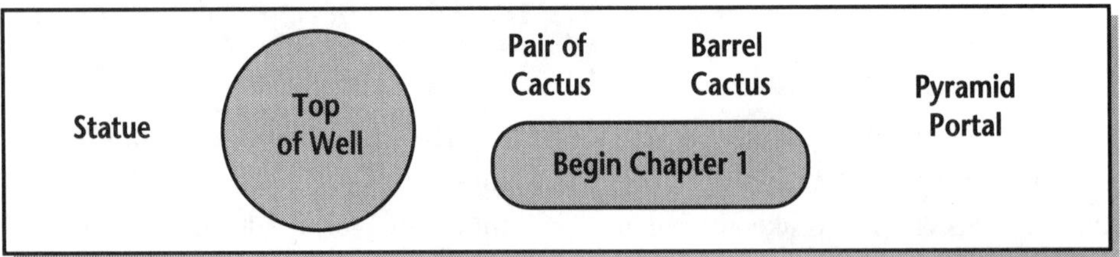

For these wide rooms, what we've mapped are the landmarks. The room above is in the Desert. With Scrolling off, it's three separate rooms, but you should have no problem moving around between them once you're there.

In computer game design lingo, each individual location is known as a room. Consider box maps as being a bunch of rooms connected by the lines.

However...

Isn't there always a however?

However; we warned you about geography. Direction often gets a bit scrambled once you are inside some rooms. Sometimes, when you get someplace, you discover that you didn't enter from the direction you were moving. And the direction back isn't always the direction from which you came.

It's time for another example:

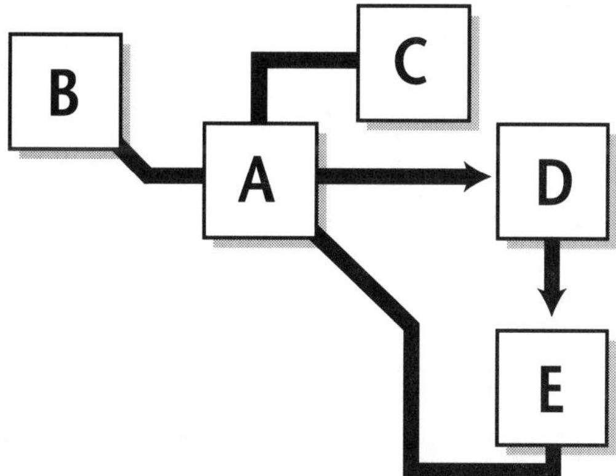

Here, you leave Room A via the top of the screen in order to get to C. But the way to return is to leave C from the left of the screen to get back to the place you started (A). It's like walking north to get to C and arriving there from the west. Leaving C is like walking west to go south. Oh, well. Nobody ever claimed that computer games are the real world.

The diagonal lines represent diagonal exits and entrances usually indicated by diagonal cursor arrows on the King's Quest screen.

Then there are the lines with arrows at one end. These are one-way arrows. You can travel in the direction the arrow is pointing, but you can't return back by that route.

That's pretty much it. A few other things appear here and there, but they follow the same rules we've just described and are usually labeled for further clarity.

Many of the rooms in King's Quest VII contain items that Valanice or Rosella need to collect in order to further their adventures. Although we have listed all of them in Chapter 6, including where they can be found, we have discovered that *knowing* that a certain item can be found in the desert is different than *seeing* just where in the desert that room exists. Therefore, next to the appropriate maps, we've included a list of what can be found in those regions.

It's a special bonus for reading this far.

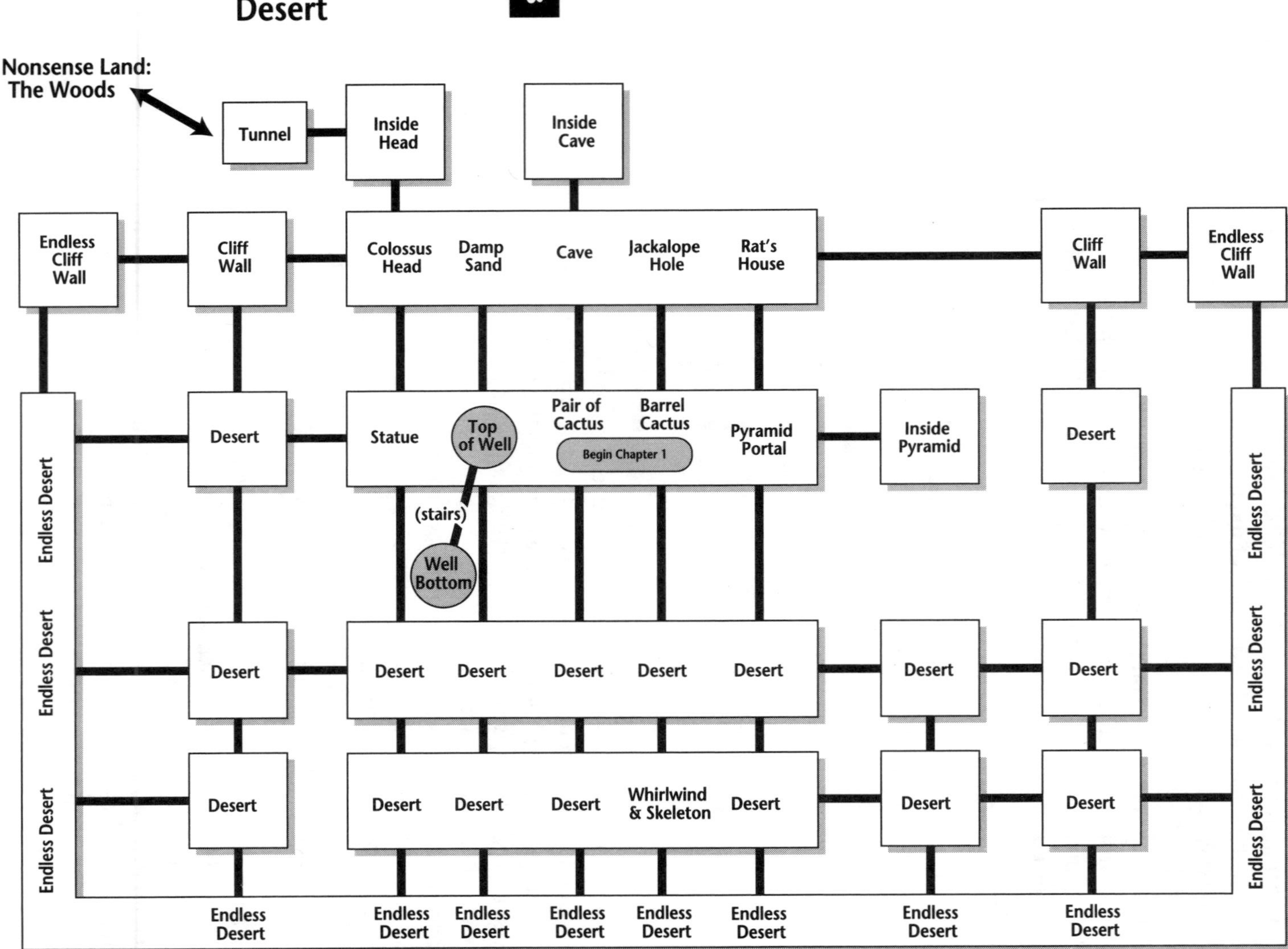
Desert
To Nonsense Land: The Woods
Tunnel
Inside Head
Inside Cave
Endless Cliff Wall
Cliff Wall
Colossus Head
Damp Sand
Cave
Jackalope Hole
Rat's House
Cliff Wall
Endless Cliff Wall
Desert
Statue
Top of Well
(stairs)
Well Bottom
Pair of Cactus
Barrel Cactus
Begin Chapter 1
Pyramid Portal
Inside Pyramid
Desert
Desert
Desert
Desert
Whirlwind & Skeleton
Desert
Endless Desert

Room	What to Get
Barrel Cactus	Piece of petticoat
Bottom of Well	Puzzle piece 2 (part of key)
Bottom of Well	Turquoise shape (false puzzle piece)
Colossus Head	Prickly pear
Damp Sand	Ear of corn (after planting kernel)
Damp Sand	Gourd seed
Inside Cave	Basket
Inside Cave	Corn kernel (inside basket)
Inside Cave	Pot
Inside Pyramid	Puzzle piece 1 (part of key)
Inside Pyramid	Beam of sunlight
Jackalope Hole	Rat's glasses (horn solution)
Jackalope Hole	Jackalope fur (horn solution)
Pair of Cactus	Rat's glasses (rope solution)
Pair of Cactus	Jackalope fur (rope solution)
Rat's House	Crook
Rat's House	Turquoise bead
Statue	Good water
Top of Well	Salt crystals
Top of Well	Salt water
Top of Well	Stick
Whirlwind (Skeleton)	Spirit's horn
Whirlwind (Skeleton)	Rope
Whirlwind (Skeleton)	Bug-reducing powder

The Troll Underground

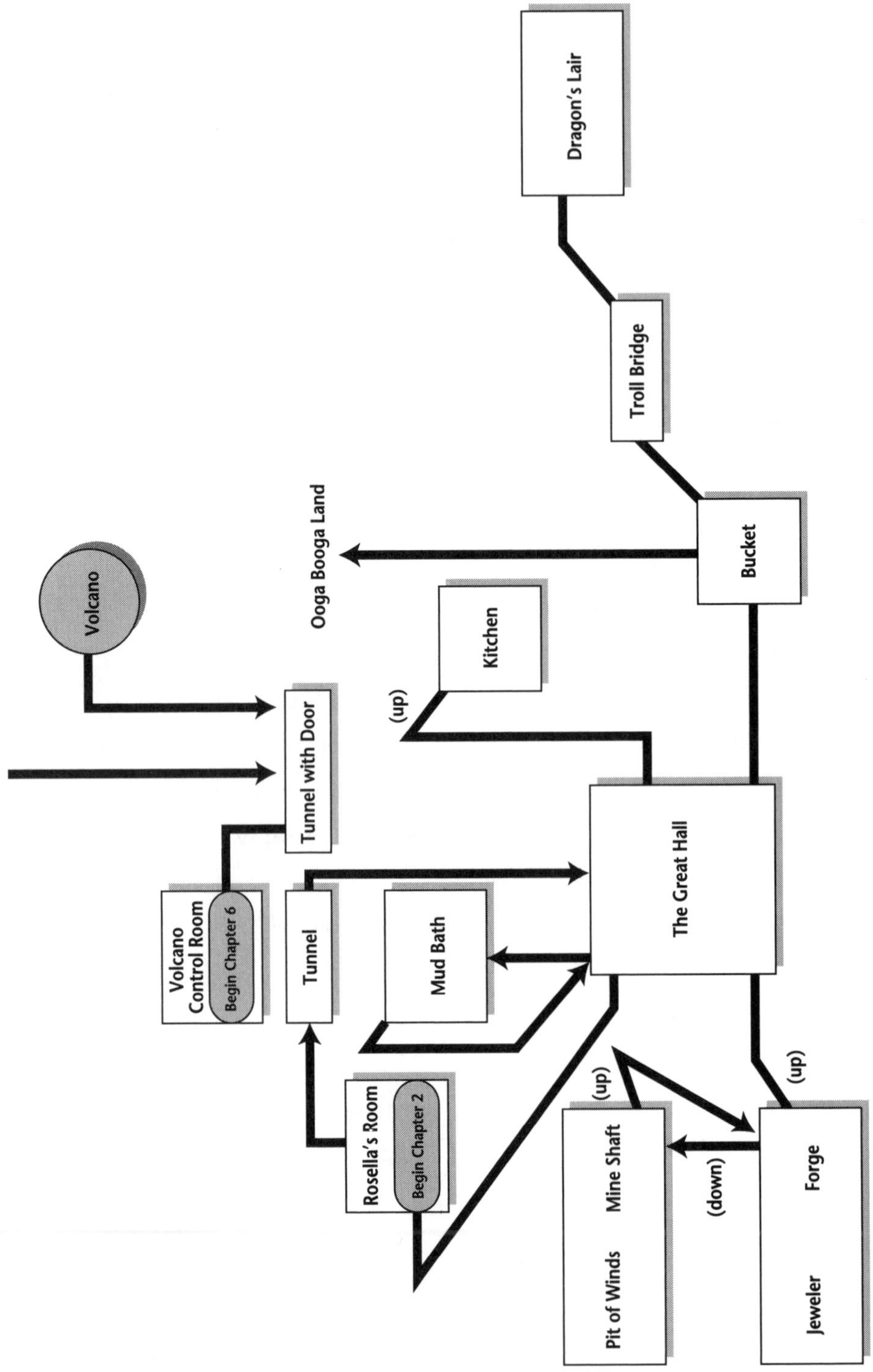

From Nonsense Land

Volcano

Volcano Control Room

Begin Chapter 6

Tunnel

Tunnel with Door

Ooga Booga Land

Rosella's Room

Begin Chapter 2

Mud Bath

(up)

Kitchen

Dragon's Lair

Pit of Winds

Mine Shaft

(up)

The Great Hall

Troll Bridge

(down)

Bucket

Jeweler

Forge

(up)

Room	What to Get
Dragon's Lair	Big gem
Dragon's Lair	Dragon (crystal) scale
Forge	Silver spoon
Forge	Spoon mold
Forge	Spark (for lantern)
Great Hall	Dragon toad
Great Hall	Enchanted rope
Great Hall	Shield
Great Hall	Silver pellet
Great Hall	Spike (taken from shield)
Great Hall	Toy rat
Jeweler	Hammer and chisel
Kitchen	Baked beetles
Kitchen	Brass bowl
Kitchen	Gold bowl
Kitchen	Toy rat (after using on chef)
Mine Shaft	Emerald (green) water
Mine Shaft	Lantern
Pit of Winds	Wet sulfur
Tunnel with Door	Fragrant flower

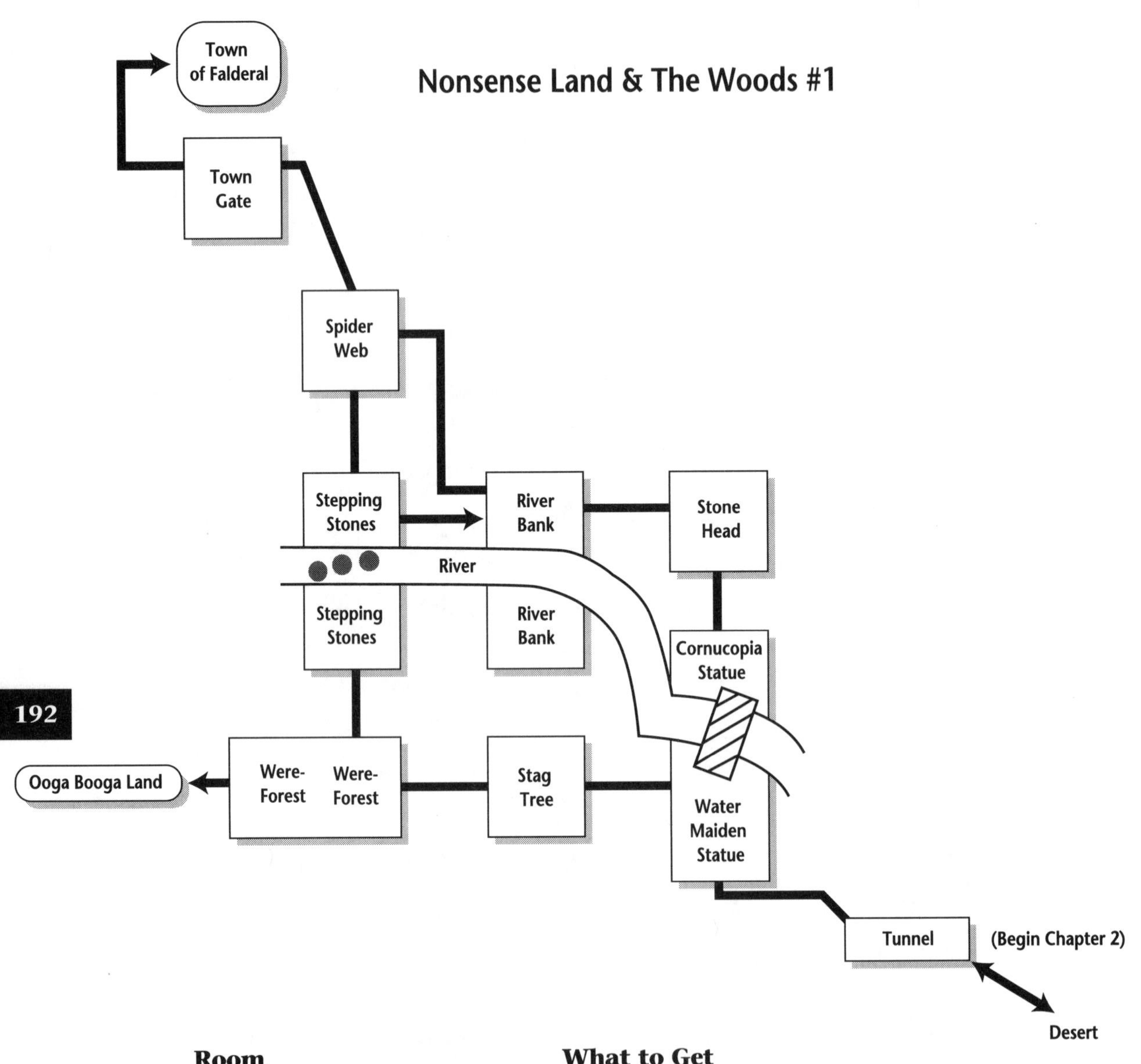

Room	What to Get
Cornucopia Statue	Pomegranate
Water Maiden Statue	Nectar

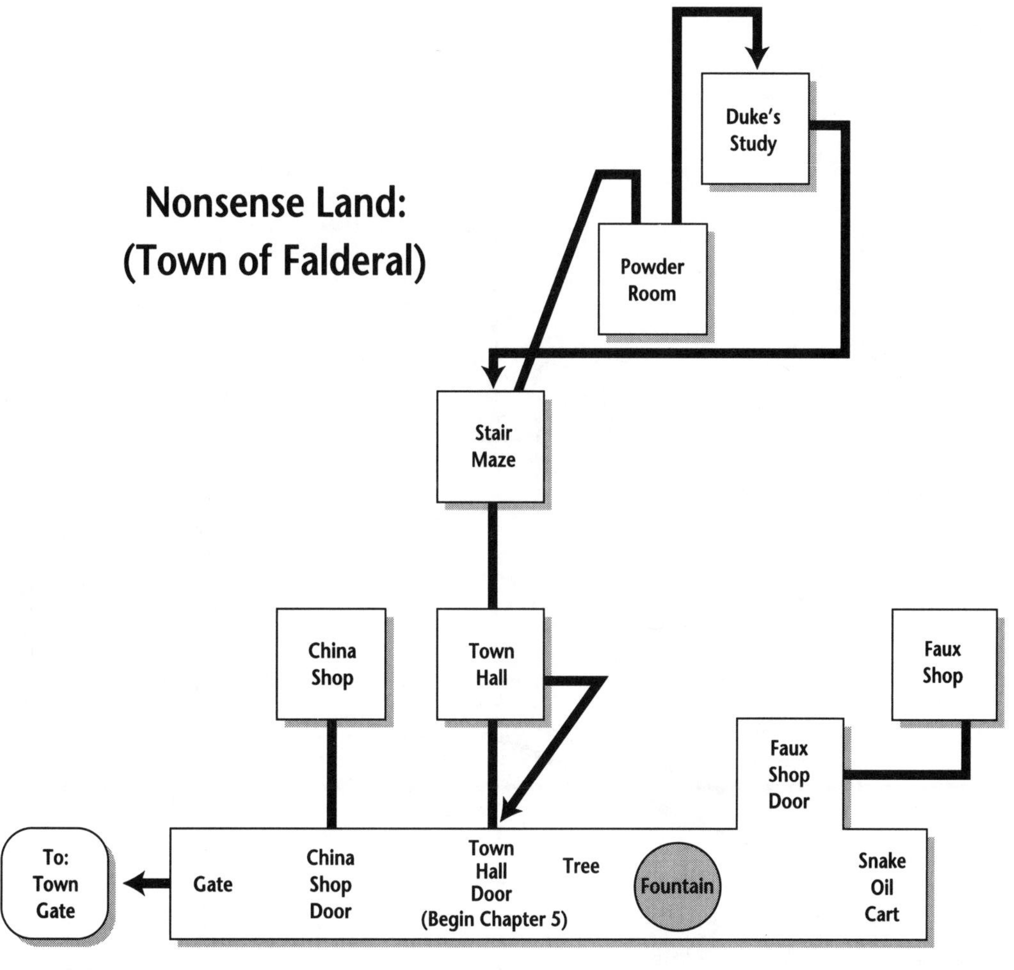

Room	What to Get
Archduke's Study	Magic statue
China Shop	Mask
Faux Shop	Book
Faux Shop	Rubber chicken
Faux Shop	Feather (from rubber chicken)
Fountain	Moon
Powder Room	Golden grape
Snake Oil Cart	China bird
Snake Oil Cart	Were-beast salve
Tree	Wooden nickel

Ooga Booga Land

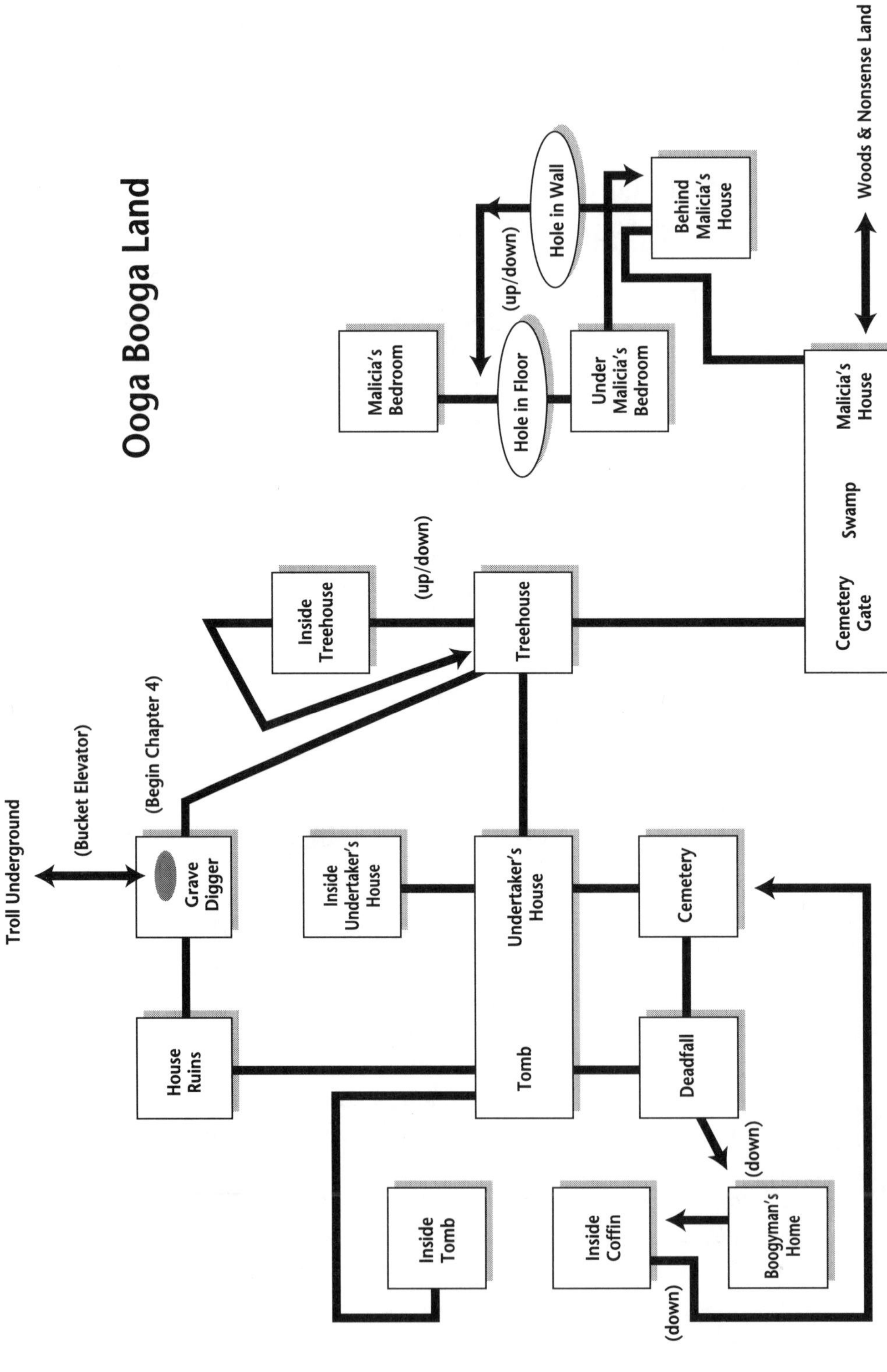

Malicia's Bedroom
Hole in Floor
Under Malicia's Bedroom
(up/down)
Hole in Wall
Behind Malicia's House
Woods & Nonsense Land
Malicia's House
Swamp
Cemetery Gate
Inside Treehouse
(up/down)
Treehouse
(Begin Chapter 4)
(Bucket Elevator)
Troll Underground
Grave Digger
Inside Undertaker's House
Undertaker's House
Cemetery
House Ruins
Tomb
Deadfall
(down)
Inside Tomb
Inside Coffin
Boogyman's Home
(down)

Room	What to Get
Cemetery	Magic wand
Cemetery	Scarab
Cemetery	Veil
Cemetery gate area	Fragrant flower
Grave Digger	Shovel
Grave Digger	Shrieking horn
Malicia's Bedroom	Crystal shaft
Malicia's Bedroom	Mysterious (Malicia-blasting) Device
Malicia's Bedroom	Woolen stocking
Tomb (outside)	Horseman's fife
Tomb (inside)	Horseman's head
Treehouse (inside)	Backbone
Treehouse (outside)	Extra life
Treehouse (inside)	Femur
Treehouse (outside)	Firecracker
Treehouse (outside)	Gravedigger's rat
Treehouse (inside)	Foot-in-a-bag
House Ruins	Headless Horseman's medal
Undertaker's House (inside)	Defoliant
Undertaker's House (inside)	Weird pet

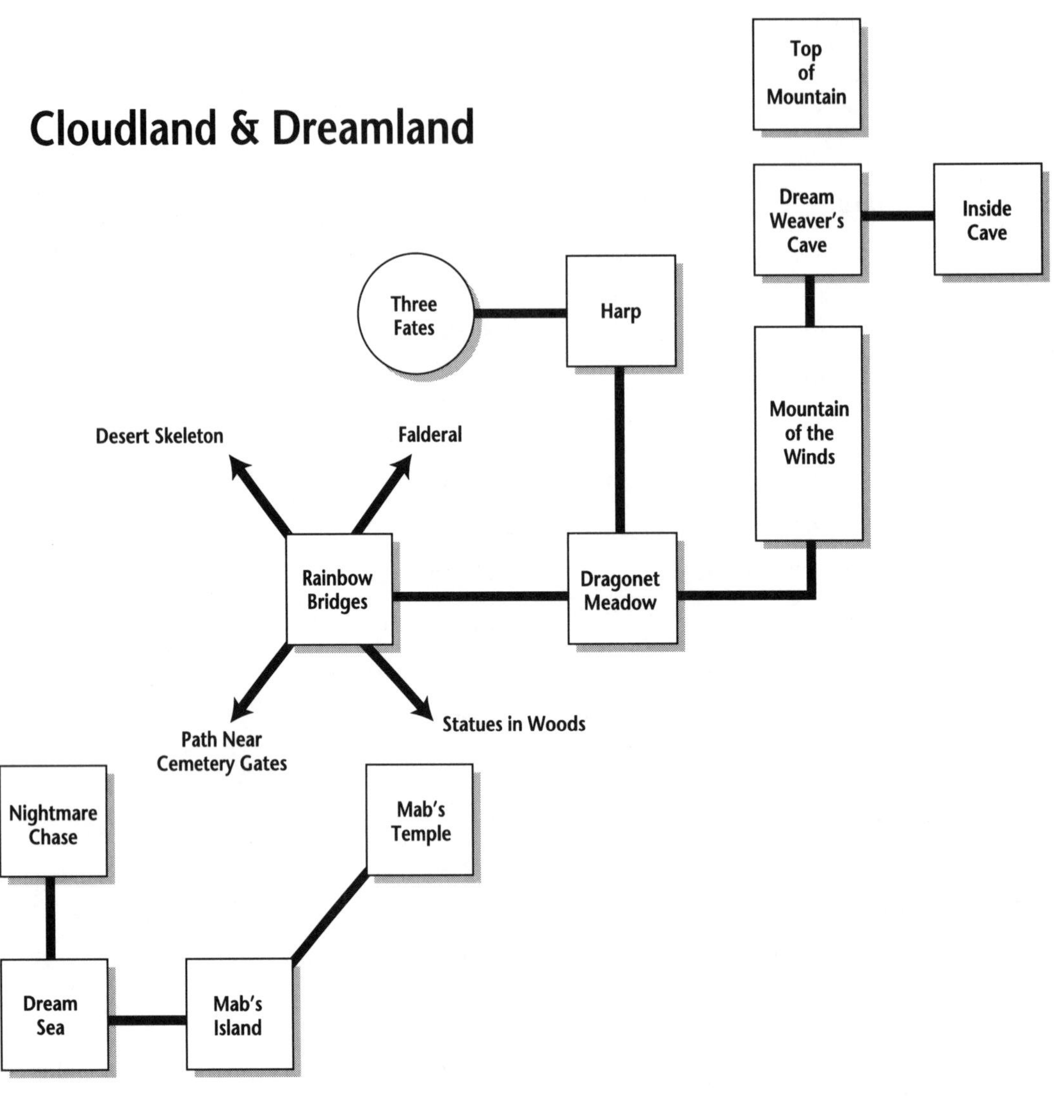

Room	What to Get
Dream Weaver's cave (outside)	Ambrosia
Dream Weaver's cave (inside)	Tapestry of Dreams
Mab's Temple	Magic bridle
Three Fates	Dream catcher

PART SIX

What's What?

As Rosella and Valanice work their way through their adventures in The Princeless Bride, they need to employ about 80 different items and objects, all of which have their specific applications. Most people think of this stuff as just *stuff*, but the strict technical terms are inventory or inventory items.

It's up to the game player, of course, to discover just what this collection of stuff does (or does not do), when it should be used (or not used), and how to use it.

Oh, you have to find all the stuff, too. In some cases, you have to make it.

So if Rosella finds a lifetime supply of belly button lint, and you just can't wait to find out what it's used for, we've put together a quick reference to help clear up the question. If you have a need to know where Valanice will find Malicia's lost car keys, that's here too. (OK. We made that up. But if Malicia owned an automobile, we know she'd misplace the keys. And she'd be really annoyed about it.)

Here's the stuff. Happy hunting.

ITEM	WHERE FOUND	CHAPTER WHEN FOUND	USE
Ambrosia	Dream Weaver's cave	5	Start cornucopia (Ch. 5) Feed Malicia's dog (Ch. 5) Feed dragonets (Ch. 5)
Backbone	Treehouse	4	Given to Dr. Cadaver in exchange for weird pet (Ch. 4)
Baked Beetles	Troll kitchen	2	Magic potion ingredient (Ch. 2)
Basket	Desert cave	1	Contains corn kernel (Ch. 1) Save hummingbird (Ch. 3)
Big Gem	Dragons lair	2	Traded for hammer and chisel (Ch. 2)
Book	Faux Shop	3	Traded for crook (Ch. 5)
Bowl (Brass)	Troll kitchen (shelves)	2	It's a decoy for the gold bowl
Bowl (Gold)	Troll kitchen (shelves)	2	To get green water (Ch. 2) Holds magic potion (Ch. 2) ("14K" inscribed on the bottom)
Bug-Reducing Powder	Desert skeleton's bag	1	Shrink scorpion in temple (Ch. 1) (Alternate solution to using flag)
China Bird	China Shop	3	Exchange for mask (Ch. 3) (Unavailable until after Valanice has spoken with China Shop owner)
Clay Pot	Desert cave	1	Collect and carry salt water (Ch. 1) Collect and carry fresh water (Ch. 1) Collect and carry nectar (Ch. 3 or 5)

ITEM	WHERE FOUND	CHAPTER WHEN FOUND	USE
Corn Kernel	Basket	1	Grow corn (Ch. 1) Traded for turquoise bead (Ch. 1) (Alternate solution to trading gourd seed for turquoise bead. A second kernel will appear in the basket after the trade.)
Crystal Shaft	Lamp in Malicia's house	5	Collect beam of sunlight (Ch. 5) Thaw Mab (Ch. 5)
Defoliant	Undertaker's house	4	Defeat Swamp Monster (Ch. 4) Defeat Malicia's dog (Ch. 4) (Unavailable until after Rosella has veil)
Dragon Scale	Dragon (in Lair)	2	Ingredient for magic potion (Ch. 2) (Hammer and chisel needed to get it)
Dragon Toad	Great Hall	2	Escape coffin (Ch. 4) (Gem from Troll King's bracelet needed to bring toad to life)
Dream Catcher	Given by the Three Fates	5	Obtain the tapestry of dreams (Ch. 5) Release nightmare in Dreamland (Ch. 5)
Ear of Corn	Corn stalk in damp sand	1	Part of sequence to turn salt water into fresh (Ch. 1) (There will be another ear of corn on the stalk as often as needed to make fresh water)
Enchanted Rope	Given by Mathilde	2	Escape Troll Underground (Ch. 2)

ITEM	WHERE FOUND	CHAPTER WHEN FOUND	USE
Extra Life	Outside treehouse	4	Resurrect Edgar (Ch. 6) (Extra life is given in return for saving black cat from being buried alive)
Feather	Rubber chicken	3 or 5	Awakens Rock Spirit (Ch. 3 or Ch. 5) (Feather will appear when rubber chicken is first examined. If not, then right after moon is shot into the sky)
Femur	Treehouse (in mummy's hand)	5	Befriend Headless Horseman's dog (Ch. 5) (Horseman's medal is the reward)
Firecracker	Outside treehouse	5	Explode lock on Headless Horseman's tomb (Ch. 5) (Firecracker will explode on its own —with terminal consequences — if carried too long)
Flag	Made from stick & petticoat	1	Stop scorpion (Ch. 1) (Alternate solution to bug powder. Warning: Scorpion can free self if Valanice remains in temple too long)
Foot-in-a-bag	Treehouse	4	Get Ooga Booga Land Fragrant Flower (Ch. 4)
Fragrant Flowers	1. Beneath hungry plant	4	Awaken real Troll King (Ch. 6)
	2. Grate in tunnel	6	Awaken real Troll King (Ch. 6) (These two flowers are mutually exclusive. If you get the one in Ch. 4, you can't get the one in Ch. 6)

ITEM	WHERE FOUND	CHAPTER WHEN FOUND	USE
Fresh Water	Created at desert statue	1	Given to Desert Spirit (Ch. 1) (Creating the fresh water, and giving it to the Spirit, are optional problems and do not need to be solved to complete the game)
Glasses	By Jackalope's hole	1	Returned to rat in desert (Ch. 1)
	Between pair of cactus	1	Returned to rat in desert (Ch. 1) (These are alternate solutions and are mutually exclusive)
Golden Comb (Rosella's Comb)	Val's Inventory	1	Make Valanice cry (all Chapters) Used with Attis and the archduke (Ch. 3 and/or Ch. 5) When combined with the magic statue, allows Valanice to see Rosella (Ch. 3 and/or 5)
Golden Grape	Powder room (on fountain)	4	Opens secret passage to Troll Underground (Ch. 4) (Need hammer & chisel to get it)
Gourd Seed	Damp sand in desert	1	Traded for turquoise bead (Ch. 1) (The seed is unavailable until the ear of corn has been taken *and* the player has left the corn screen and returned)
Gravedigger's Horn	Gravedigger	4	Summon gravedigger (Ch. 4) (Unavailable until rat is returned to gravedigger. If horn is blown when Boogeyman is home, Rosella will die)
Gravedigger's Rat	Treehouse	4	Exchanged for gravedigger's horn and shovel

ITEM	WHERE FOUND	CHAPTER WHEN FOUND	USE
Hammer and Chisel	Jeweler in Forge room	2	Remove scale from the crystal dragon (Ch. 2) Remove gem from Troll King's bracelet (Ch. 4) Remove gilded grape in powder room (Ch. 4)
Horseman's Fife	Outside Horseman's tomb	5	Summon Horse (Ch. 5)
Horseman's Head	Inside Horseman's Tomb	5	Befriend Horseman (Ch. 5)
Horseman's Medal	Ruined house	5	Given to Horseman's wife (Ch. 4) (Given by the Horseman's dog in exchange for giving it the femur)
Hunting Horn	Next to desert skeleton	1	Blow Jackalope out of his hole to obtain rat's glasses (Ch. 1) (Alternate solution to using rope)
Jackalope Fur	Between pair of cactus	1	Combined with were-beast salve (Ch. 5)
	Outside	or	
	Jackalope's hole	1 or 3	Combined with were-beast salve (Ch. 5) (If player begins game at Ch. 3, the fur will be available, free for the picking, at the jackalope's hole)
Lantern	Mine Shaft	2	Carry fire (spark) (Ch. 2)
Lantern with Spark	Forge	2	Put some spark in the crystal dragon's life (Ch. 2)
Magic Bridle	Mab's temple	5	Harness wind horse (Ch. 5)
Magic Statuette	Archduke's office (desk drawer)	3	Exchange for were-beast salve (Ch. 5) Combined with comb to see Rosella (Ch. 3 and/or 5)

202

ITEM	WHERE FOUND	CHAPTER WHEN FOUND	USE
Magic Wand	Cemetery (from Troll King)	4	Transform Troll King to himself (Ch. 4) Transform false Troll King (Ch. 6) (The magic wand has two settings: T and F. Only the F setting will restore Edgar, the false Troll King. Warning: If magic wand is used any other time, Rosella will die.)
Mask	China Shop	3	Allows entry to Masquerade Ball (Ch. 3) Traded to obtain rubber chicken (Ch. 3 or Ch. 5)
Moon	Fountain in Falderal	3	To get Val arrested (Ch. 3) Shot into sky (Ch. 5)
Mysterious Device	Malicia's house (dresser)	4	Transform Malicia (Ch. 6) Transform Malicia's dog (Ch. 6)
Pomegranate	Cornucopia statue	5	Turns oak tree into Ceres (Ch. 5)
Prickly Pear	Next to colossus head	1 or 3	Get past giant gila monster (Ch. 3)
Puzzle	Made by combining the two turquoise pieces.	1	Key to open colossal head statue (Ch. 1)
Ripped Petticoat	Barrel cactus	1	Combined with stick to make flag (Ch. 1) (Alternate scorpion solution)
Rope	Desert skeleton's bag	1	Trip Jackalope (Ch. 1) (Alternate jackalope solution) (If rope is taken from bag instead of the bug-reducing powder, Val must make the flag to defeat the scorpion)
Rubber Chicken	Faux Shop	3 or 5	Shoot moon back into sky (Ch. 5)

ITEM	WHERE FOUND	CHAPTER WHEN FOUND	USE
Sacred Nectar	Flowers by water maiden statue	3 or 5	Start River of Life (Ch. 3 or Ch. 5)
Salt Crystals	Desert well	1 or 3	Enter Faux Shop (Ch. 3)
Salt Water	Desert well	1	Ingredient for fresh water (Ch. 1)
Scarab Beetle (Troll King as Scarab)	Cemetery	4	Carry around the Troll King (Ch. 4) (The scarab is his disguise)
Shield	Great Hall	2	To make a wheel for cart (Ch. 2) (The shield contains a spike)
Shield Spike	On Shield	2	To secure shield to the cart (Ch. 2) (Spike must be removed from shield to be used)
Shovel	Gravedigger	4	Enter Malicia's house (Ch. 4) Pry rock free for stool (Ch. 6) Dig out from volcano (Ch. 6) (Shovel is unavailable until after Rosella returns to the gravedigger's area *after* she has returned the gravedigger's rat)
Silver Pellet	Great Hall	2	Combined with woolen stocking to make sling (Ch. 4) (After Rosella drinks the magic potion, the silver spoon melts and becomes the pellet)
Silver Spoon	Forge	2	Magic-potion ingredient (Ch. 2)
Sling	Made from silver pellet and woolen stocking	4	Knock out the were-bear (Ch. 4)

ITEM	WHERE FOUND	CHAPTER WHEN FOUND	USE
Stick	Desert well	1	Combined with ripped petticoat to make flag (Ch. 1) Get prickly pear (Ch. 1 or Ch. 3)
Tapestry of Dreams	Dream Weaver's cave	5	Fly to Dreamland while awake (Ch. 5)
Toy Rat	Great Hall	2	Send cook on a wild goose chase (Ch. 2) Scare Malicia (Ch. 2)
Turquoise Bead	Rat's house	1	Exchanged for Turquoise Piece 2 at bottom of well (Ch. 1)
Turquoise Piece 1	Temple in desert	1	Combined with Turquoise Piece 2 to create key (Ch. 1)
Turquoise Piece 2	Bottom of well	1	Combined with Turquoise Piece 1 to create key (Ch. 1)
Turquoise Shape	Bottom of well	1	This piece is merely a wrong choice to trip up players (Ch. 1)
Veil	Cemetery	4	Disguise to hide from Boogeyman and Malicia (Ch. 4)
Weird Pet	Undertaker's house	4	Exchanged with ghoul kids for gravedigger's rat (Ch. 4)
Were-beast Salve	Snake oil salesman	5	Combined with Jackalope fur, it turns Valanice (temporarily) into a jackalope
Wet Sulfur	On wall in Pit of Winds	2	Put forger troll to sleep (Ch. 2) (The sulfur will not work until Rosella has overheard the troll women discussing it in the hot pool. Rosella has to return to the pool before this conversation happens)

ITEM	WHERE FOUND	CHAPTER WHEN FOUND	USE
Wooden Nickel	Tree by fountain (mockingbird's nest)	3	Exchanged for book in Faux Shop (Nickel is unavailable until after the moon has splashed down)
Woolen Stocking	Malicia's room (dresser)	4	Combined with silver pellet to create sling (Ch. 4)

PART SEVEN

Who's Who

It is very easy to get submerged in the seductive technological dazzle of a state-of-the-art computer game. Sharp, clean, colorful, smoothly animated graphics can make us say "Wow!" and pause for a few admiring moments before continuing on. It's a reaction for which game designers strive. It's where they get their jollies. And its one of the places where they fiercely compete with other companies in "my game is cooler looking than your game" one-upsmanship. But in doing so, we often lose something.

Behind all the gee-whiz flash and glitter, oft-times lost is the art and craftsmanship that goes into the game's characters before they're shrunk, digitized, and animated.

In the course of their adventures through The Princeless Bride, Rosella and her mother Valanice will encounter and interact with scores of different characters, some human, many not, and the others...well, we'll let you decide. All of these characters began their screen life as pencil drawings on pieces of paper. Artist Marc Hudgins is responsible for the original designs. It was his job to give physical form to these individuals, and to shape and render individualities. The final sketches were then used by the game's animators as the basis for their giving the characters life and movement.

In practice, 100 pixels or so may be enough to reproduce the drawing of, for example, the rat Valanice trades with, but it doesn't always reflect the work put into creating it. And it doesn't reflect all of the physical personality of, say, the guard at the gate of Falderal, or the ghoul kids, or Chicken Petite. Stories move so quickly at times that secondary characters often get visually slighted in the passing.

So if you're tired of squinting at the computer screen to get a closer look at the Boogeyman (yuk!) or the China Shop owner or the oily features of the snake-oil salesman...

Oh, the heck with what we have to say. Have a look at the drawings. You'll get the picture.

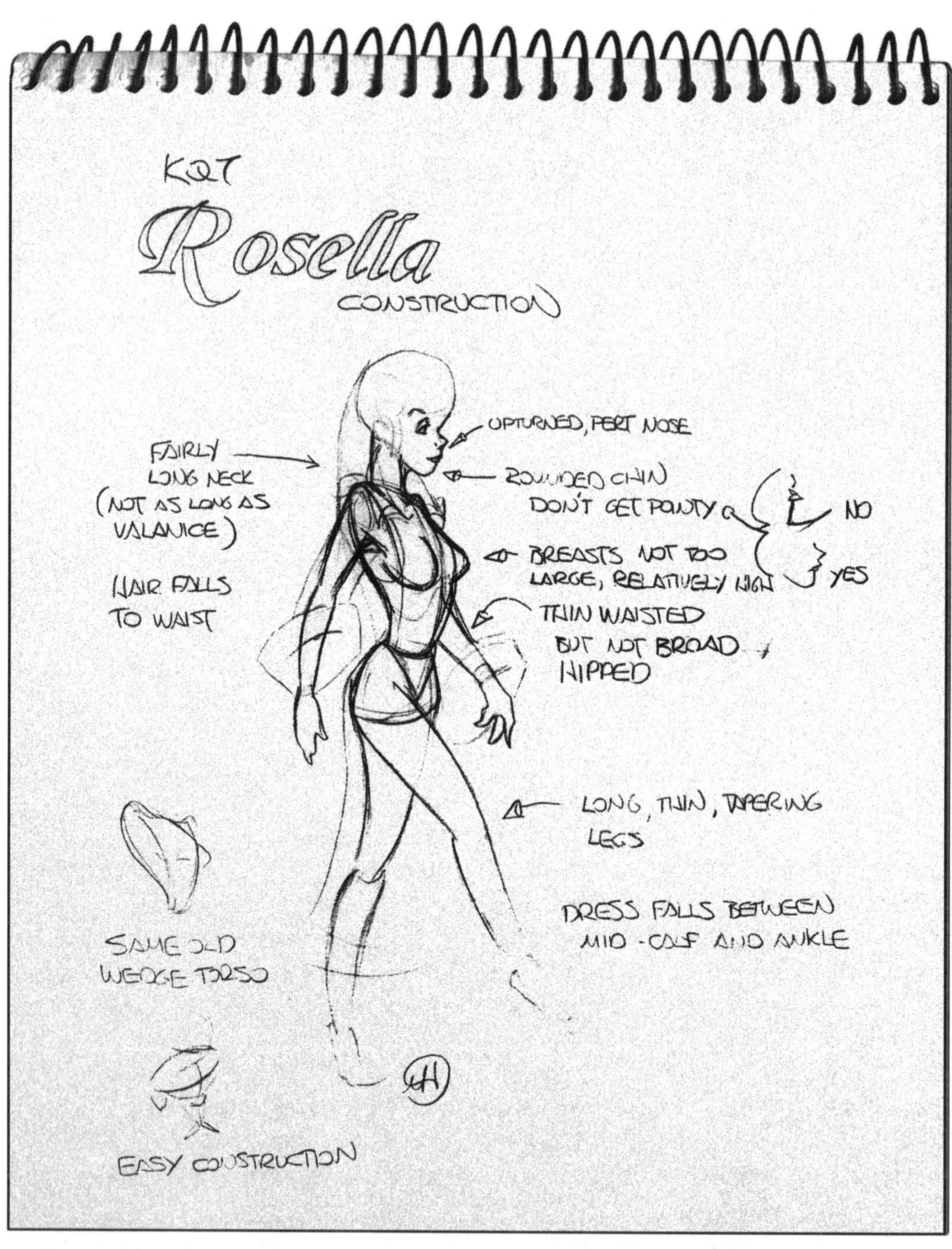

This drawing of Rosella is a "construction" and tells animators how a character should move. Constructions are usually only done for major characters.

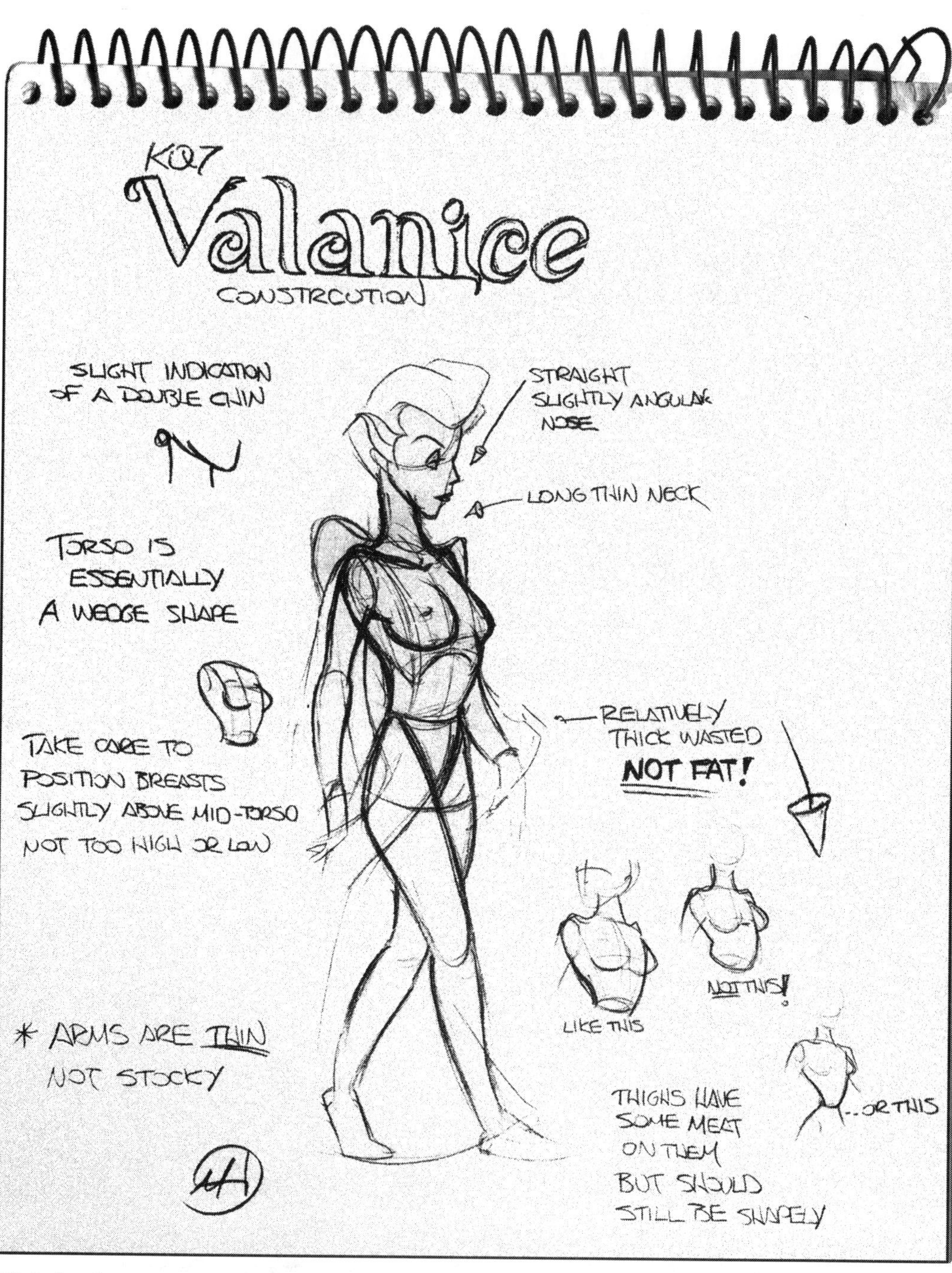

This is the construction for Queen Valanice. As you can see, she is not fat.

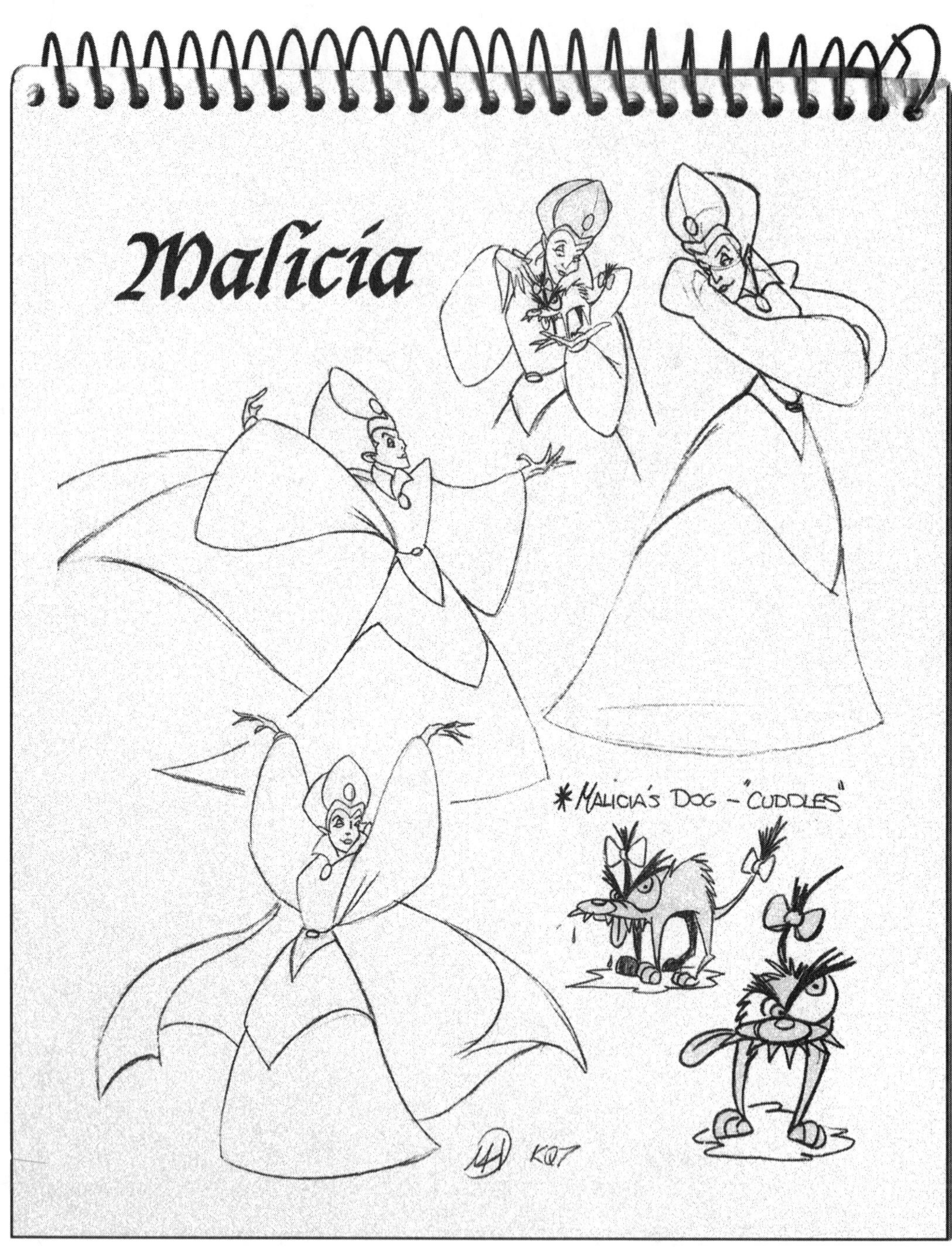

Malicia and her "adorable" pooch, Cuddles.

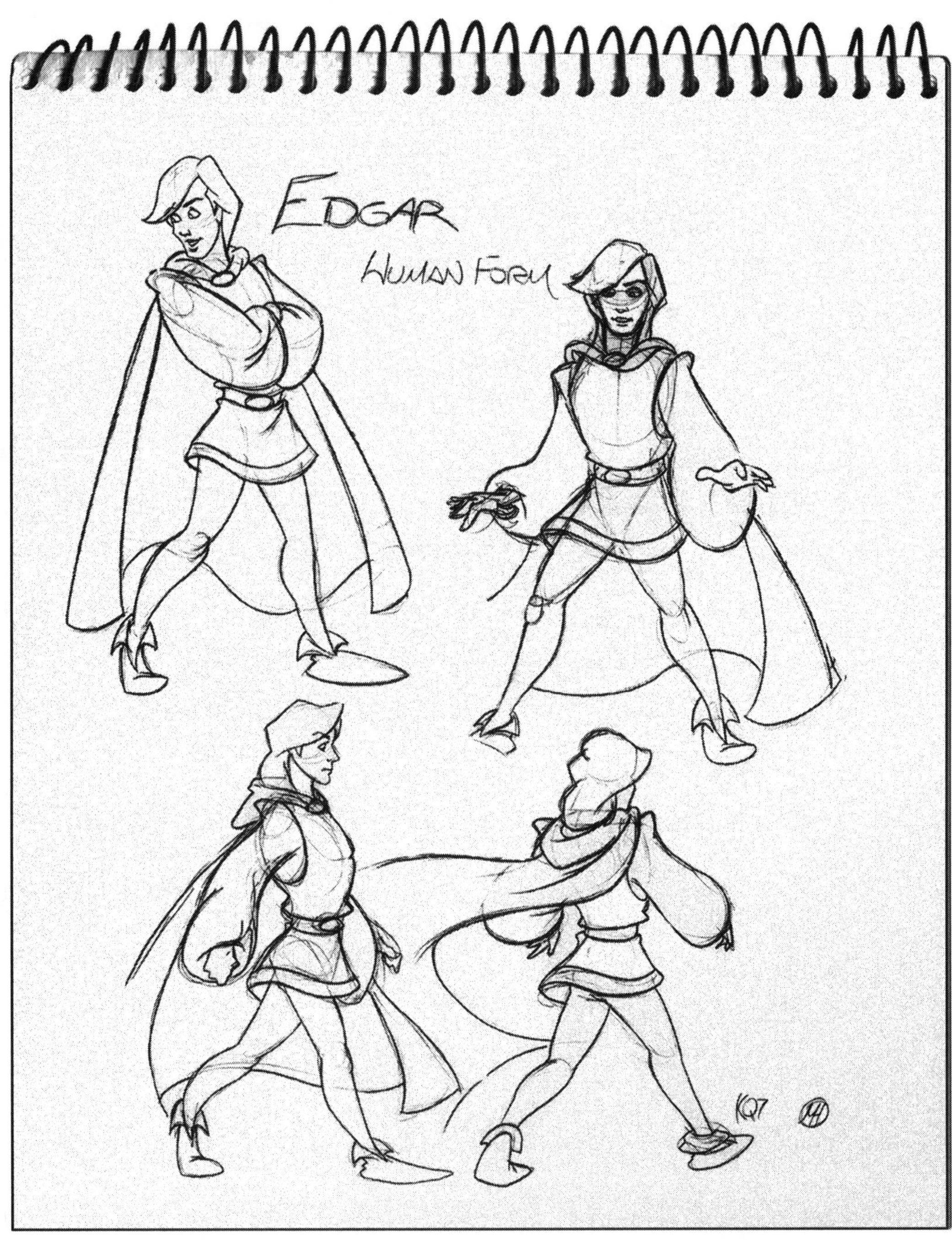

Artist Marc Hudgins, who drew the sketches for every one of the 60 or so characters in King's Quest VII, was told to make Edgar "not too bland and a little goofy."

The same illustration is used for both the real and fake Troll Kings.

The Kangaroo Rat is the desert trader, but we know he's a pack rat.

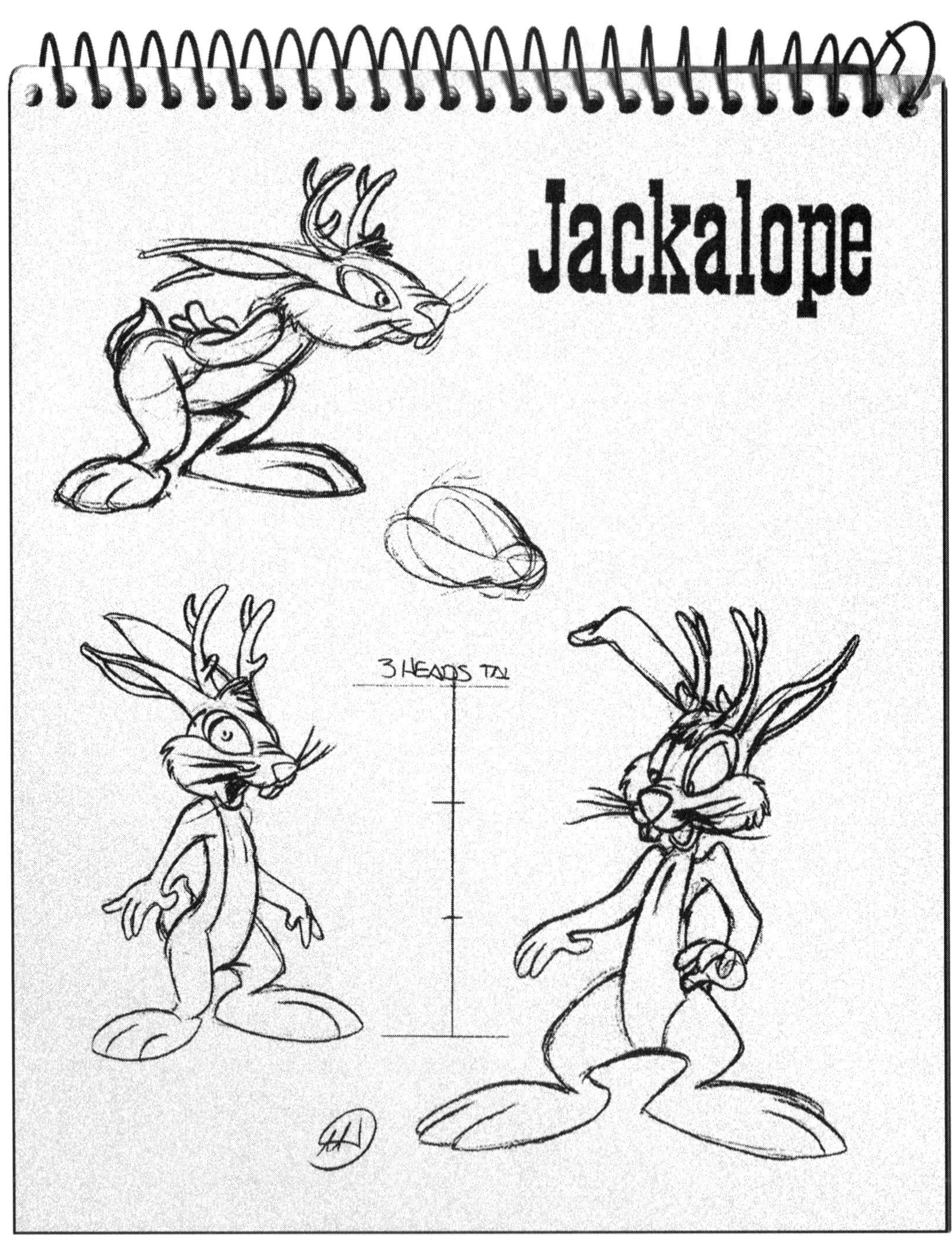

The Jackalope is half jackrabbit and half antelope. He Bugs folks.

Attis and Ceres, who is also known as Mother Nature to artist Marc Hudgins, in human form.

The Snake-Oil Salesman is slick, and eel take you every time.

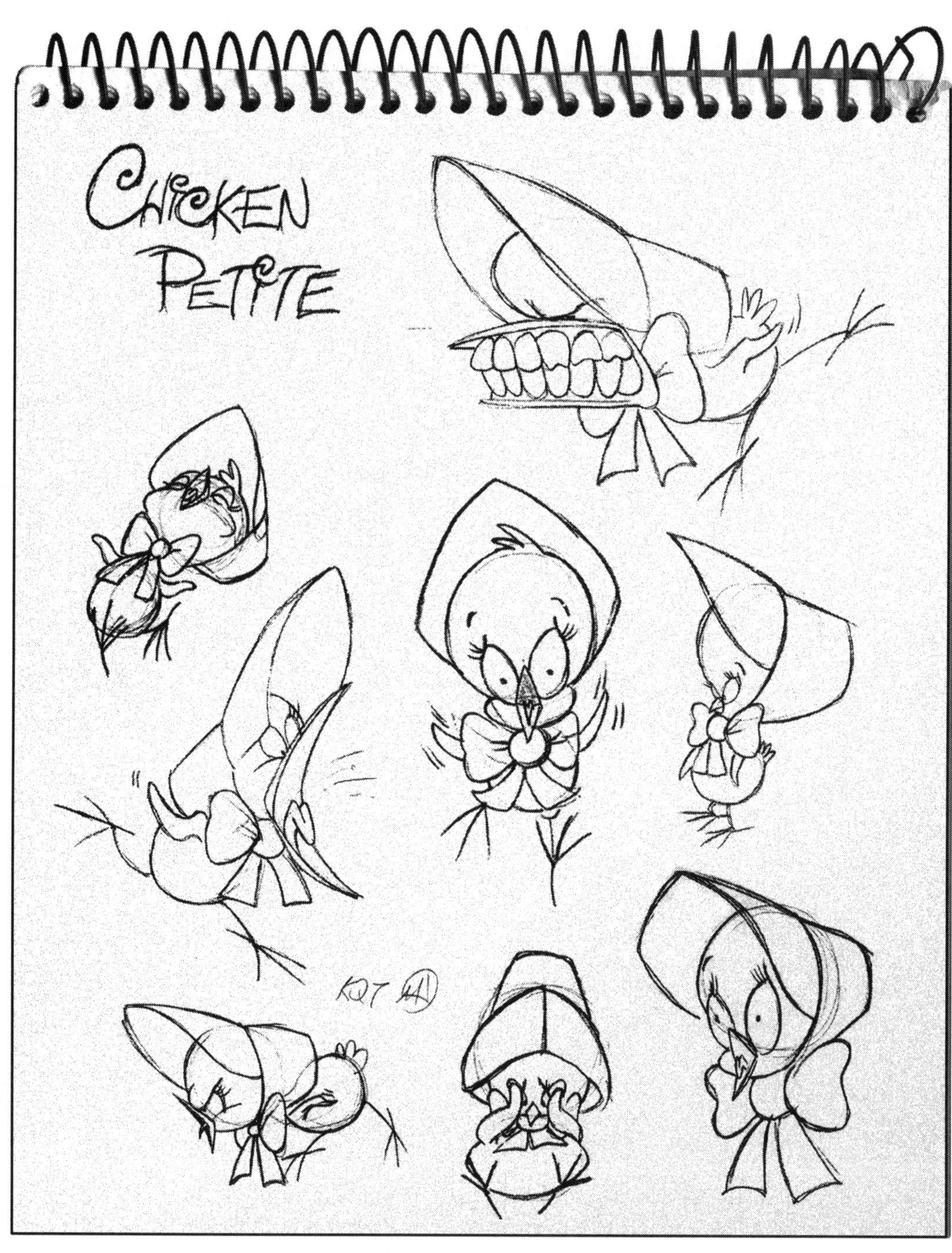

Could is be that Chicken Petite is Chicken Little's evil twin?

Falderal's Chamber of Commerce.

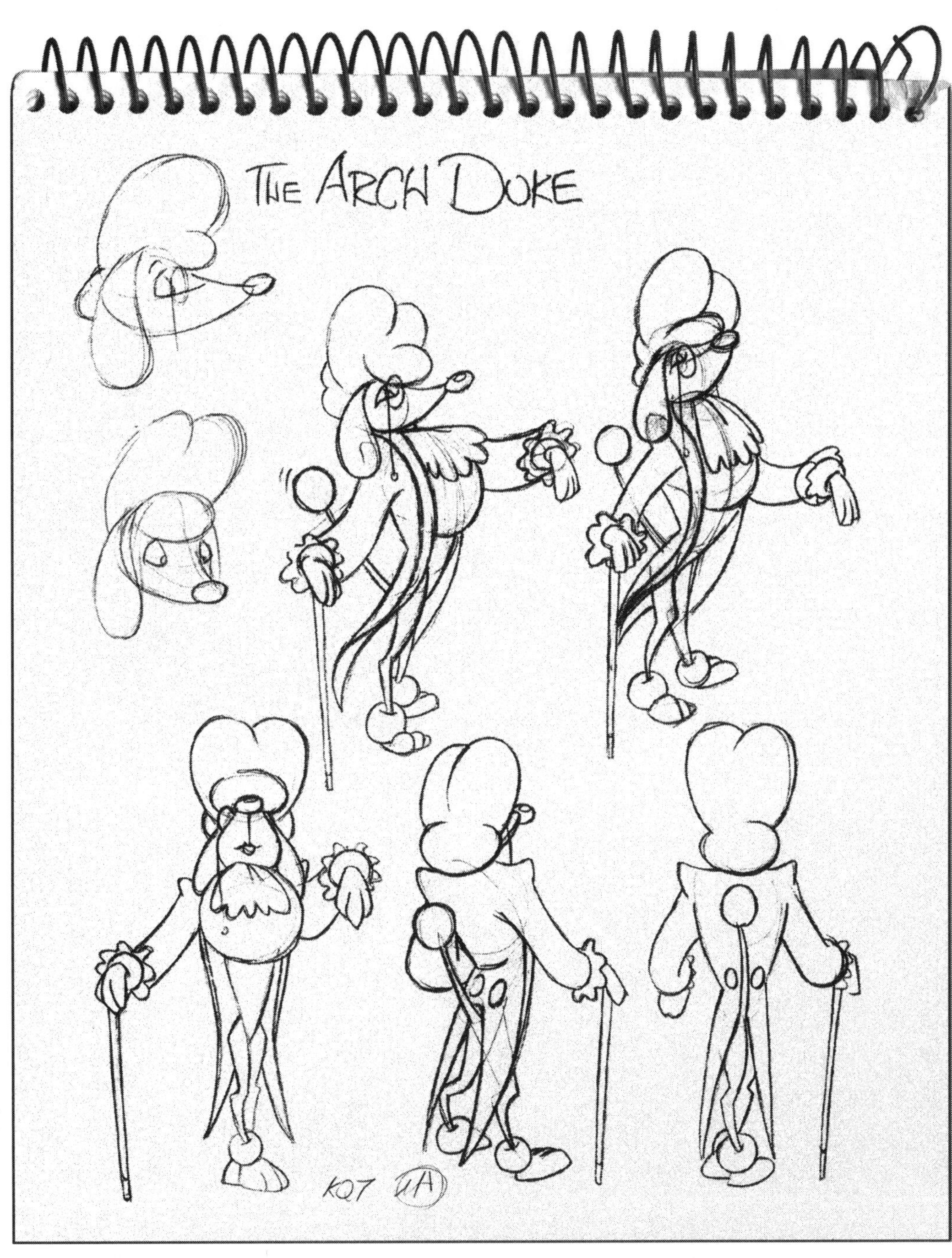

He is the Arch Duke because that's the way he acts.

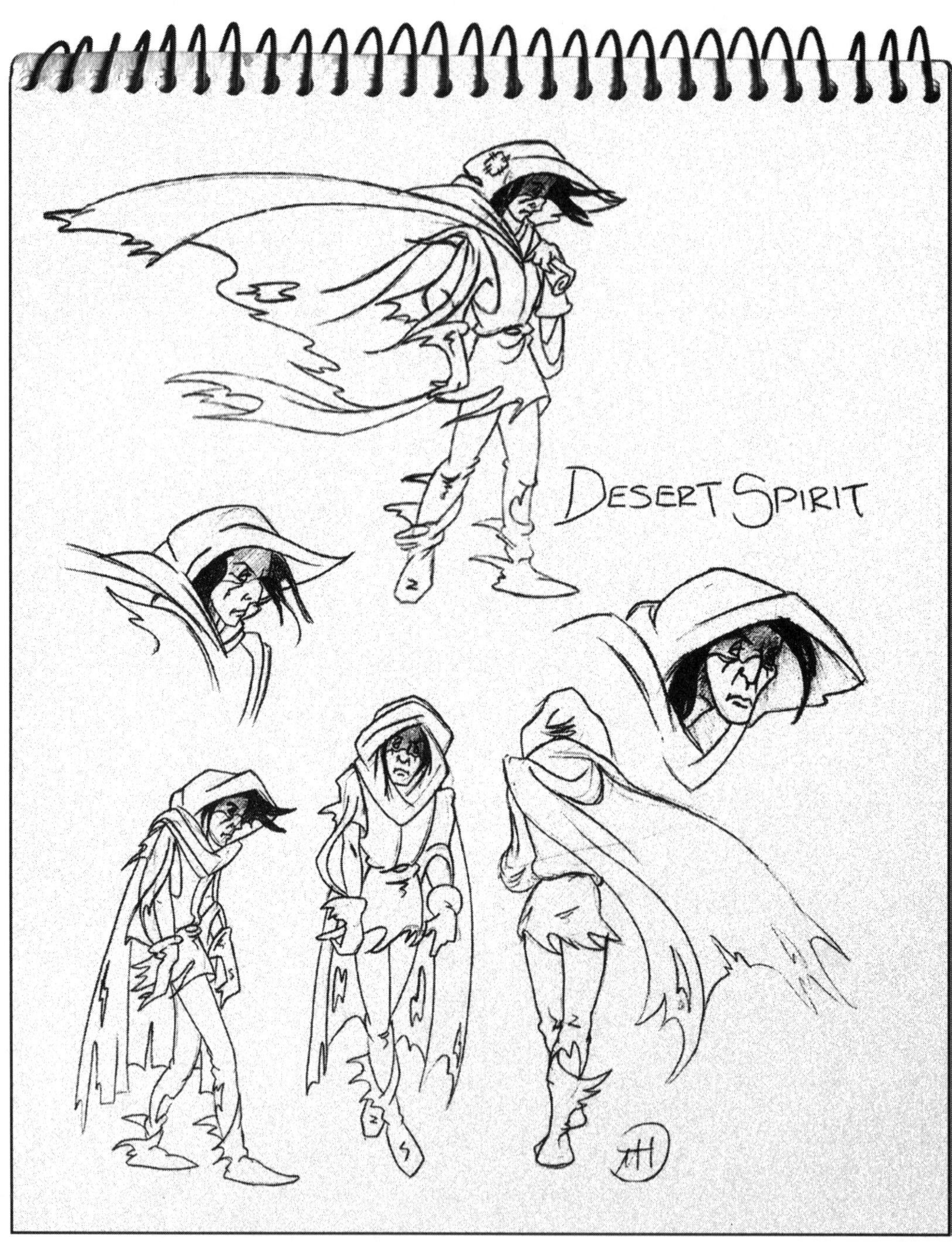

It's such a drag being dead.

The Troll Jeweler, the Troll Forger, and Mathilde, the Troll King's nursemaid. It's not true that if you've seen one troll, you've seen them all.

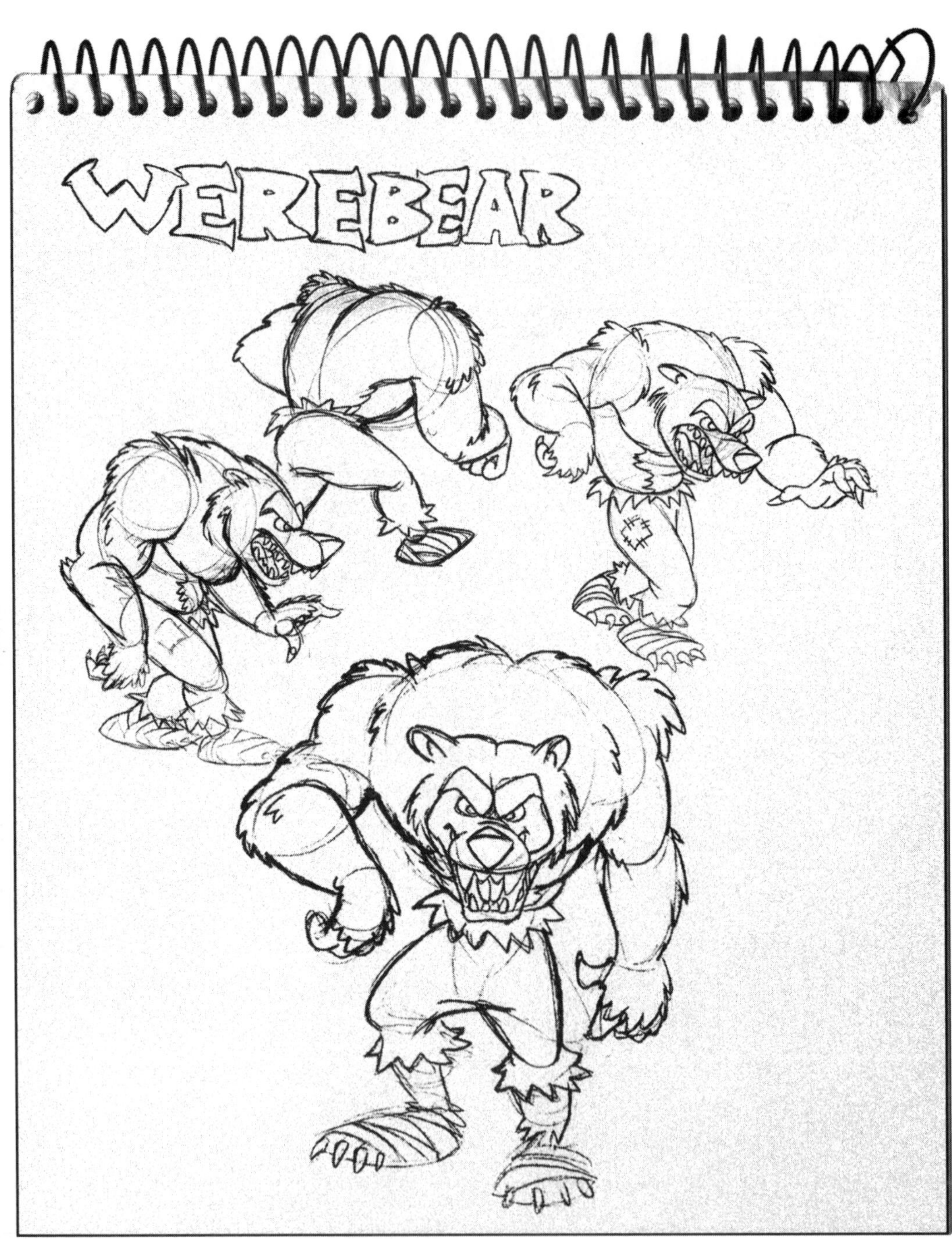

"I'm the were-bear — gotta problem with that?"

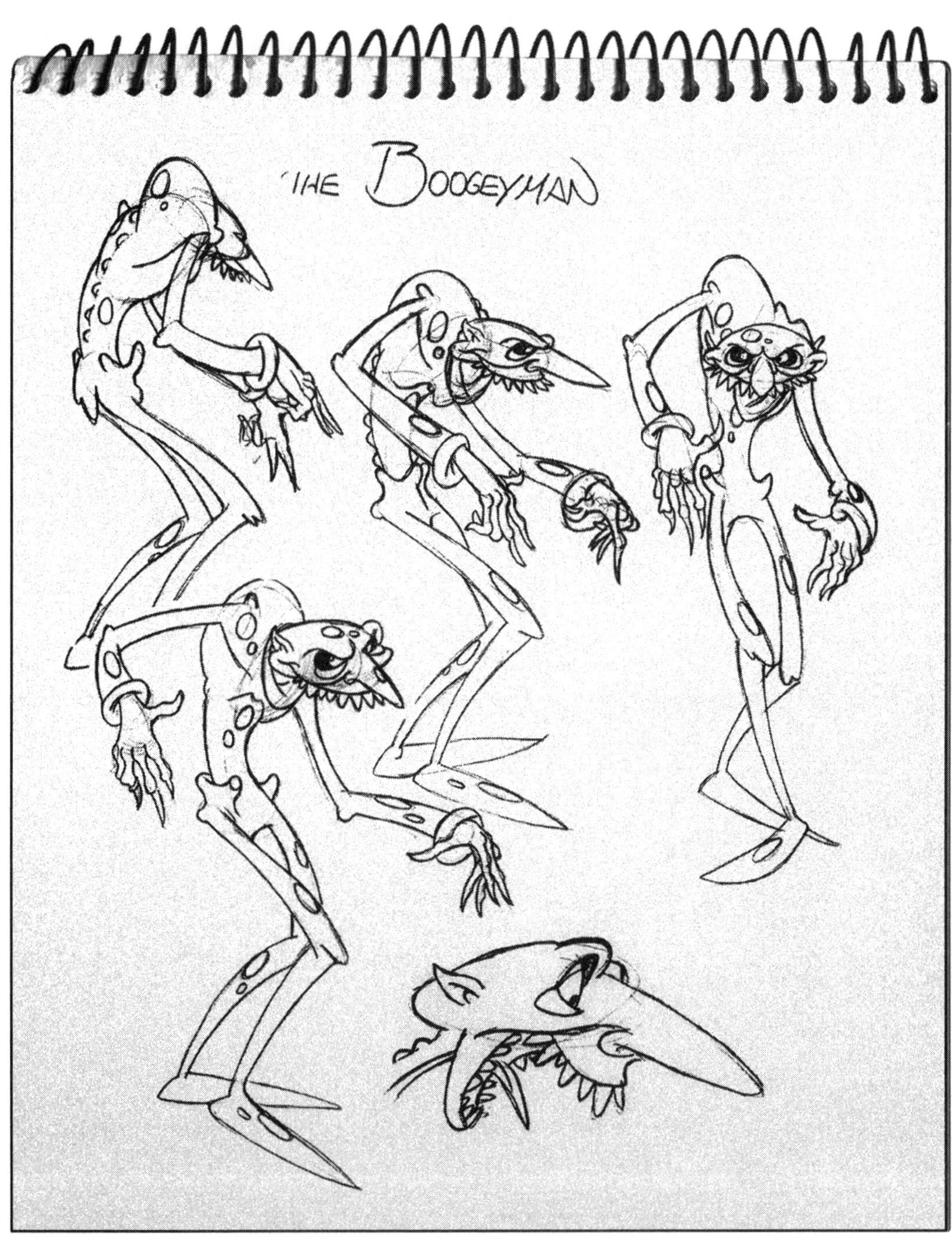

Marc Hudgins describes the Boogeyman as "sick and diseased with worms in the brain. He's not evil, just hideous and sick — a real twisted individual."

The Undertaker: spined and unspined.

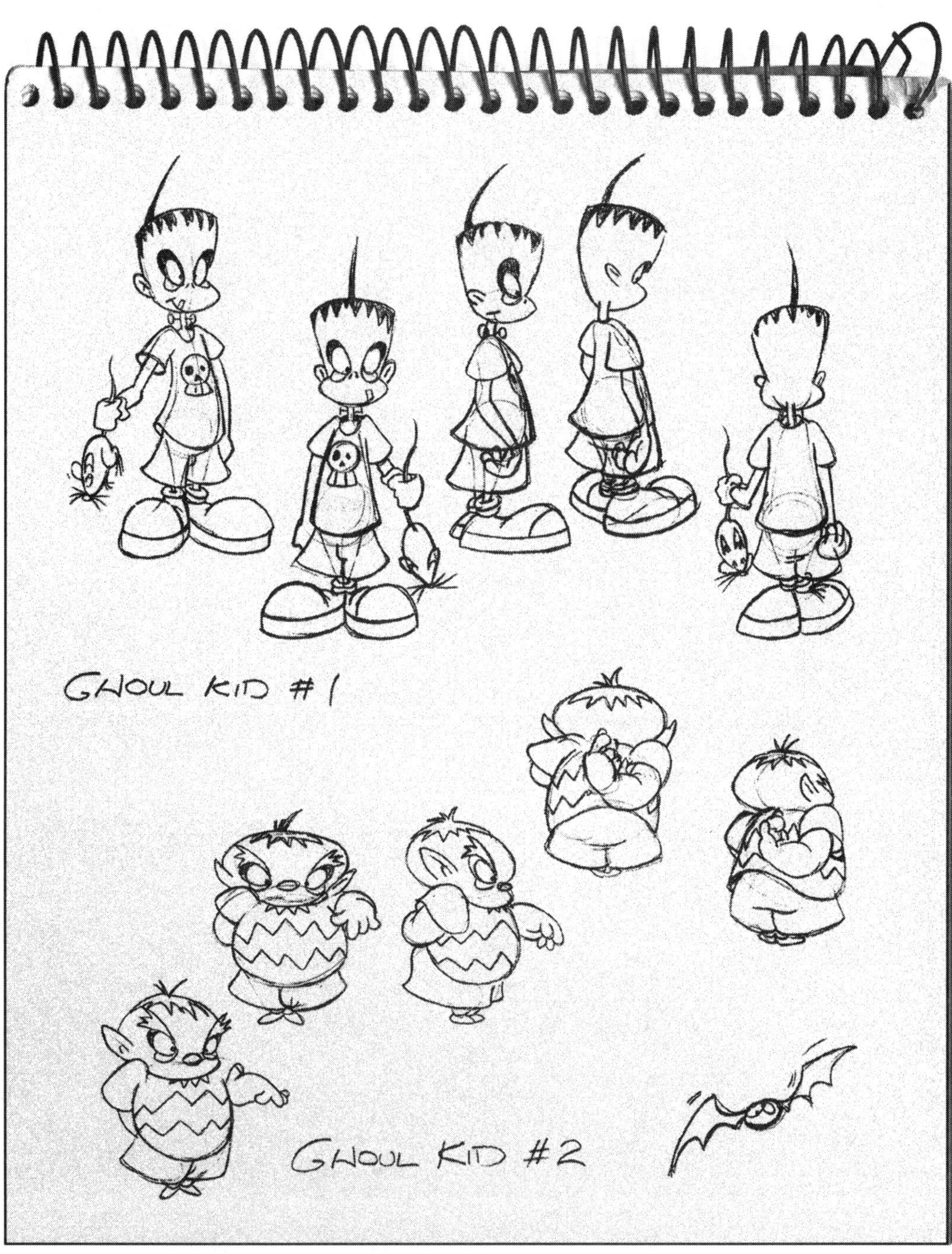

Your friendly neighborhood ghoul kids, Nasty and Nsatier.

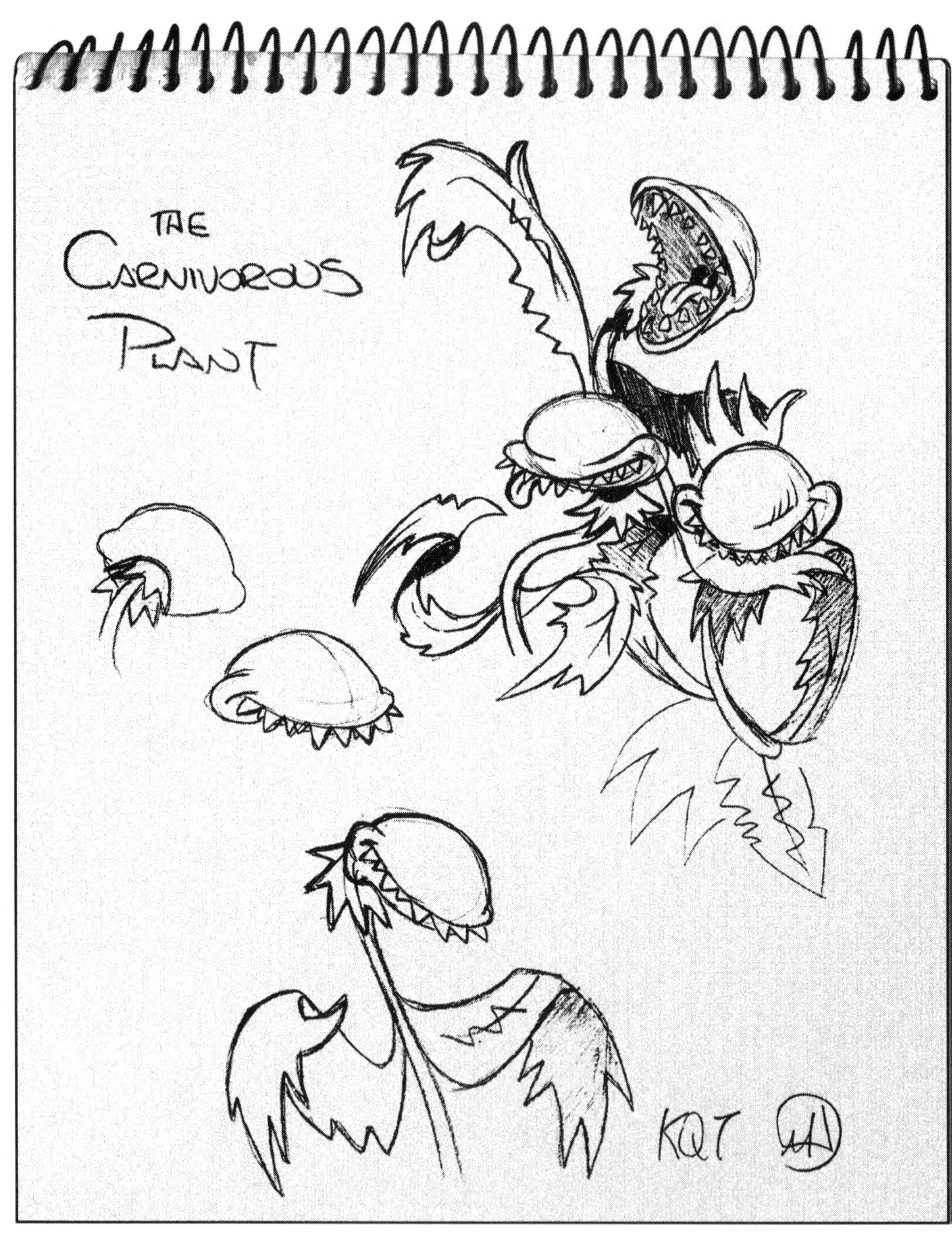

"Feed me."

Oberon and Titania, Edgar's parents.

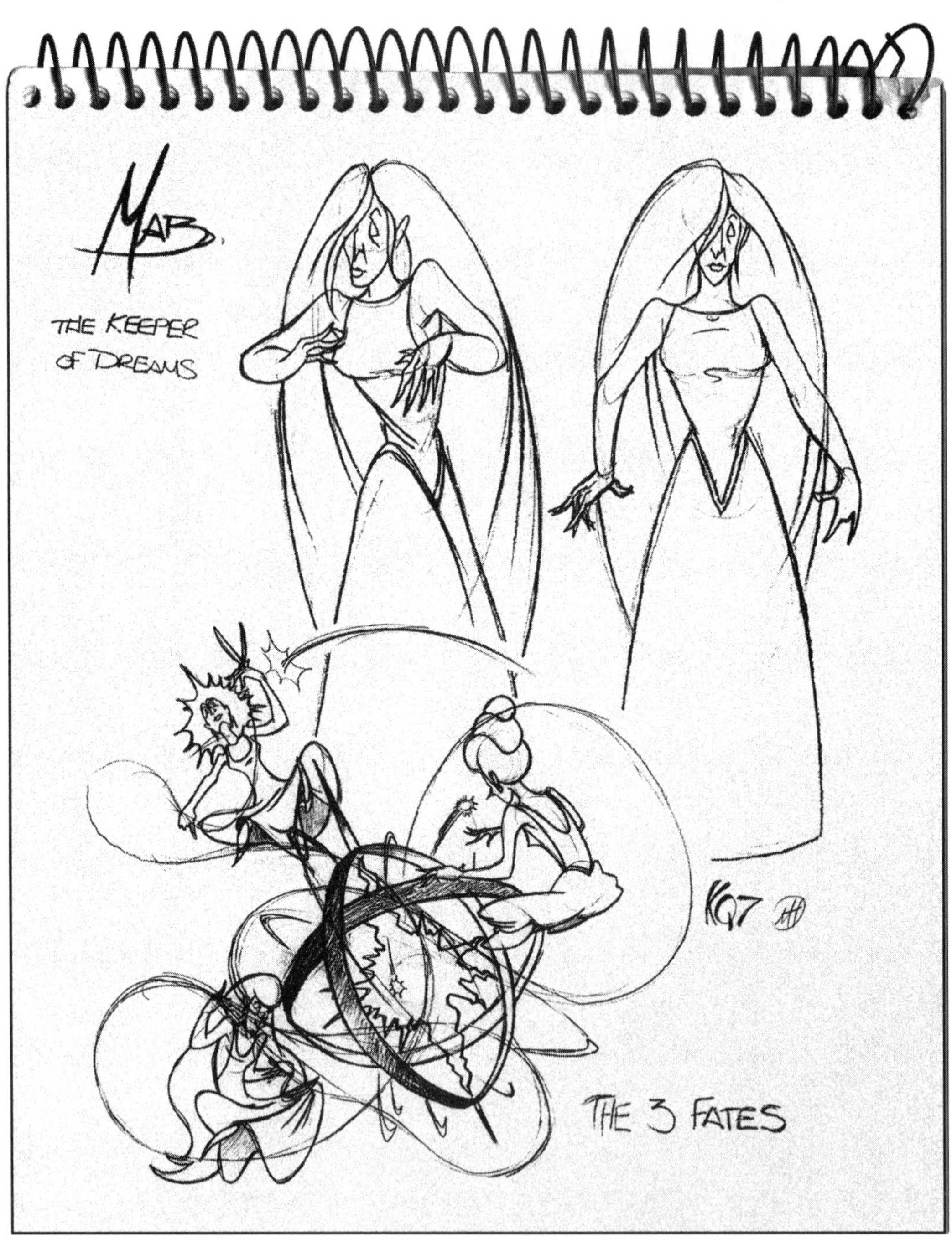

Mab, unfrozen, and the conceptual sketch of the Three Fates weaving destinities.

These aren't ghosts, they're the winds named Borasco and Scirocco.